THAT WE MAY BE
MUTUALLY
ENCOURAGED

THAT WE MAY BE ⟆MUTUALLY⟅ ENCOURAGED

Feminism and the New Perspective in Pauline Studies

KATHY EHRENSPERGER

T&T CLARK INTERNATIONAL
A Continuum imprint
NEW YORK • LONDON

T & T Clark International, Madison Square Park, 15 East 26th Street, New York, NY 10010

T & T Clark International, The Tower Building, 11 York Road, London SE1 7NX

T & T Clark International is a Continuum imprint.

Design: Corey Kent

Library of Congress Cataloging-in-Publication Data

Ehrensperger, Kathy, 1956–
    That we may be mutually encouraged : feminism and the new perspective in Pauline studies / Kathy Ehrensperger.
        p. cm.
Includes bibliographical references and index.
    ISBN 0-567-02640-X (pbk.)
    1. Bible. N.T. Epistles of Paul—Criticism, interpretation, etc.
    2. Feminist theology.   I. Title.
BS2650.52.E39 2004
225.9'2—dc22

                                                                            2003021377

Printed in the United States of America

04 05 06 07 08 09   10 9 8 7 6 5 4 3 2 1

ᨒᨔ CONTENTS ᨒᨔ

Part 2—Paul in Contemporary Studies and Theologies

To the memory of my father,
to my mother,
and to Rahel, Joachim, and Aurelia

✑ ACKNOWLEDGMENTS ✑

This book was originally submitted as my PhD thesis to the University of Wales, Lampeter, UK, in March 2002. The project could not have come to completion without the support and help of a network of people around me on both sides of the English Channel. I would like to thank my two supervisors for their support: Dr. William S. Campbell has been a critically encouraging source of inspiration, and Professor Dan Cohn-Sherbok's questions helped to clarify many sections of the thesis. Professor Mary Grey on several occasions has been a dialogue partner in feminist issues. The Department of Theology and Religious Studies at the University of Wales, Lampeter, has been a friendly and welcoming place for a guest from abroad. I would like to thank them for their hospitality and for providing an excellent academic experience.

I could not have succeeded in my research without the never-ending support of the network on the Basel side, both in university and church, especially all my friends and family. Many could be mentioned here—such as Professor Ekkehard Stegemann—who have encouraged and supported me during the difficult years when I had to combine work and research. The list of names would be too long, but I include them all in my grateful appreciation.

I would like to express my special gratitude to my brother Urs—a supportive and critical partner in conversation, and whose encouragement means so much to me—and to my children. Rahel, Joachim, and Aurelia are the sunshine of my life. They were unbelievably supportive and patient throughout these years. I know this has not always been easy for them as they had to put up with a mother not only working but also studying! But they kept on inspiring and challenging me and always brought me back to the "real world" through their stimulating conversations, and even more through their lives. They are just fine young people—it is to them, to my lovely mother, and to the memory of my father that this book is dedicated.

PART 1

Hermeneutics and Presuppositions

1

Introduction

Over the last thirty years major shifts have been transforming Pauline studies, feminist theologies on Paul, and theologies dealing with the Shoah. But these changes often did not have an impact on other strands of theological research outside the boundaries of their respective disciplines. This study has emerged from a deep concern about how different strands of research in theology and biblical studies proceed in isolation from each other. From a feminist perspective, which emphasizes relationality in life and faith, such unrelatedness raises particular concerns.

In this book I insist that relating insights of research—particularly of Pauline studies, feminist theologies, and theologies dealing with the Shoah— would lead to illuminating and fruitful interactions and new insights for each of these theologies and would prove especially relevant for understanding Paul from a radically new perspective. From such interaction should emerge an image of Paul beyond traditional male scholarship's image of him as the first Christian theological thinker of a law-free Gentile church, and beyond traditional feminist scholarship's image of him as the father of misogyny and dominating power.

Part 1 of this study concentrates on hermeneutics and different ways of thinking as the presuppositions behind any interpretation. Part 2 concentrates on the study of Paul, applying insights gained from the first part. I elaborate particularly on the question of the consistency of Paul's way of thinking, taking consciously into account that there are different ways of perceiving and interpreting life and events. In chapter 6, then, I take the insights on Paul emerging from this analysis and compare them to issues emphasized in feminist theologies.

The changes in theologies dealing with the Shoah, in feminist theologies, and in Pauline studies are part of wider changes in perspectives that have questioned traditional ways of acting and thinking generally. Chapter 2 gives an overview of changing perspectives in different areas, starting with changes in philosophies and in hermeneutics, which to a vast extent set the agenda for changing perspectives in other disciplines. I outline the development that caused the shift from hegemonic ways of thinking and interpretation, to forms of thinking involving diversity and difference: postmodern/postcritical approaches. Then I describe the shift that has been evoked by theological approaches stressing that we cannot theologize after the Shoah as if nothing had happened, because anti-Judaism and thus anti-Semitism have their roots in specific interpretations of the Christian tradition.

At the beginning of the 1970s feminist theologies were prominently involved in the hermeneutical paradigm shift from hegemony to diversity. With their focus on patriarchal patterns of domination in biblical texts, however, feminist interpretations often unconsciously transmitted other patterns of domination in interpretation—anti-Judaism, for example. Therefore, I investigate aspects in the history of feminist theologies that are relevant in the context of the anti-Judaism debate. I argue that feminist theologians have often uncritically reapplied hermeneutical patterns of traditional mainstream/ *malestream* interpretation in their perspectives rather than developing their own entirely new approaches to the biblical texts.

An overview of the history of the interpretation of Paul's letters demonstrates that patterns of hierarchical domination, and particularly of anti-Jewish patterns of interpretation, have been dominant for centuries. During the last thirty years perspectives have begun to change significantly only with the emergence of the "New Perspective on Paul," which has sought to overcome the anti-Jewish tradition in Pauline studies. Feminist research on Paul has long concentrated on the issue of women and Paul, which led to feminist theologians limiting themselves to a small number of relevant texts of the Pauline Letters. Though in feminist studies of Paul this restrictive situation has changed significantly in the last few years, feminist research on the whole scope of Paul's writings is still rather slight.

Again and again scholars prominently address one problem in the interpretation of Paul's letters: Where do the contradictions in Paul come from, and how can they be resolved? Chapter 3 addresses this question by showing that apparent contradictions in Paul have something to do with the patterns of thinking from within which one tries to understand Paul and his letters. Traditional interpretations locate Paul at the margins of Judaism or already outside it, and emphasize Paul's opposition to the faith of his ancestors. The Pauline Letters are viewed as expressions of Western rational logic. Several scholars have asked whether this is an appropriate description of Paul and his thinking. An overview of different and differing ways of thinking in antiquity and in the contemporary world, as relevant for the study of Paul, supplies insights into different and differing perceptions and interpretations of life. I demonstrate that differing perceptions have run along parallel to the dominant Western perceptions of life. Often such perceptions arose from the edges of society and were kept marginalized because they interpreted life from the fringes of the dominant society, perceiving life and events from a different perspective and stressing different things. I concentrate on ways of thinking in different subgroups of first-century Judaism by analyzing their differing patterns of interpretation of Scriptures as indicative of their ways of thinking: the Pharisaic/pre-rabbinic styles of interpretation, including Qumran, apocalyptic, and Hellenistic patterns of interpretation. Can we discover similarities to Paul's ways of thinking within these groups? Is our perception of Paul's ways of thinking influenced by dominant ways of thinking in the majority society around us? If so, to what extent?

The next section of chapter 3 concentrates on feminism. In various disciplines, feminism has emphasized the limited perspective of the dominant Western perception. They concentrate instead on a "thinking from the margins," most prominently from the perspective of women, a marginalized half of humanity. The analysis of contemporary approaches that differ radically from mainstream/malestream rationality focuses on feminist theories. This leads into part 2, designed to consider what the outcome of an interaction between feminist research and Pauline studies might be. Three issues emerge as central in feminist theory as well as feminist theology: identity, diversity, and relationality.

In chapter 4, I analyze and reflect on the image of Paul that emerges when we take into account that Paul might have been thinking and acting in a way that differs from Western Enlightenment modes of rational thinking. Most recent strands of research notice that hermeneutical presuppositions significantly shape the patterns by which Paul's letters are interpreted. Interpreters are stressing different aspects in a New Perspective on Paul and leading to a consideration of such things as the context of his letters, the scriptural reasoning of Paul within first-century Judaism, the apocalyptic dimension in Paul's theologizing, the political context of the first-century Roman Empire. The leading question is, What difference does it make to view Paul with different hermeneutical presuppositions and from differing perspectives?

Feminist theology strongly emphasizes the need to analyze critically and to be aware of hermeneutical presuppositions in interpretation. Since the dominant pattern of interpretation has been unchallenged for centuries, it is almost impossible to escape completely from its influence. In chapter 5, with an analysis of three feminist commentaries on Romans, I ask what the hermeneutical presuppositions are on which their interpretation is based. I demonstrate that in some aspects they are not critical enough of their own hermeneutical presuppositions since their interpretations unwittingly are still based on traditional malestream interpretations of Romans.

In chapter 6, then, I apply aspects of the image of Paul emerging from the most recent strands of research of the New Perspective and even beyond it in an analysis of Rom 14–15.[1] I demonstrate that from such a perspective an interpretation of these chapters emerges that addresses issues which feminist theories and theologies also prominently handle somewhat differently.

This study shows that the interaction and positive relation of different strands of research on Paul—feminist interpretation, Pauline studies, and theologies dealing with the Shoah—actually lead to a fresh view of Paul and his letters. The consequences of such interaction between different strands of research on Paul open the door for significant new avenues of research, particularly in relation to issues of power.

---

1. For details, see Part 2, Chapter 4, 123ff.

꩜ 2 ꩜

Changing Perspectives

On Hermeneutics

To live is to interpret. There is no such thing as a pure event that speaks for itself. "In the beginning there is hermeneutics," as Jacques Derrida has expressed it.[1] Even such a basic event as the birth of a child does not speak for itself. We can see it as the happiest moment in the parents' life, but one family may barely notice that a new human being has arrived among them, and another family may view the birth as a catastrophe, a disaster. How they perceive the birth depends on the context into which a child is born. Any interpretation involves psychological, social, economic, political, and cultural factors, as in understanding the birth of a child. This is not to claim that there is nothing out there beyond our minds, that it is all in our heads; instead, the stance I advocate here opposes a naive empiricism claiming that what we experience, see, and understand is the objective reflection of "reality."

---

1. Jacques Derrida states: "The necessity of commentary, like poetic necessity, is the very form of exiled speech. In the beginning is hermeneutics. But the *shared* necessity of exegesis, the interpretive imperative, is interpreted differently by the rabbi and the poet. . . . The original opening of interpretation essentially signifies that there will always be rabbis and poets. And two interpretations of interpretation. The Law then becomes question and the right to speech coincides with the duty to interrogate. The book of man is a book of question." From "Edmond Jabès and the Question of the Book," in *Writing and Difference* (Chicago: University of Chicago Press, 1978), 67; original, *L'écriture et la différence* (Paris: Editions du Seuil, 1967). Also see Seyla Benhabib, *The Reluctant Modernism of Hannah Arendt* (Thousand Oaks, Calif.: Sage Publications, 1996), 3.

5

Nothing can be real to us without interpretation. Experiences of the physical world are given shape and meaning by interpretive acts.[2]

Religious traditions are one way of shaping and interpreting life and finding meaning in it. They provide specific matrices for believers to understand their lives in the present and in the future.

Christianity, like Judaism and Islam, is a religion based on forebears of faith and on written traditions, which are regarded as holy and therefore have authority attributed to them. The interpretation of "Holy Scriptures" as the basis for one's understanding of life is of primary importance for Christianity, as it is for all three monotheistic religions. Just as life itself is not self-explanatory, so also we need to interpret the Scriptures for the present situation. In Western culture Jewish and Christian traditions of interpretation developed over the centuries, and such biblical hermeneutics form one of the two main foundations of modern hermeneutical approaches, alongside the pattern of interpretation of Greek philosophy.[3] Later we will turn to this aspect. Interpretation does not question the authority of the scriptural tradition; instead, interpretation is the means by which the tradition of the past attains relevance for the present and the future.[4]

In Jewish and Christian tradition, Scripture is the record of earlier traditions of interpreting life in the light of the people's relationship to the one God. This record has been passed on within communities that, in a complex process, both shaped these traditions and were shaped by them. The Bible, the so-called Old and New Testaments, or the Hebrew Scriptures and the New Testament, are the basic texts for Christian self-understanding. To come to understand our own life in the light of this tradition, we necessarily have to enter into an interpretative dialogue with its written form.[5] Since these are the living traditions of communities of faith, we cannot enter into this dialogue without being in dialogue also with such communities.

As interpreters we are not entering the dialogue of interpretation as a tabula rasa. We enter this dialogue in the specific social, cultural, political, and personal context we live in, from our own specific and thus also limited

---

2. See also Pamela Dickey Young: "The experience we have, whatever 'the externality of many facts,' is filtered, interpreted through the lens of who we are, reflected upon in light of 'the internality of this experiencing,' what our cumulative experience of the past has made us. . . . But whatever these experiences in their immediacy, the articulation and understanding of them change as factors such as culture, gender, race, and class, mold one's expectations and reflections." In *Feminist Theology/Christian Theology: In Search of Method* (Minneapolis: Fortress, 1990), 51.

3. See Susan Handelman, *The Slayers of Moses: The Emergence of Rabbinic Interpretation in Modern Literary Theory* (Albany: State University of New York Press, 1982), xiii.

4. See Sylvia Keesmaat, *Paul and His Story: (Re)Interpreting the Exodus Tradition* (Sheffield: Sheffield Academic Press, 1999), esp. chap. 1.

5. On this see the refreshing and profound analysis of Paul M. van Buren, *A Theology of the Jewish-Christian Reality.* Part 1: *Discerning the Way* (San Francisco: Harper & Row, 1980), chaps. 6 and 7.

perspective. There is also no "view from nowhere."[6] There is only a view from a specific location and from within the limits of a specific perspective; "There is only a perspectival seeing, only a perspectival knowing," as Friedrich Nietzsche emphasized.[7] This specific and selective perspective cannot be neutral or innocent. Any perspective is entrenched in social, political, and personal interests and thus is centrist to some degree, even in its most honest attempts to do justice to all.[8] This means that we enter the dialogue of interpretation as embodied human beings, not as detached from the concrete world in which we live. The feminist philosopher Seyla Benhabib has thus declared:

> Understanding always means understanding within a framework that makes sense for us, from where we stand today. In this sense, learning the questions of the past involves posing questions to the past in the light of our present preoccupations. . . . Every interpretation is a conversation, with all the joys and dangers that conversations usually involve: misunderstandings as well as ellipses, innuendos as well as surfeits of meaning.[9]

These statements about presuppositions and conditions in the process of interpreting are indications of the sociopolitical situation in which interpretation takes place at the beginning of the twenty-first century. Since there is no generally agreed term for this situation, it is often subsumed under the term "postmodernism," indicating that the period of so-called modernity, dominated by objective positivism, has come to an end. As the Old Testament scholar Walter Brueggemann has expressed it, "The great new fact of interpretation is that we live in a pluralistic context, in which many different interpreters in many specific contexts representing many different interests are at work on textual (theological) interpretation."[10] The diversity of these different and differing readings cannot be subsumed into any kind of universal common assumption about a "truth behind the text."

---

6. On this see, e.g., Peter J. Tomson's excellent formulation: "The process of reading is more complicated than is often assumed. One always 'reads,' that is, understands a written text from a preconception of what one expects to find written there. . . . In other words, nobody reads without tradition or 'canon,' without an a priori understanding within which that which is read is situated. Reading is always interpreting." *"If This Be from Heaven . . ." : Jesus and the New Testament Authors in their Relationship to Judaism* (Sheffield: Sheffield Academic Press, 2001), 15–16. See also Susan Bordo, "Feminism, Postmodernism, and Gender-Scepticism," in *Feminism/Postmodernism* (ed. Linda Nicholson; New York: Routledge, 1990), 136.

7. Quoted in Bordo, "Feminism, Postmodernism, and Gender-Scepticism," 140.

8. Ibid., 140.

9. Benhabib, *The Reluctant Modernism of Hannah Arendt*, xxxiv.

10. Walter Brueggemann, *Theology of the Old Testament: Testimony, Dispute, Advocacy* (Minneapolis: Fortress, 1997), 62.

In the field of theological interpretation several approaches—mainly from
the margins of mainstream scholarship, such as feminism, poststructuralism,
and postcolonialism, as well as from a theology dealing with Auschwitz—
have contributed to the questioning of objective positivism, which granted
privilege to certain interpretive perspectives. These approaches convincingly
demonstrate the impossibility of neutral objectivity and thus show that, in
reality, any claim to an interest-free interpretation is an illusionary ideal.
"Interpretation . . . is an ongoing process of negotiation, adjudication, and
correction."[11] No approach therefore can claim to be "the right one" or "the
ultimate one." There can only be different, provisional, and possibly conflicting readings, for which the interpreter is ethically responsible. The purpose of this enterprise thus cannot be to achieve "assured results" but to come
to adequate conclusions that in themselves raise new questions asking for
new responses. This requires interpreters to remain engaged in an ongoing
and open adjudicating, dialogical process.

Some voices in contemporary theological discourses warn that different
perspectives are related to, and may influence, each other. With regard to
feminist hermeneutics, Elisabeth Schüssler Fiorenza has emphasized that
"feminist scholars are in danger of collaborating with the continuing patri-
kyriarchal silencing and marginalizing of feminist theoretical accomplish-
ments."[12] Being aware of such a warning, I nevertheless consider it of
primary importance for feminist as well as other theologians to be involved
in an open dialogue with other and differing strands of scholarly research.
Entering an open and mutual dialogue has nothing to do with submitting to
the domination of another perspective, even when this might be a main/
malestream perspective. Instead, it means simply recognizing that we can
develop neither feminist theology nor any other type of theology from within
an ivory tower, detached from others, nor can we adequately develop theology
only from within the boundaries of one separated interpretive community.

A dialogue is a process of mutual influencing that is supposed to be fruitful for all those involved in it. Research—particularly biblical interpretation
from whatever perspective—developed in isolation can do nothing but lead
to distortions and deprive itself of insights others have gained. This applies,
for example, to main/malestream theologians, who are still frequently ignoring the insights and ongoing processes of feminist theologies. But it applies
likewise to feminist theologians ignoring insights and ongoing processes in
post-Shoah theologies and Pauline studies.

---

11. Ibid., 63.
12. Elisabeth Schüssler Fiorenza, "Liberation: A Critical Feminist Perspective," in *Theology Digest*
46.4 (winter 1999): 335.

The purpose of this study is to engage in a dialogue between different strands of research, to relate interpretive insights from certain perspectives (the so-called New Perspective on Paul, and Beyond the New Perspective) to others (feminist perspectives on Paul). Insights gained in Pauline studies over the last thirty years have led to a paradigm shift via the New Perspective, to a perspective Beyond the New Perspective. From a different perspective, feminist theologies have provoked a paradigm shift on the methodological level generally, as well as in biblical studies in particular. Both these paradigm shifts indicate similar tendencies, though emerging from different perspectives. However, there is hardly any recognition of these similar trends across the boundaries of disciplines and interpretive communities, and thus these paradigm shifts cannot illuminate each other. This study is a contribution to such a dialogue that, if fully engaged in, could prove mutually beneficial.[13]

Hermeneutical Presuppositions: From Hegemony to Diversity

The philosophical program of rationalism, particularly identified with René Descartes and the Enlightenment, generally provides the theoretical framework for the scientific perception of the world of modernity. Rationalism has perceived the human being as the knower who by objective reason can achieve knowledge of truth. One has to keep in mind that this program— associated with reason, objectivity, autonomy, and positivism, and culminating in the work of Immanuel Kant and Georg Wilhelm Friedrich Hegel[14]—developed as a reaction against the domination of the churches' claims to truth. After the Reformation, people were confronted not only with one claimant to truth but by differing ones, which moreover resulted in the absurdity of a war that went on for thirty years, leaving most of Europe devastated. Descartes wrote during these years, seeking for ways out of such brutal nonsense.[15]

But despite the Enlightenment's liberationist point of departure, to free people from church domination, its project of rationality quickly developed into a new instrument of domination. Human reason was perceived as the one universal human essence, the common ground of sameness of all humankind, beyond particularity and differences. Hence, rationalists had to

---

13. E.g., Elisabeth Moltmann-Wendel, *A Land Flowing with Milk and Honey* (New York: Crossroad, 1986); Christa Mulack, *Jesus: der Gesalbte der Frauen. Weiblichkeit als Grundlage Christischer Ethik* (Stuttgart, 1987); Elsa Tamez, *The Amnesty of Grace: Justification by Faith from a Latin-American Perspective* (Nashville: Abingdon, 1993).

14. On the different stages of the development of the "discourse of modernity," see, e.g., Brueggemann, *Theology*, 6–15.

15. On this see, e.g., Sheila Greeve Davaney, *Pragmatic Historicism: A Theology for the Twenty-First Century* (Albany: State University of New York Press, 2000), 5f.

overcome or suppress any particularities and differences that did not conform to this ideal of humanity. The ideal of this rational human being had
close similarities to the white European man (bourgeois), leaving little room
for those who were different—women and Jews in particular, as well as people
from non-European cultures. It is not necessary here to discuss the implications of the Enlightenment in detail. Nevertheless, in the aftermath of the
Enlightenment, political imperialism and anti-Semitism seem to be more
than merely historical accidents.

In the wake of the Enlightenment, the enterprise of interpretation developed the critical approach, which dealt with the biblical text not as privileged
by tradition or church authority. Criticism had great confidence in objective,
detached scholarship: human rationality was the lawcourt to which any
interpretation had to adjust. This ideal of scholarly objectivity supposedly
left the interpreter personally uninvolved in the process of interpretation.

Amid the critical assumptions of modernity, one could sustain theological claims only by adjusting theology and the enterprise of interpretation to
the academic institution's standards of critical scholarship. According to
Brueggemann, these were committed to

> (a) historicism that could determine "what happened," for there could be no
> meaning beyond "what happened"; (b) evolutionism, so that religious devel-
> opment occurred in a straight line of unilateral progress from the primitive to
> the sophisticated; and (c) a rationalism that felt a need to explain away much
> of the contradiction that violated "reasonableness" or that made claims
> beyond a naturalistic, scientifically available world.[16]

In Brueggemann's view, it was through the combination of triumphalist
Christendom with critical positivism that "a pattern of hegemonic interpretation" was established.[17]

Hans-Georg Gadamer's *Wahrheit und Methode* (1960) is regarded as a
watershed between such traditional objectivist perceptions of interpretation
and the growing awareness of the complexity of interpreting processes.[18]
Anthony C. Thiselton describes this shift:

> Traditionally, hermeneutics entailed the formulation of rules for the under-
> standing of an ancient text, especially in linguistic and historical terms. The

---

16. Brueggemann, *Theology*, 708.
17. Ibid., 709.
18. Hans-Georg Gadamer, *Truth and Method* (rev. trans. Joel Weinsheimer and Donald G. Marshall;
2d, rev. ed.; New York: Crossroad, 1989); first published as *Wahrheit und Methode* (Tübingen: Mohr,
1960).

interpreter was urged to begin with the language of the text, including its grammar, vocabulary, and style. He examined its linguistic, literary, and historical context. In other words, traditional hermeneutics began with the recognition that a text was conditioned by a given historical context. However, hermeneutics in the more recent sense of the term begins with the recognition that historical conditioning is two-sided if not even multifaceted: the modern interpreter, no less than the text, stands in a given historical context and tradition.[19]

Preceding Gadamer's work, however, were earlier fundamental critiques of traditional Western discourse by philosophers such as Walter Benjamin, Max Horkheimer, and Theodor Adorno.[20] As early as 1914, Benjamin criticized the idea of evolutionism as well as the notion to reconstruct "what happened" from an objectivist position of detached scholarship. Instead, he emphasized that history is always reconstructed, and the reconstruction is thus dependent on the position of the scholar in the present.[21] Whether and to what extent the most prominent representatives of the Frankfurter school, Horkheimer and Adorno,[22] were influenced by Benjamin is a matter of debate. Nevertheless, in their *Dialectic of Enlightenment,* the two developed an analysis of the perception of history and culture that anticipated postmodern approaches in several ways. They stated that the dominant discourse of rationality had turned into its opposite by producing new rationalized forms of domination to the extent of becoming totalitarian: it eliminated other patterns of thinking and claimed to be the only path to truth and validity.[23]

Since Walter Benjamin and many members of the Frankfurter school were Jews, these critiques of the Enlightenment discourse in Germany emerged at

---

19. Anthony C. Thiselton, *The Two Horizons: New Testament Hermeneutics and Philosophical Description with Special Reference to Heidegger, Bultmann, Gadamer, and Wittgenstein* (Grand Rapids: Eerdmans), 1980), 11.

20. Naming these philosophers does not provide a definitive list of early critics of the discourse of modernity and positivist historicism; one could mention many more "masters of suspicion." See Paul Ricoeur, *Freud and Philosophy: An Essay in Interpretation* (trans. Denis Savage; New Haven: Yale University, Press 1970), 32–36.

21. On this see Stéphane Mosès, *Der Engel der Geschichte: Franz Rosenzweig, Walter Benjamin, Gerschom Scholem* (Frankfurt: Jüdischer Geschichte, 1994), 87ff.; translation of *L'ange de l'histoire: Rosenzweig, Benjamin, Scholem* (Paris: Editions du Seuil, 1992).

22. It is noticeable that already in 1931 Adorno had developed a radical critique of traditional philosophy: "Whoever chooses philosophy as a profession today must first reject the illusion that earlier philosophical enterprises began with [the belief] 'that the power of thought is sufficient to grasp the totality of the real.'" Adorno goes on to state that all "ontological blueprints" and any attempt to conceptualize the totality of being are illusions. "True being," according to Adorno, only appears in traces and ruins (Theodor Adorno, "The Actuality of Philosophy," *Telos* 31 [spring 1977]: 120–33, quote from 120.)

23. See Steven Best and Douglas Kellner, *Postmodern Theory: Critical Interrogations* (London: Macmillan, 1991), 217ff.; Max Horkheimer and Theodor W. Adorno, *Dialectic of Enlightenment* (trans. John Cumming; New York: Herder & Herder, 1972), translation of *Dialektik der Aufklärung*, originally published as *Philosophische Fragmente* (Amsterdam: Querido, 1944).

the margins of the dominant culture of the West. Furthermore, the totalitarian regime of the Nazis came to power in Germany and played a significant role in Horkheimer and Adorno's critique of the dominant discourse.

There were other critical approaches that paved the way to what now is generally termed "postmodern" thinking.[24] Beginning with the late 1960s, however, a series of new philosophical approaches evolved, particularly in France, which queried the traditional claim of objectivity in the process of scholarly research and knowledge.[25] Yet it was only near the end of the twentieth century that Brueggemann could say, "Dissidence and hegemony have become so deep and so broad as to challenge the hegemony [of the Enlightenment discourse] in serious and effective ways."[26]

Feminist theory as well as feminist theology played a significant role in the emergence of postmodern approaches.[27] For our purpose, it is significant to note that these approaches oppose any kind of closure in totalizing, centralized theories and systems. Such systems require as their foundation a secure knowledge of truth. The new approaches regard any claim to obtain or have unmediated access to "true reality" as illusionary: truth and meaning can only be produced in "a never-ending process of signification . . . within the infinite, intertextual play of signifiers."[28]

Postmodern approaches have implications for biblical interpretation, especially for exegesis as a hermeneutical process, since it is about understanding a text. As for any scholars, there is no absolute objective viewpoint for exegetes. Even in science the "new physics" questions the validity of the subject-object dichotomy and recognizes that "the conductor of an experiment is not a purely independent observer, but an active participant whose input directly influences the experiment's result."[29] One can hardly find a solitary true or original meaning of a literary text.[30] Though this seems to be

---

24. There is no room in this study to deal with these here in detail, but see Best and Kellner, *Postmodern Theory,* 3–33, the introduction.

25. With utmost caution, one might compare the "breach of civilization" that the events of the Shoah eventually caused for many European intellectuals, with the damage the Vietnam War caused to the confidence in the dominant discourse and the legitimacy of established institutions in the United States. See Brueggemann, *Theology,* 709 n. 8.

26. Ibid., 709.

27. See my more detailed outline in chapters 2 and 3; cf. Davaney, *Pragmatic Historicism,* 17–18: "Thus while many liberation, African American and feminist theologians proclaimed their distance from the dominant modes of theologizing, they nonetheless altered the entire theological scene in profound ways. For they introduce, in a manner previously unheard of in theology, the issue of power and how it was deployed throughout religious worldviews and theological symbol systems. The seeming innocence of theology, for everyone, was over."

28. Best and Kellner, *Postmodern Theory,* 21.

29. David Rutledge, *Reading Marginally: Feminism, Deconstruction, and the Bible* (Leiden: Brill 1996), 46.

30. Wendy Dabourne explained: "The basic exegetical tool is the question, What does this text mean? It is shattering to realize that exegetical experiment and hermeneutical study over several decades have broken it. The concept 'the meaning of the text' has been relativized. Is it the meaning of what the writer intended to say? Does meaning inhere in the structures of a text itself, independently of the writer's

a rather pessimistic statement, I do not mean it to be so. All those techniques of interpretation that have been developed in the aftermath of the Enlightenment—such as the historical-critical, sociological, linguistic, literary-critical methods—are useful and necessary tools to help us come to understandings of biblical texts as adequately and as historically responsible as possible. They might help the interpreter to come to well-based arguments to support an interpretation that has its basis in the text and in its historical context and is not mere fantasy. But none of these valuable tools will reveal to us the "true meaning" of Scripture generally and of Paul's letters in particular.

These tools, nevertheless, are used by human beings, bringing with them their own presuppositions and their specific context, which inevitably influence the process of interpretation. Thus the statement that we cannot find the "true meaning" of a literary text is not meant to lead to the conclusion that it makes no sense at all to try to understand such a text, especially a text of our religious tradition. As far as is possible, however, we should become aware of the presuppositions that influence our own interpretations. We therefore must recognize that every interpretation is contextual and driven by certain specific interests.[31] Moreover, recognizing the limits of any particular interpretation implies the recognition that there are different and differing interpretations of the same texts, and that any one interpretation can only be provisional and has to remain open to questions and adjudication.

Thus interpretation always is a dialogical process: "The practice of understanding proceeds as it does and will, as dialogue."[32] It is also in a concrete context that includes the personal situation of the interpreter,[33] never merely in an academic ivory tower. People entering a dialogue enter into relationships. Relating to each other means influencing each other. This applies to relationships generally and for interpretation as a dialogical process in particular. Entering this process means influencing and being influenced by others, altering and being altered by others. Interpretation understood in such a way thus also implies being in, and remaining involved in, a conflictual conversation about different adequate conclusions. Conflict belongs to the core of the enterprise of interpretation in a pluralistic context.

---

intention? Does meaning arise in the encounter between text and reader? . . . A text is a series of conventional marks on a sufficiently smooth surface. All our language about meaning is metaphor. In reading a text in general we conceive the meaning in different ways, depending on the nature of the text and what we want to do with it." In *Purpose and Cause in Pauline Exegesis: Romans 1.16–4.25 and a New Approach to the Letters* (SNTS Monograph Series 104; Cambridge: Cambridge University Press, 1999), 4.

31. On this see Craig A Evans, James A. Sanders, eds., *The Function of Scripture in Early Jewish and Christian Tradition* (Sheffield: Sheffield Academic Press, 1998), 15: "A tradent of necessity is limited to the terms of the culture, no matter how 'advanced' or refined, in which the tradent and his community live."

32. R. Barry Matlock, *Unveiling the Apocalyptic Paul: Paul's Interpreters and the Rhetoric of Criticism* (Sheffield: Sheffield Academic Press, 1996), 337.

33. On this aspect in the process of biblical interpretation, see the excellent volume of essays from Ingrid Rosa Kitzberger, ed., *The Personal Voice in Biblical Interpretation* (London: Routledge, 1999).

Moreover, ethical responsibility for the practical implications of any one interpretation is of vital significance in this process of interpretation, for the individual as well as for the community and the society.[34] This has not been recognized in the course of history, and in addition negative implications were also accepted and justified as inevitable to the extent that they were in accordance with God's will. There is a long history of negative results from specific biblical interpretations. Since political imperial power often reinforced and supported these negative effects, they frequently caused incredible suffering for innumerable people. Jews and women are among those most prominently wronged.

To a vast extent in Western culture, Christians and Jews have generally determined the history of interpretation by each group maintaining different interpretations of Scriptures. This history includes numerous debates about "the proper" interpretation of the text. Christianity claimed to have found "the proper and final true understanding" of Scriptures: it claimed to possess truth in an absolute way, a claim that has had tragic consequences, especially for the Jewish people.[35]

In universalizing its particular interpretation, triumphalist Christendom did not allow for any differing notion alongside its own. Moreover, the continuing existence of the Jewish people was a constant threat to any such claims and could not be tolerated. Thus, almost from its beginnings, Christianity formulated its own identity through using Judaism and Jews as a negative foil. Christians could not come to terms with the fact that there was a group of people who related to the same tradition of Scriptures as they themselves did, but who adhered to a different interpretation of them and therefore claimed legitimacy for their different lifestyle and distinctiveness generally. Christian tradition was unable to find another way to cope with this difference than through teaching contempt for these others who wanted to remain different in keeping their distinct identity as Jews. For centuries Christians used hegemonic claims for their interpretation to teach contempt against Jews, thus preparing the ground for the rise of political and racist anti-Semitism in the nineteenth century, which as a consequence led to the Shoah in the twentieth century.

After the Shoah the question is whether or not we can define Christian identity without anti-Judaism, whether or not Christians can interpret

---

34. See Elisabeth Schüssler Fiorenza, "The Ethics of Interpretation: De-Centering Biblical Scholarship," *Journal of Biblical Literature* 107 (1988): 3–17; also David Tracy, *Plurality and Ambiguity: Hermeneutics, Religion, Hope* (San Francisco: Harper & Row, 1987), 36–37: "There is no such thing as an unambiguous tradition; there is no innocent reading of the classics."

35. On this see William S. Campbell, "Millennial Optimism for Jewish-Christian Dialogue," in *The Future of Jewish-Christian Dialogue* (ed. Dan Cohn-Sherbok; Lampeter, U.K.: Mellen, 1999): 215–37.

Scriptures without absolute claims and teaching contempt against Jews. It is actually the question of whether or not anti-Judaism is inherent in Christianity: Is it possible, from a Christian perspective, to accept that alongside the Christian interpretation there has been and is a different and Jewish interpretation of Scriptures? Can the acceptance of diversity in a pluralistic context be a Christian option?

In her book *Faith and Fratricide: The Theological Roots of Anti-Semitism*, Rosemary Radford Ruether has strongly argued for a perception of Christendom in which anti-Judaism is an inherent and essential part.[36] Accepting her argument would mean that hegemonic claims were and are inherently and essentially Christian. Whether or not other scholars agreed with her analysis and the conclusions she drew from them, a number of them from the 1970s onward became more and more aware of the connections between the Christian teaching of contempt for Jews and anti-Jewish interpretations of Scripture. These scholars had committed themselves to dialogue with Jews, realizing that theology and interpretation after Auschwitz could never be the same as it had been before. One of its leading representatives in Germany, Roman-Catholic scholar Johann Baptist Metz, wrote: "As Christians, we can never get behind Auschwitz; but considered properly we can never get beyond Auschwitz just by ourselves, but only together with the victims of Auschwitz."[37] What Walter Brueggemann wrote with regard to Old Testament theology is valid for Christian theology as such:

> One must avoid trivializing the Holocaust by "taking a lesson" from it. Nonetheless a crucial learning . . . is a sharp measure of suspicion toward, or even resistance to, the triumphalist story of faith that is too easily recited on the basis of the Bible. Any triumph is made thin by this event, and every triumph is made unstable by this reality. . . . We do not yet know how to do even disruptive interpretation in light of this break, but whatever we are now able to do is profoundly and irreversibly qualified by this break.[38]

This strand of research has insistently emphasized that something had to change radically in Jewish-Christian relations after World War II.

---

36. Rosemary Radford Ruether, *Faith and Fratricide: The Theological Roots of Anti-Semitism* (New York: Seabury, 1979), 226.

37. Johann Baptist Metz, "Kirche nach Auschwitz," in *Israel und Kirche heute: Beiträge zum christlich-jüdischen Dialog: Für Ernst Ludwig Ehrlich* (ed. Marcel Marcus, Ekkehard W. Stegemann, and Erich Zenger; Freiburg: Herder, 1991), 112: "Wir Christen kommen niemals mehr hinter Auschwitz zurück; über Auschwitz hinaus aber kommen wir, genau besehen, nicht mehr allein, sondern nur noch mit den Opfern von Auschwitz."

38. Brueggemann, *Theology*, 329.

Hermeneutical Consequences from Post-Shoah Theology

Scholarship and the enterprise of biblical interpretation in particular are contextual, "conducted by real people who are concretely located in the historical process."[39] Therefore, we cannot ignore the fact that this enterprise is undertaken in a post-Shoah situation. Since theological supersessionism and practical Christian teaching of contempt for Jews contributed to the emergence of political anti-Semitism and its unthinkably brutal realization in the Third Reich, Christian theology has lost its innocence and cannot go on doing business as usual.

Although the Shoah was not the sole impetus, it certainly was the decisive event that made Christians aware of the urgency of radical changes in their teaching and preaching vis-à-vis Judaism. It has been a courageous step for Jewish participants to enter into dialogue with Christians during and immediately after World War II. Small groups began to meet regularly, convinced that only through serious dialogue as equal partners, and without any hidden missionary agenda on the Christian side, could they take steps to overcome anti-Judaism in church and theology. In the beginnings of dialogue the main issue was to get to know and understand each other as different but equal religions. Later the Christian partners in dialogue began to realize how deeply Christianity was entrenched in stereotyped views of Judaism and the teaching of contempt. Research by both Christian and Jewish scholars led people to have increasing awareness and recognition of the Jewishness of Jesus.

There is a still ongoing debate about the "rehabilitation of Paul in Judaism"[40] and more generally about the reformulation of Christian identity without any kind of anti-Judaism. This agenda has developed over the last fifty years of dialogue. It is surprising that it was only from the mid-1960s that Christians, and then mainly those at the margins rather than in mainstream theology, began to realize that theology after Auschwitz can never be the same as it had been before.[41] Johann Baptist Metz has stated: "No longer

---

39. Ibid., 734.

40. On this see W. S. Campbell, "Millennial Optimism," 217–37; Stefan Meissner, *Die Heimholung des Ketzers: Studien zur jüdischen Auseinandersetzung mit Paulus* (Tübingen: Mohr, 1996).

41. Rolf Rendtorff, "Nach Auschwitz," *Kirche und Israel: Neukirchener theologische Zeitschrift* 10 (1995): 7: "As the Christian perception of Judaism has led to Auschwitz and as this perception of Judaism has been a basic part of Christian self-understanding (and still is), Christian identity has to be reformulated, 'after Auschwitz.' It has taken almost fifty years until some Christians have come to this insight, or rather, have been urged to it." This is my translation of the German: "Weil die christliche Sicht des Judentums nach Auschwitz geführt hat, und weil diese Sicht des Judentums bisher ein grundlegender Bestandteil des christlichen Selbstverständnisses gewesen ist (und weitgehend noch ist), muss die christliche Identität 'nach Auschwitz' neu formuliert werden. Es hat fast fünfzig Jahre gedauert, bis einige Christen zu dieser Einsicht vorgedrungen—oder besser gedrängt worden sind." On this see also Rolf Rendtorff and Ekkehard Stegemann, eds., *Auschwitz—Krise der christlichen Theologie* (Munich: Chr. Kaiser, 1980), 178.

[is it possible] to pursue any theology that is so conceived that it remains untouched by Auschwitz or could remain untouched by it."[42]

Although these insights are gained in the encounter between Christians and Jews, they are by no means limited to this encounter or to a theology specific to this encounter. As Christianity and Judaism share a long and often closely intertwined history, Christian theology cannot avoid reflecting on this relationship in order to find and formulate its own identity.[43] Over the centuries theologians have done this by formulating a stance over against Judaism. This anti-Judaism permeates all areas of Christian theology as well as biblical studies. Peter von der Osten-Sacken goes as far as to say:

> In this sense Christian theology can fundamentally *only* be theology in Christian-Jewish dialogue. . . . The Jewish-Christian encounter (as the *Sitz im Leben* under discussion), whether it takes place directly or indirectly, will therefore continue for a long time to have a primarily heuristic function, the function to help Christians undergo the undoubtedly wearisome and lengthy transformation of theology, proclamation, and instruction in its present largely anti-Jewish form.[44]

In this process the interpretation of biblical texts plays a crucial role as both religious traditions rely basically on written texts to formulate their identity. In the process of the parting of the ways, the church, according to its own perception, had replaced Israel as the people of God. Thus Christians claimed to be the sole inheritors of Scripture, which in the early church meant the Hebrew Bible in its Greek translation, the Septuagint.[45] They regarded their own interpretation of Scripture as the true and only true one, which meant that supersessionism and triumphalism from then on served as main hermeneutical guidelines for understanding the sacred texts. In this view there could not be any future for a different (Jewish) interpretation of Scripture after the coming of Christ; there was actually no reason for Judaism to exist after the coming of Christ.

---

42. Quoted in Peter von der Osten-Sacken, *Christian-Jewish Dialogue: Theological Foundations* (Philadelphia: Fortress, 1986), 6.

43. On this see Daniel Boyarin and Judith Lieu. For the period up to the fourth century, they both argue for a much more closely related history of what later became two separate religions. See Daniel Boyarin, *Dying for God: Martyrdom and the Making of Christianity and Judaism* (Lancaster/Yarnton Lectures in Judaism and Other Religions; Stanford: Stanford University Press, 1999); Judith M. Lieu, "'Impregnable Ramparts and Walls of Iron,' Boundary and Identity in Early 'Judaism' and 'Christianity,'" main conference paper read at the 56th Annual General Meeting of Society for New Testament Studies, Montreal, Aug. 2001, published in *New Testament Studies* 48.3 (July 2002): 297–313.

44. On this see Osten-Sacken, *Christian-Jewish Dialogue,* 16.

45. See Justin Martyr, *Dialogue with Trypho,* quoted by van Buren, *According to the Scriptures: The Origins of the Church's Old Testament* (Grand Rapids: Eerdmans, 1998), 150–51.

As Christian tradition formulated its self-understanding, it was influenced particularly by Graeco-Roman interpretations of the Platonic-Aristotelian tradition. To a vast extent it developed a pattern of thinking in dichotomies, a dualistic mentality that constructed a far from innocent hierarchy of values—such as subject-object, appearance-reality, reason-nature, men-women—thus excluding and devaluing the inferior terms of the dichotomies. Christianity set up dichotomies such as old/new, letter/spirit, law/gospel, God of wrath/God of love, judgment/promise, particularistic/universal, Judaism/Christianity—in each pair regarding the first term as inferior and identified with Judaism, and the second term as higher and referring to Christianity. Through such patterns, which were also at work in interpretation, the teaching of contempt for Judaism became widespread. Later theological developments added to this early anti-Jewish pattern of interpretation by reading into biblical texts more of their own contemporary debates. Through Bible studies and interpreting Romans, Luther found his basic doctrine of righteousness of faith over against works. This was mainly influenced by his criticism of the Roman Catholic church, in which he put Jews and Roman Catholics into the same devalued categories.[46]

The interpretation of Scriptures is a crucial issue that we must address in the process of reformulating Christian identity without anti-Judaism. Theologies grappling with Auschwitz have developed several general hermeneutical rules as guidelines for looking afresh to our biblical heritage, to find meaning and guidance for contemporary problems of everyday life as well as world politics:

1. Christians should never again forget that the Scriptures first and above all were and still are the Scriptures of the Jewish people.[47] As Christians, we share the Jewish Bible, the "Tanach," in the form of the First or Old Testament of our Scriptures, with the Jews. As Brueggemann has put it, "Christians are able to say of the Old Testament, 'It is ours,' but must also say, 'It is not ours alone.'"[48]

2. In the church any form of displacement theory concerning Israel, or the Jewish people, has to be abandoned. The church and its scholars have to realize that there is and always has been an ongoing history of Israel and the Jewish people up to the present: they have been and are contemporaries of the Christians.[49]

3. Recognizing this implies that there is not only one way to interpret Scriptures, but several and differing ones. The Jewish people had and have their own distinctive way of interpreting Scriptures. Christians need to appreciate

---

46. On this see W. S. Campbell, "Martin Luther and Paul's Epistle to the Romans," in *The Bible as Book: The Reformation* (ed. Orlaith O'Sullivan; London: British Library, 2000), 103–14.

47. On this see van Buren, *A Theology*, part 1: *Discerning the Way*, 120–46.

48. Brueggemann, *Theology*, 735.

49. See also van Buren, *Discerning the Way*, 141.

this situation and to listen to this other voice of interpretation. As early as 1958 the German theologian Helmut Gollwitzer formulated a key principle: "If it is impossible to understand the New Testament without the Old, then it is impossible to understand the Bible as a whole without a discussion with the Jews. What arrogance for Christians to believe that [Jews] have nothing to say to us!"[50] Brueggemann also asserts: "Jewish imaginative construal of the text is a legitimate theological activity, to which Christians must pay attention."[51]

4. Since over the centuries the church has used Scripture and its interpretation to teach contempt toward the Jews, Christians are obliged to investigate all of this tradition for elements of anti-Judaism in order to prevent any further bias resulting from them.

According to these main guidelines, theologians have to reinterpret the New Testament writings as well as the First Testament. This implies that Christians have to seek to formulate their identity in a new and different way without using Judaism as a negative foil. The change of perspective required is *radical* in the real sense of the word: it affects the roots of Christian identity.

Just as in the aftermath of the Shoah the anti-Judaism in Christian theologies and traditions became a serious issue, feminist research has made us aware of the misogynist tendencies in Christian theologies and traditions. This led to the emergence of new perspectives in both disciplines. But since these two strands of research have seldom related their work to each other, the history of their interaction has been rather complicated and conflictual.

This need not necessarily be so. Although the shifts in perspectives are not identical, they show similarities in that they both emphasize the need to move beyond dominating and oppressive patterns of interpretation.

Feminist Hermeneutics and the Feminist Debate on Anti-Judaism

By the end of the nineteenth century Elizabeth Cady Stanton with a group of women started developing *The Woman's Bible*.[52] This project arose from the insight that society had used the biblical tradition to legitimate the supposed

---

50. Helmut Gollwitzer, *Israel—und wir* (Berlin: Lettner, 1958), 23.

51. Brueggemann, *Theology,* 735; he goes on to state: "I have no doubt that Christian supersessionism, enforced as it is by classical modes of Hellenistic thought, has made it nearly impossible for Christians to attend to the riches of Judaism. Once [we have] recognized that theological construal and imagination other than our own is legitimate, however, we may take it into serious account. I do not imagine that attention to this primal alternative construal of the text will lead to an abrupt overthrow of distinctive Christian claims. But I also do not imagine that such attention would leave Christian claims untouched, certainly not untouched in their fearful, destructive aspects, but perhaps also not untouched in good-faith exclusivism, rooted in a text that remains elusive as its Subject and that relentlessly resists closure."

52. Elizabeth Cady Stanton et al., *The Woman's Bible* (2 vols.; New York: European Publishing Co., 1895–98; reprint, Boston: Northeastern University Press, 1993).

inferior status of women and oppression against them. Cady Stanton and her coauthors thus eliminated texts they regarded as biased against women and created a new canon suitable for women. Thus, when Elisabeth Schüssler Fiorenza introduced her mold-breaking method of "feminist critical hermeneutics of suspicion" in her *Bread Not Stone: The Challenge of Feminist Biblical Interpretation* (1984), she did so as part of an already-exisiting feminist hermeneutical tradition.

Different strands of religious feminism have emerged over the last thirty years: some feminists moved beyond Christianity, perceiving it as hopelessly patriarchal; some of them found enough liberationist potential in this tradition to render it worthwhile to remain within it.[53] In any case, many women assert with Ursula King, "Feminism is about a different consciousness and a vision, a radically changed perspective."[54]

To a significant extent feminism as well as feminist theology in particular have contributed to the hermeneutical shift from hegemony to diversity, as outlined above. Feminist theologians have demonstrated that the "objective" human perspective in research has almost exclusively been the perspective of white European men; therefore, in no way could it be regarded as universal. It is as particular as any other perspective. In its first stage, feminism generally, as well as feminist theology in particular, has emphasized that scholarly research, as any other human activity, is based on experience. Since human beings exist in the mode of male and female, gender is thus one crucial aspect that shapes human experience.[55] Feminist theology was born out of the struggle to overcome the oppression and subordination of women. It is rooted in visions of equality, justice, and liberation, and its intention is to do theology from a completely new and critical perspective, questioning especially the tendencies of universalization, hierarchical dualisms, and idealized abstractions.[56]

---

53. For an overview see, e.g., Luise Schottroff, Silvia Schroer, and Marie-Theres Wacker, *Feminist Interpretation: The Bible in Women's Perspective* (trans. Barbara and Martin Rumscheidt; Minneapolis: Fortress, 1998); ET of *Feministische Exegese: Forschungsbeiträge zur Bibel aus der Perspektive von Frauen* (Darmstadt: Wissenschaftliche Buchgesellschaft, 1995). Cf. also Adela Yarbro Collins, ed., *Feminist Perspectives on Biblical Scholarship* (Atlanta: Scholars Press, 1985).

54. Ursula King, *Woman and Spirituality: Voices of Protest and Promise* (London: Macmillan Education, 1989), 15.

55. I am aware of the ongoing debate in feminist theory about the question of body and gender. I cannot add to that debate, but Adriana Cavarero's theory of human beings as two, created in God's image as male and female, is most convincing to me. In this definition nothing is said yet about what male and female means; Cavarero does not go back to traditional or biologically based definitions. She says that what it means to be female is still to be discovered, since traditional definitions have been definitions by men. So what it means to say that human beings are twin ("der Mensch ist zwei") is what still is to be discovered, the not yet of feminist theory. See Adrianna Cavarero, "Der Mensch ist zwei," in *Der Mensch ist zwei: Das Denken der Geschlechterdifferenz* (ed. Diotima, Philosophinnengruppe aus Verona; Vienna: Wiener Frauenverlag, 1989).

56. On this see Ursula King, "Feminist Theologies in Contemporary Contexts," in *Is There a Future for Feminist Theology?* (ed. Deborah F. Sawyer and Diane M. Collier; Sheffield: Sheffield Academic Press, 1999), 100–114.

This "first-stage feminism"[57] assumed that there is a common and universal character to women's experience, based on what is assumed to be the essence of femininity. In fact, however, first-stage feminist theology as such was based on the theoretical framework of modernity, with its belief in a coherent self, which by means of objective rationality could explain the structure of existence. Rebecca S. Chopp thus emphasized: "In this stage, both feminist theory and feminist theology simply extended and stretched the modern frame to make it more equitable in its inclusion of women."[58]

From within this general context, Elisabeth Schüssler Fiorenza has developed the "feminist hermeneutics of suspicion."[59] She looked at biblical texts with critical eyes, questioning traditional interpretations in the light of women's experience, which has meant and often still means enduring contempt and oppression. Based on the insight that biblical texts are inherently patriarchal/kyriarchal, Schüssler Fiorenza developed methods to uncover the hidden history and voices of women in these texts.

Schüssler Fiorenza and other feminist theologians following her approach have stressed that the processes of writing and of canonization were male dominated, produced from a patriarchal perception of the world and of religious tradition. The fact that these texts hardly mention women and hardly reflect women's experience is not proof that "there were no women present." The hermeneutics of suspicion was the method applied to uncover the hidden and silenced history of women in these patriarchal/kyriarchal texts. Feminist scholars began to look for the impact of silencing on women in terms of history: Where are women's lives in biblical texts? Likewise, how did silencing impact women's thinking? Where are women's thoughts and expressions of faith in Scripture? After the beginnings of feminist theology and feminist hermeneutics, scholars did substantial research in the early 1970s. Feminist theologians have reformulated the main theological issues from a feminist perspective in order to develop a theology that would support the liberation of women. The feminist quest, taken seriously, requires as deep a shift in theological thinking as does the quest to eradicate anti-Judaism.[60]

---

57. This term comes from Rebecca S. Chopp, "Theorizing Feminist Theology," in *Horizons in Feminist Theology: Identity, Traditions and Norms* (ed. Rebecca S. Chopp and Sheila Greeve Davaney; Minneapolis: Fortress, 1997), 216–17.

58. Ibid., 217.

59. As mentioned above, the fundamental theory was formulated by Elisabeth Schüssler Fiorenza: see *In Memory of Her: A Feminist Theological Construction of Christian Origins* (New York: Crossroad, 1983); and *Bread Not Stone: The Challenge of Feminist Biblical Interpretation* (Boston: Beacon, 1984).

60. Cf. also Elisabeth Schüssler Fiorenza, in *The Power of Naming: A Concilium Reader in Feminist Liberation Theology* (ed. Elisabeth Schüssler Fiorenza; London: SCM, 1996), xxix: "Feminist theological studies in particular underscore both that wo/men must be recognized as theological subjects and that the practices and institutions of theology must be changed. They want to engender a paradigm shift . . . from malestream scholarship produced by kyriarchal academic institutions, to feminist comprehension of the world, human life, and Christian faith. Such a paradigm shift would not only produce different emancipatory knowledges but also a different kind of theology."

Despite the undoubted merits of the earlier feminist theological approaches, feminists from different perspectives, especially from different cultural backgrounds, have questioned some of the basic presuppositions implicit within them. They asked whether the notion of an essential, universal nature of women, as well as the category of experience as the root of women's thinking, was not in fact a universalization of white middle-class women's nature and experience. These critics pointed out that the thinking and theologizing of women from different backgrounds living in different cultures are shaped by experiences that might differ radically from those of white middle-class women living in the Western world. In such experiences, women could find racism, anti-Semitism, and other prejudices to be as threatening as sexism.[61] The perception and rethinking of diversity and difference became an issue in feminist theology.

At the end of the 1970s, in the context of such critical negotiations about more differentiation in feminist theology, Jewish feminists made Christian feminist theologians cognizant of the inherent anti-Judaism in most current feminist theological concepts. Nevertheless, until the late 1980s there was hardly any dialogue between those involved in the reformulation of Christian theology from a feminist perspective and those involved in the project of reformulating Christian theology to avoid anti-Judaism. Where there is no dialogue, there is no exchange of knowledge; thus, feminist theologians often unconsciously based their research on traditional theological patterns of interpretation that were inherently anti-Jewish. In formulating liberation theology for women, they repeated anti-Jewish stereotypes and continued teaching contempt for Jews.[62] Jewish feminists Judith Plaskow and Susannah Heschel first made Christian feminists aware of the trap they had fallen into.[63]

In her article "Blaming the Jews for the Birth of Patriarchy," Plaskow showed that in order to find an image of Jesus and Christian origins that is liberating for women, feminist theologians had used Judaism as a negative foil. They depicted it as the religion that had imposed and maintained patriarchal dominion over women. Christian feminist theologians had just added "a new slant to the old theme of Christian superiority."[64] Following these pioneering articles by Plaskow and Heschel, there has been an intensive debate

---

61. See Katharina von Kellenbach, *Anti-Judaism in Feminist Religious Writings* (Atlanta: Scholars Press, 1994), 17; Doris Strahm, *Vom Rand in die Mitte: Christologie aus der Sicht von Frauen in Asien, Afrika und Lateinamerika* (Lucerne: Edition Exodus, 1997), 24–56.

62. Kellenbach gives an excellent and detailed analysis of this debate in *Anti-Judaism*.

63. Judith Plaskow, "Blaming the Jews for the Birth of Patriarchy," in *Nice Jewish Girls* (ed. Evelyn T. Beck; Watertown, Mass.: Persephone, 1982), 250–54; Susannah Heschel, "Jüdisch-feministische Theologie und Antijudaismus in christlich-feministischer Theologie," in *Verdrängte Vergangenheit, die uns bedrängt* (ed. Leonore Siegele-Wenschkewitz; Munich: Chr. Kaiser, 1988), 54–103; ET, "Anti-Judaism in Christian Feminist Theology," *Tikkun* 5.3 (1990): 25–28, 95–97.

64. Plaskow, "Blaming the Jews," 250.

about these crucial issues, first in the United States and then, from the second half of the 1980s, also in Germany.[65]

Although the issues debated were identical, the debates themselves were not. The fact that the context was quite different played a significant role: in the United States there is a "vibrant Jewish feminist community and feminist organizations where Jews and non-Jews collaborate."[66] In Germany, however, the Jewish-Christian dialogue and the debate about anti-Judaism in particular are often carried on without Jewish participants. This is the legacy of the Shoah, which left Germany practically *judenrein* (cleared of Jews). This legacy is a far more significant feature in central Europe than in other parts of the world, and it renders it exceedingly difficult to point to anti-Judaism and anti-Semitism without provoking intensive emotional denial.[67]

In the United States, in response to Plaskow and Heschel's critique, Christian feminist scholars such as Bernadette Brooten, Ross Kraemer, and Elisabeth Schüssler Fiorenza began to focus on the problem of anti-Judaism in feminist theology. Wide-ranging historical research on Jewish, Christian, and pagan women's lives of the Second Temple Period became an important aspect of feminist research, in order to reformulate the image of the Jesus movement, to see it not so much in opposition to Judaism but rather as an "alternative option."[68] Christian feminists also became aware of the growing volume of research done by Jewish feminists on women's lives, and more aware of Jewish research generally.

In Germany, the feminism and anti-Judaism debate has taken longer to bear fruit in academic research. This is partly due to the fact that it is exceedingly difficult for feminist scholars to obtain appointments to ordinary academic lectureships. Feminist theologians are in a position that renders them vulnerable. Therefore, the critique from Jewish feminists as well as from scholars involved in Jewish-Christian dialogue, at least during the initial period, could hardly be seen as a full-fledged and constructive critique. It was rather perceived as questioning feminist theology as such. Nevertheless, in

---

65. See *Schlangenbrut* 16–18 (1987); *Kirche und Israel: Neukirchener theologische Zeitschrift* 5.1–2 (1990); and *Journal for the Feminist Study of Religion,* especially 7.2 (1991). Kellenbach, *Anti-Judaism,* 28–36.

66. Kellenbach, *Anti-Judaism,* 32.

67. This became obvious in the different debate on Jewish gold in the Swiss banks; see Pierre Weill, *Der Milliarden-Deal* (Zurich: Weltwoche ABC, 1999).

68. See Bernadette J. Brooten, *Women Leaders in the Ancient Synagogue: Inscriptional Evidence and Background Issues* (Chico, Calif.: Scholars Press, 1982); idem, "Jewish Women's History in the Roman Period: A Task for Christian Theology," in *Christians among Jews and Gentiles: Essays in Honor of Krister Stendahl on His Sixty-Fifth Birthday* (ed. G. W. E. Nickelsburg and George W. MacRae; Philadelphia: Fortress, 1986), 22–30; Schüssler Fiorenza, *In Memory of Her;* Ross Shepard Kraemer, *Maenads, Martyrs, Matrons, Monastics: A Sourcebook on Women's Religions in the Greco-Roman World* (Philadelphia: Fortress, 1988); idem, *Her Share of the Blessings: Women's Religions among Pagans, Jews, and Christians in the Greco-Roman World* (New York: Oxford University Press, 1992).

the aftermath of the debates in the feminist journal *Schlangenbrut* (snake fry) and the Neukirchener theological journal *Kirche und Israel,* which is committed to Jewish-Christian dialogue, Luise Schottroff and Marie-Theres Wacker in particular further developed their feminist approaches in careful awareness of the traps of anti-Judaism.[69]

There are four main traps into which certain feminist theologians had fallen and on which the debate mainly focused:

1. They saw Judaism as the antithesis of the early Christian church, depicted as a liberation movement, freeing people from the bonds of particularism and oppression, and in the case of women mainly from patriarchal oppression. Feminist theologians had regarded as Jewish all the particularism, patriarchy, and quite often, whatever did not conform to the idea of early Christianity as a liberation movement of equals. The liberationist and universalist components, on the other hand, they ascribed to the open-minded Hellenistic influence, especially on Paul. Thus von Kellenbach stated: "The pro-Gentile bias is evident in the presupposition that egalitarian and feminist customs and beliefs found in the New Testament originated in Greco-Roman Gentile culture rather than in Jewish tradition. . . . The 'good' Jesus and Paul are claimed as Christian while the 'bad' Jesus and Paul are rejected as Jewish."[70]

2. They saw Jewish images of God as inferior to Christian images of God, regarding the Jewish image of God as that of a God of wrath, and the Christian God as the God of love and mercy. They took the New Testament use of *abba* as typical for Jesus' image of God as a nonpatriarchal parent, encompassing paternal as well as maternal love. In contrast, they depicted the "Jewish God" as authoritarian and patriarchal, whose love was not as perfect as that of the Christian God.[71] In her essay "Abba Isn't Daddy,"[72] the German feminist theologian Martina Gnadt pointed to the inherent anti-Judaism of this imagery. Again, now in a feminist form, this image formulated Christian identity over against Judaism, not taking into account that God is depicted as righteous and merciful both in the Hebrew Bible and in the New Testament. Moreover, she also showed that the use of *abba* is not as unusual and extraordinary as feminist theologians (who had based their concepts mainly on the work of Joachim Jeremias[73]) claimed it to be. Scholars

---

69. See especially Luise Schottroff and Marie-Theres Wacker, eds., *Von der Wurzel getragen: Christlich-feministische Exegese in Auseinandersetzung mit Antijudaismus* (Biblical Interpretation 17; Leiden: Brill, 1995).

70. Kellenbach, *Anti-Judaism,* 66, 69.

71. Ibid., 75–86.

72. Martina Gnadt, "Abba Isn't Daddy—Aspekte einer feministische-befreiungstheologische Revision des Abba Jesu," in *Von der Wurzel getragen,* 115–31.

73. Joachim Jeremias, *Abba: Studien zur neutestamentlichen Theologie und Zeitgeschichte* (Göttingen: Vandenhoeck & Ruprecht, 1966).

such as Ulrich Luz and James Barr had shown that *abba* is "a more solemn, responsible, adult address to a Father,"[74] not uncommon in the Judaism of Jesus' day. Gnadt also doubts that feminist liberation theology can rely on such a male-oriented image of God as "Jesus' *abba*" as one pillar of their (feminist) Christian identity.[75]

3. A reappearance of the old accusation that the Jews murdered God (in Jesus' execution) was the variation that the monotheistic religion of the Jews murdered the Goddess. The idols against which the prophets had been fighting were not just mere idols but, among others, symbols of the great Goddess. Under the influence of the prophets, Israel suppressed her worship, and the male God pushing to power replaced and banned her. Alongside this replacement theory goes the depiction of Hebrew society as patriarchal, submitting women to oppression and depriving them of rights:

> It was inevitable that together with the development of patriarchal religion, the position of woman in society would also be upset. . . . The scope of misogynist polemic in the Old Testament reaches from instructions of petty restrictions of women's rights in everyday life to the justification of the brutal murder of women.[76]

Feminist theologians based these arguments on the theory of matriarchy as a primary stage in history, a sort of a utopian, ideal golden age of women's reign, where all evil is banned. This is not to criticize feminist research on matriarchal societies in general; nevertheless, there is a tendency in some parts of this stream of research rather easily to transfer utopian dreams of an ideal society too uncritically into a remote past. The inherent danger is the creation of a dualistic worldview, which blames mainly the Old Testament and Hebrew society for the evil of the murder of the Goddess, overlooking the marginality of the Israelites in the Near East between 2500–1000 B.C.

4. We find a less obvious anti-Jewish trap in the feminist variation of replacement theology and in the inclusion of Judaism in Christian theological concepts. To demonstrate awareness of the Jewish origins of Christianity, people use the term "Judeo-Christian tradition,"[77] usually not merely to designate two different religious traditions but simply to recognize that the Christian faith is rooted in the Jewish one. Yet this particular term designating

74.   James Barr, "'Abba, Father' and the Familiarity of Jesus' Speech," *Theology Today* 91 (1988): 173–79. See also Barr, "Abba Isn't Daddy," *Journal of Theological Studies* 39 (1988): 28–47.

75.   Gnadt, "Abba Isn't Daddy," 125–28.

76.   Gerda Weiler, *Ich verwerfe im Lande die Kriege* (Munich: Frauenoffensive, 1984), 386.

77.   See, e.g., Elisabeth Moltmann-Wendel, *A Land Flowing with Milk and Honey: Perspectives on Feminist Theology* (trans. John Bowden; New York: Crossroad, 1986), 106; Susanne Heine, *Matriarchs, Goddesses, and Images of God: A Critique of Feminist Theology* (trans. John Bowden; Minneapolis: Augsburg, 1988), 20.

Christian tradition is an expression of the assumption that the Jewish tradition has now become part of the Christian; hence, it is nothing but a variation of the traditional supersessionist concept: Judaism is the prologue, Christianity the fulfillment. These concepts do not demonstrate sufficient awareness of Jewish traditions and contemporary Jewish people as distinct and self-determining while based on the same biblical tradition as Christians.

There are examples of feminist theologians who include Jewish symbols or theological issues in their theologies without referring to their origin. For example, Virginia Mollenkott integrates the concept of God's Shekinah into her interpretation of the New Testament, claiming that the "body of Christ . . . is the perfect dwelling place" for the Shekinah. As von Kellenbach has noted, this "reasserts traditional replacement theology and dispossesses a Jewish concept for Christian purposes. It fails to preserve the Jewish interpretation of the *Shekinah* in its integrity and distinctiveness."[78]

Another example of an unconscious reintroduction of traditional anti-Jewish patterns of interpretation is Carter Heyward's depiction of Jesus as the man who had made relationship the core of his message. This, she claimed, implied a radical change "from an emphasis on ritual to right relation; from an understanding of salvation as 'escaping from enemies' to an understanding of salvation as 'just relation with God.'"[79] Here we find the traditional oppositions of law/gospel, body-bound Jew/spiritual Christian. Also, Heyward does not mention the fact that a main characteristic of Judaism is its stress on the relational aspects of life, whether the relationship to God or among human beings; from a Jewish perspective, therefore, Jesus' attention to relationships is nothing exceptional or innovative.

Since this anti-Judaism debate began in feminist theology, feminist research has increasingly become aware of these issues. This applies especially to research on the history of women of the Second Temple period and on the Jesus movement.[80] A fruitful and constructive dialogue with Jewish feminists has led to new and more appropriate insights into the developments and relationships of Judaism and Christianity in the early days of the church. But, as the Swiss feminist theologian Silvia Schroer has put it, "The task to develop a historically appropriate model for a feminist reconstruction of history without anti-Judaistic implications is not yet solved."[81]

---

78. Kellenbach, *Anti-Judaism,* 128.

79. Carter Heyward, *The Redemption of God: A Theology of Mutual Relation* (Washington D.C.: University of America Press, 1982).

80. Tal Ilan, *Jewish Women in Greco-Roman Palestine: An Inquiry into Image and Status* (Tübingen: Mohr/Siebeck, 1995); Kraemer, *Her Share of the Blessings;* Amy-Jill Levine, ed., *Women Like This: New Perspectives on Jewish Women in the Greco-Roman World* (Atlanta: Scholars Press, 1991).

81. Silvia Schroer, "Feminismus und Antijudaismus: Zur Geschichte eines konstruktiven Streits," in *Antijudaismus—christliche Erblast* (ed. Walter Dietrich, Martin George, and Ulrich Luz; Stuttgart:

Until recently Paul and his letters have not been central for feminist theology and research. This difficult brother in Christ has either been ignored or been regarded primarily as the one who reimported patriarchy into the Jesus movement of equals. Feminists may also count him as the one who created a new universalistic religion, beyond particularity and contextuality.[82] Feminist research on Paul and his letters has been growing during the last few years, but feminist approaches to Paul[83] have hardly yet taken into account the shift in Pauline studies initiated by the New Perspective and by perspectives Beyond the New Perspective.[84]

I will elaborate further on this question in chapters 5–7 of this study. Now I turn to aspects of the history of Pauline studies and feminist studies on Paul before we deal with different hermeneutical presuppositions and their relevance for the interpretation of Paul and his letters.

Pauline Studies and Feminist Theology: Some History of Research

Albert Schweitzer surveyed the history of Pauline research from the Reformation up to 1911. More recently, Peter J. Tomson (1990) has studied Paul's relationship to the Jewish law and its halakah.[85] These and other resources help us to assess what feminist theology needs to deal with in Pauline studies.

The Traditional Perspective on Paul

In church and academy, people have traditionally regarded Paul as the one who had overcome Judaism in favor of a universalistic Christian faith. They

---

Kohlhammer, 1999), 28–39, with my translation of the German: "So ist die Aufgabe, ein historisch tragfähiges Modell feministischer Geschichtsrekonstruktion ohne antijudaistische Implikation zu entwerfen, keineswegs gelöst."

82. On this see, e.g., Elisabeth Schüssler Fiorenza, *Rhetoric and Ethic: The Politics of Biblical Studies* (Minneapolis: Fortress, 1999), esp. 165–67; Elisabeth Castelli, "Romans," in Elisabeth Schüssler Fiorenza (ed.), *Searching the Scriptures*, vol. 2: *A Feminist Commentary* (New York: Crossroad, 1994), 272–300.

83. Luise Schottroff is an exception to this as she emphasized throughout her work that a differentiated approach to Paul from a feminist perspective is necessary. See, for instance, Christine Schaumberger and Luise Schottroff, *Schuld und Macht: Studien zu einer feministischen Befreiungstheologie* (Munich: Chr. Kaiser, 1988), 15–36; Luise Schottroff, "Wie berechtigt ist die feministische Kritik an Paulus? Paulus und die Frauen in den ersten christlichen Gemeinden im Römischen Reich," in her *Befreiungserfahrungen: Studien zur Sozialgeschichte des Neuen Testaments* (Munich: Chr. Kaiser, 1990), 229–46; and most recently Claudia Janssen, Luise Schottroff, and Beate Wehn, eds., *Paulus: Umstrittene Traditionen—Lebendige Theologie* (Gütersloh: Chr.Kaiser/Gütersloher Verlagshaus, 2001); ET, *Journal for the Study of the New Testament* 79 (2000).

84. W. S. Campbell introduced this term in his paper "The Interpretation of Paul: Beyond the New Perspective," given at the New Testament Postgraduate Seminar, Oxford, 2001. On this further, see chap. 4, below.

85. See Albert Schweitzer, *Geschichte der paulinischen Forschung von der Reformation bis auf die Gegenwart* (Tübingen: Mohr, 1911); ET, *Paul and His Interpreters: A Critical History* (New York: Macmillan, 1951); Peter J. Tomson, *Paul and the Jewish Law: Halakha in the Letters of the Apostle to the Gentiles* (Minneapolis: Fortress, 1990), 5–19.

regarded the center of Paul's theology as a polemic against the law, which to him no longer had any positive theological or practical meaning. The Protestant Reformation emphasized this view in its conviction that a Christian is saved "by faith alone, without works of the law."[86] The theology of justification by faith gained fundamental importance in Reformation theology and became the key for interpreting the Pauline Letters, and even the whole New Testament.

Ferdinand Christian Baur, the founder of the Tübingen school of New Testament historical criticism, emphasized this implicitly anti-Jewish interpretation of Paul in a new way. Baur's interpretation still influences recent scholarship.[87] It is based on Hegel's philosophy of history: Baur claimed that in history an idea only can become real in a dialectical way.[88]

As Susannah Heschel has stressed, Baur was the first scholar to see that Jewish Christianity played a significant role during the first two centuries and that there has been some sort of continuity between Judaism and Christianity. He described the history of early Christianity as experiencing an antithesis between the Jewish "Petrine" and "Pauline" factions, from which the genuine Christian self-consciousness arose as a new synthesis. For this depiction of history, Baur "needed" Jewish Christianity to represent "the narrow, nationalist, conservative tendency of adherence to Old Testament law among early Christians."[89] Thus, although he saw no discontinuity between the two religions, their relationship was one of opposition and negation. In Baur's view, Paul advocated "a total renunciation of the compulsoriness of the Mosaic Law" and revealed the fundamental "antithesis between Judaism and Pauline Christianity."[90] He regarded the essence of Christianity as a moral universalism already present in Jesus' teachings, but there it was still bound to Jewish particularism.

Paul's achievement, according to Baur, was that he brought Christianity to its own self-understanding, to universalism. Thus, he regarded Paul as the one who formulated the Christian truth in clear opposition to Judaism, with its narrowness and particularity. He saw this antithesis not only as a historical

---

86. On this see Susannah Heschel's excellent analysis in her *Abraham Geiger and the Jewish Jesus* (Chicago: University of Chicago Press, 1998), especially 106–26, chap. 4, where she emphasizes the significant role Judaism played in German Protestant interpretations of Christian origins in which a "construct of Jewishness" served to depict so-called legalism as opposing nascent Christianity (107). See also Tomson in the introduction to his *"If This Be from Heaven,"* 1ff.

87. Daniel Boyarin himself notes that the image of Paul he depicts in his *A Radical Jew: Paul and the Politics of Identity* (Berkley: University of California Press, 1994), is related to Baur's approach (11, 212).

88. See Heschel, *Abraham Geiger*, 112–13.

89. Ibid., 112.

90. Ferdinand Christian Baur, "Die Christuspartei in der korinthischen Gemeinde, der Gegensatz des paulinischen und petrinischen Christentums in der ältesten Kirche," *Tübinger Zeitschrift für Theologie* 4 (1831): 61–206; reprinted in vol. 1 of *Ausgewählte Werke in Einzelausgaben* (ed. Klaus Scholder; Stuttgart-Bad, Cannstatt: Frommenn, 1963), 49, 74–75.

event of early Christian history but also as a necessary stage in the process of history being interpreted as the dialectical unfolding of the Spirit:

> Christianity in itself wants to be only a spiritualized Judaism, and goes back with the deepest roots of its origins in the ground of the Old Testament religion. . . . In its God-consciousness Christianity knows itself to be above all united with Judaism; the God of the Old Testament is also the God of the New Testament. . . . But the Old Testament concept of God has, on the other side, also such a genuinely nationalist imprint [that] the whole stands in its particularism in the most distinct opposition to Christianity.[91]

The church had to liberate the concept of God from this narrow nationalism and particularism, Baur claimed, so that the concept of God in its universal meaning could become the pure concept of religion as such. Whenever "Jewish particularism raised its head in a hierarchical or dogmatic way,"[92] Baur needed Paul and his insights, again and again, to protest against this.

It is no accident that Baur, like Luther, used the same categories in his characterization of Catholicism and Protestantism as he used in his characterization of Judaism and Christianity. The primary focus for Baur was not contemporary Judaism as such but rather contemporary issues of debate between Catholicism and Protestantism in Germany. Nevertheless, his perception and use of Judaism in these debates was such that it became a movement essentially and in principle opposed to Christianity. This deprived Judaism of any positive identity in ongoing history. The logic inherent in this reconstruction of early Christian history is that contemporary Judaism is an anachronism. The Jews are and remain the "others." Baur's reconstruction made Paul into the man who freed Christianity from the limits of Jewish particularity as a religion of the law. Mainstream theology after Baur can never seem to rid itself of this particular perception of Paul.

At the beginning of the twentieth century, Adolf von Harnack saw the history of early Christianity more in terms of a development rather than a dialectical process of antitheses, as Baur had done. Therefore, he placed Paul closer to Judaism, perceiving Jesus and Paul more in terms of different stages of a development than as being separated by a gap. He saw Jesus as the one who opposed the Pharisees and other Jewish leaders, as the renewer of the

---

91. Ferdinand Christian Baur, *Das Christenthum und die christliche Kirche der drei ersten Jahrhunderte* (2d ed.; Tübingen: Fues, 1860); reprinted as vol. 3 of *Ausgewählte Werke* (1966), 16; cited in Heschel, *Abraham Geiger*, 113.

92. Heschel, *Abraham Geiger*, 77, with my translation of the German: "Den jüdischen Partikularismus hierarchisch oder dogmatisch auf's Neue sein Haupt . . . erheben."

ancient message of the prophets. Jesus, therefore, was a reformer who revealed the real essence of Judaism. From this perspective actual Judaism is only the distortion of its true self, a tradition that should have come to an end with the gospel of Jesus. With regard to the history of the separation of Christianity and Judaism, Harnack sees a somewhat revolutionary tendency, whose most splendid representative was Paul. But the progressive religious thinker Paul, according to Harnack, was in some respect still struggling with "the Jew in himself."[93] Nevertheless, he perceived Paul's position as genuinely Pauline, though only formulated in full clarity by apostolic fathers such as Justin. Thus, Harnack arrived at an image of Paul and early Christianity that does not differ much from Baur's: Paul had transformed the still-"Jewish" teachings of Jesus into the universal Christian religion.[94]

A new strand of New Testament studies emerged in the powerful religions-geschichtliche school, with Wilhelm Bousset as one of its main representatives. His influence is of lasting importance. Yet, it is clear that a biased view of the opposition between Paul and Judaism implicitly structured his work. Judaism to him was nothing but a degenerated outcome of preexilic Israel. He saw the Judaism contemporary to Jesus as entirely decadent and indicated that by the term *Spätjudentum* (*late* Judaism). One of his main works, *Die Religion des Judentums* (1903), informs thoroughly about apocalyptic and mystical aspects of ancient Judaism. Yet, Bousset perceived Judaism as entirely decadent and in absolute opposition to Christianity: "With Judaism and its perception of the world, one can never get to the figure of Jesus, since these are complete contrasts. . . . Judaism was the test tube within which the different elements were collected. Following this, in a creative miracle the new creation of the gospel emerged."[95]

Through Rudolf Bultmann, Bousset's work and perceptions "gained decisive and lasting influence, especially in German research."[96] Bultmann further developed the interpretation of Paul but changed nothing in the perception of Paul with respect to Judaism. He thus appreciated Paul's achievement of succeeding in his fight for a law-free gospel and bringing the Christian communities into a united church. "Indeed, the main importance of Paul has not been mentioned yet. It is to be found in the fact that as a theologian he provided

---

93. See Adolf von Harnack. "Die Stellung des Apostels Paulus zum Judentum und Judenchristentum nach seinen Briefen; seine jüdischen Schranken," in *Beiträge zur Einleitung in das Neue Testament,* vol. 4: *Neue Untersuchungen zur Apostelgeschichte und zur Abfassungszeit der synoptischen Evangelien* (Leipzig: Hinrich, 1911), 43–44.

94. Cf. Ekkehard Stegemann, "Der Jude Paulus und seine antijüdische Auslegung," in *Auschwitz— Krise der christlichen Theologie* (eds. Rolf Rendtorff and Ekkehard Stegemann; Munich: Chr. Kaiser, 1980), 126.

95. Quoted in ibid., 128; my translation of the German: "Vom Judentum aus und seiner Weltanschauung erreicht man niemals die Gestalt Jesu, hier liegen vollständige Gegensätze vor. . . . Das Judentum war die Retorte, in welcher die verschiedenen Elemente gesammelt wurden. Dann erfolgte durch ein schöpferisches Wunder die Neubildung des Evangeliums."

96. Tomson, *Paul and the Jewish Law,* 13.

Christian faith with the adequate understanding of itself."[97] That Judaism and Christianity are in opposition to each other is presupposed and implicit in his *Existenztheologie:* Jews and their religion represent the old type of man who misses his true existence. "Jew" and "Christian" are types of false or true existence respectively. Jewish writings contemporary to Paul are of no significance for understanding Pauline thoughts and arguments. Bultmann, like Baur and Bousset, saw hardly any connections between Paul and Jewish apocalyptic tradition.[98]

This brief overview of aspects of the history of Pauline studies is limited and incomplete in order to focus more on the recent tendencies in research that have led to the changing perspectives in Pauline studies now known as the New Perspective. These tendencies are part of, and have to be seen in the context of, the major hermeneutical changes of the last thirty years. After identifying some theologians who are developing alternatives to traditional mainstream perceptions of Paul that have their roots in earlier approaches, I conclude this chapter with a summary of some feminist approaches on Paul.

Early Alternatives

Albert Schweitzer presented a completely different view of Paul in *Die Mystik des Apostels Paulus* (1930). Schweitzer radically opposed mainstream interpretation. Two decades earlier, in *Die Geschichte der paulinischen Forschung von der Reformation bis zur Gegenwart* (1911), he had already given an outline of his approach. He intended to demonstrate the connection of Paul's eschatological thoughts with Judaism and traced this back to exilic and preexilic prophecy. Rather than interpreting Paul from within a Hellenistic perspective, he did not hesitate to "understand him exclusively in the light of his Jewish and Jewish-Christian background."[99] He saw this background not in rabbinic traditions but in apocalyptic mystical traditions. Schweitzer regarded it as necessary to compare Paul's letters with ancient Jewish writings, especially apocalyptic literature, to come to a more adequate understanding. He was a lone voice in the desert, and his approach remained without much influence at this time.

Only a few scholars developed similar approaches. George F. Moore, as early as 1921, published a study demonstrating how inadequate was the description of ancient Judaism as a religion that needed to earn salvation

---

97. Rudolf Bultmann, "Paulus," in *Religion in Geschichte und Gegenwart,* vol. 4 (ed. H. Gunkel et al.; 2d ed.; Tübingen: Mohr/Siebeck, 1930), 1026, with my translation of the German: "Indessen ist damit noch nicht die eigentliche Bedeutung des P. genannt. Sie liegt darin, dass er als Theologe dem christlichen Glauben das sachgemässe Verständnis seiner selbst gegeben hat."

98. Tomson, *Paul and the Jewish Law,* 13.

99. Ibid., 11.

through works of the law.[100] This is an indirect critique of traditional interpretations of Paul, which presupposed a negative depiction of first-century Judaism in comparison to a positive depiction of Paul and early Christianity. Moore further developed his approach in *Judaism in the First Centuries of the Christian Era: The Age of the Tannaim* (1927–30). In these three volumes he described ancient rabbinic Judaism positively.

Another early approach emphasizing the importance of studying first-century Jewish sources was W. D. Davies in *Paul and Rabbinic Judaism* (1947). Unlike Schweitzer, he argued that scholars needed to include rabbinical literature in their study of contemporaneous Jewish sources in order to understand Paul. In his detailed comparison of Paul's letters with rabbinic literature, Davies came to the conclusion that Paul remained within Jewish tradition and did not object to the Jewish-Christian tradition. He declared that the doctrine of justification by faith was not the center of his thought; instead, the center is in Christology, in Paul's "awareness that with the coming of Christ, the age to come had become present fact."[101]

After the singular voices of Moore, Schweitzer, and Davies, Johannes Munck presented an important critique of Baur's Tübingen school by showing how it failed to take into account that Paul lived in, and was rooted in, a specific historical and religious context: Judaism. In *Paulus und die Heilsgeschichte* (1954)[102] he depicted an image of Paul as a Jew who had not converted to a new religion on the road to Damascus, but had received a call (similar to the prophets) as a missionary to the Gentiles. Paul never ceased to have positive relations with the Jewish Christ-believing groups in Jerusalem. But, like Schweitzer's low initial influence, Munck's approach was slow to find acceptance in New Testament scholarship.[103]

Krister Stendahl

It was Krister Stendahl's lecture "Paul and the Introspective Conscience of the West," given in 1961 for psychologists, that provoked wider reaction among Pauline scholars.[104] Stendahl's thesis was that Paul's questions had nothing to do with the pangs of conscience of Lutheran and Calvinist piety

100. George F. Moore, "Christian Writers on Judaism," *Harvard Theological Review* 14 (1921): 197–254.

101. W. D. Davies, *Paul and Rabbinic Judaism: Some Elements in Pauline Theology* (50th anniversary ed.; Mifflintown, Pa.: Sigler, 1998), 222.

102. Johannes Munck, *Paulus und die Heilsgeschichte* (Copenhagen: Munksgaard, 1954); ET, *Paul and the Salvation of Mankind* (London: SCM, 1959).

103. See W. S. Campbell, *Paul's Gospel in an Intercultural Context: Jew and Gentile in the Letter to the Romans* (Berlin: P. Lang, 1992), 10 nn. 23–24.

104. See Campbell, "Beyond the New Perspective."

but in fact were rooted in Augustine's interpretation of Paul. Augustine, the "first modern man," referred to Paul's "justification by faith" as the way of salvation for the troubled soul, but he did not take into account the historical situation for which Paul had made that formulation. Paul had tried to solve problems emerging from concrete questions about the relation of Jews and Gentiles (after the Christ event).[105] He had no intention of writing abstract general messages about the situation of man and his soul. Augustine generalized Paul's concrete statements into a timeless interpretation of the human situation. Thus Stendahl wrote:

> Where Paul was concerned about the possibility for Gentiles to be included in the messianic community, his statements were now read as answers to the quest for assurance about man's salvation out of a common human predicament.[106]

Luther took up and differentiated this introspective or Augustinian emphasis in the interpretation of Paul. The image of Paul thus created has dominated Pauline studies up to the present. What Luther depicted in his image of Paul was an image of his own pangs and worries of conscience. Therefore, Luther did not understand Paul's experience on the road to Damascus as a call for the mission to Gentiles but as an inner conversion, and thus as a transfer to a new religion, from Judaism to Christianity. However, this conversion also meant salvation from despair.[107]

Ernst Käsemann reacted with some intensity to this thesis. In his public lecture "Rechtfertigung und Heilsgeschichte im Römerbrief,"[108] he argued that Stendahl's interpretation threatened Protestantism at its heart because it questioned justification theology as the center of it. He did not deny that "die Rechtfertigungsbotschaft eine antijudaistische Kampfeslehre ist (the message of justification is a teaching in the struggle against Judaism)."[109]

---

105. See also W. S. Campbell, "Divergent Images of Paul and His Mission," in *Reading Israel in Romans: Legitimacy and Plausibility of Divergent Interpretations* (ed. Cristina Grenholm and Daniel Patte; Harrisburg, Pa.: Trinity Press International, 2000), 206.

106. Krister Stendahl, "Paul and the Introspective Conscience of the West," in his *Paul among Jews and Gentiles and Other Essays* (Philadelphia: Fortress, 1976), 78–96.

107. See also Stanley K. Stowers, *A Rereading of Romans: Justice, Jews and Gentile* (New Haven: Yale University Press, 1994), 327: "But Augustine, in the heart of the Pelagian controversy, made Paul's argument about God's plans for the Gentiles into a timeless theology that placed human agency in opposition to divine agency. This made doing good or keeping God's law into a complex religious and psychological problem that doing the good and keeping the law was not for Paul himself." He also states: "Augustine and Luther view Romans as both an attack on human pride, epitomized by Jewish keeping of the Law, and a defense of the gospel of God's grace. Romans has become a polemical theological treatise about humanity in which Jews and Gentiles serve only as examples of human depravity" (14).

108. Ernst Käsemann, "Rechtfertigung und Heilsgeschichte im Römerbrief," in his *Paulinische Perspektiven* (Tübingen: Mohr/Siebeck, 1969), 108–39.

109. Ibid., 125.

Käsemann did not see any problem in this as such. In 1961 there was hardly any awareness of the possible consequences of such a theological statement; there was hardly any consciousness of the significance of the Shoah for theology. Thus he could state that "Israel has exemplary significance for Paul"; at the same time Käsemann had a tendency to spiritualize "the Jew" and "the law" as the example of the ungodly, stating that "in and with Israel he strikes at the hidden Jew in all of us."[110]

The New Perspective

Several scholars had followed the emphasis of the above-mentioned approaches to Paul as being rooted in Judaism. Nevertheless, it was E. P. Sanders's *Paul and Palestinian Judaism: A Comparison of Patterns of Religion* (1977)[111] that led to a broad debate in Pauline studies on whether and how Paul was rooted in Judaism and what this meant for theology in general. In this book Sanders relied mostly on modern Jewish research for his description of ancient Judaism. He convincingly deconstructed the image of ancient Judaism as a religion of works-righteousness. Although this image is widespread among Christian exegetes, Sanders demonstrated that it is a distortion of first-century Judaism.

Instead, he described the pattern of first-century Judaism as "covenantal nomism." After investigating Palestinian Jewish literature from 200 B.C. to A.D. 200, Sanders came to the conclusion that, although this literature is quite heterogeneous, there is a common pattern in which the different types of Judaism they represent are rooted. This pattern is based on the view that one's place in God's plan is established on the basis of the covenant; as the proper response of the people, the covenant requires obedience to its commandments, while providing means of atonement for transgression.[112]

---

110. Ernst Käsemann, "Paul and Israel," in his *New Testament Questions of Today* (London: SCM, 1969), 182–87. Although Käsemann had seen the challenging significance of Stendahl's essay, there was little debate about it in German-speaking theology, and it had hardly any influence on theological research there. One exception was Markus Barth, who criticized Käsemann's view that "the apostle's essential adversary is the pious Jew." M. Barth, "St. Paul—a Good Jew," *Horizons in Biblical Theology* 1 (1979): 7–8). Stendahl's essay (see n. 105, above) was not published in German until 1996: "Der Apostel Paulus und das 'introspektive' Gewissen des Westens," *Kirche und Israel: Neukirchener theologische Zeitschrift* 11 (1996): 19–33.

111. E. P. Sanders, *Paul and Palestinian Judaism: A Comparison of Patterns of Religion* (Philadelphia: Fortress, 1977).

112. Sanders, ibid., 422, describes covenantal nomism as follows: "The 'pattern' or 'structure' of coventanal nomism is this: (1) God has chosen Israel and (2) given the law. The law implies both (3) God's promise to maintain the election and (4) the requirement to obey. (5) God rewards obedience and punishes transgression. (6) The law provides for means of atonement, and atonement results in (7) maintenance or re-establishment of the covenantal relationship. (8) All those who are maintained in the covenant by obedience, atonement and God's mercy belong to the group which will be saved. An important interpretation of the first and last points is that election and ultimately salvation are considered to be by God's mercy rather than human achievement."

This means that the only way to obtain salvation is by God's merciful election. Torah is not the way to salvation but the means through which the relationship within the covenant is maintained. Sanders thus showed that first-century Judaism is by no means a religion of works-righteousness but rather a religion of grace.

This description of ancient Judaism made it clear that mainstream Christian theology was wrong in depicting Paul and his gospel in such an opposition to Judaism, and in teaching that Paul advocated a religion of grace in contrast to a religion of works-righteousness. Sanders stated that Paul was not opposing Judaism as such, and that he did not see anything wrong with its practices and beliefs. But Sanders portrayed Paul as a man who, in his ecstatic experience "in Christ," had found something that was beyond and different from Judaism. Thus, according to Sanders, the only thing Paul found wrong in Judaism was that it was not Christianity.[113] But this implied that Paul had left behind the pattern of "covenantal nomism."

Sanders's research on first-century Judaism introduced a paradigm shift in Pauline studies, though other scholars such as Davies and Stendahl with their research had already been pointing in a similar direction. Nevertheless, his perception of Paul was not all that different from the classical interpretation of Paul in that he saw a fundamental difference between the apostle and the Judaism he knew.

There was a wide response to Sanders's approach, coming in different ways. Scholars such as Heikki Räisänen supported Sanders's view that Paul had left Judaism. Räisänen saw Paul drawing a distorted image of the Judaism of his time as a result of overreacting against his opponents. According to Räisänen, he therefore constructed a theological contrast between faith in Christ and works of the law. Without being aware of what he was doing, Paul had created a break between Judaism and the new faith in Christ. This sociological perspective suggests that the "theologizing" of a conflict led to all the inconsistencies in Paul's attitude toward the law.[114]

Jacob Neusner did not criticize Sanders's main thesis concerning first-century Judaism as being held together in "coventantal nomism." But he regarded his use of rabbinic literature as not differentiated enough. Sanders did not take into account that this literature encompassed traditions dating back to the first century, although rabbinic Judaism as such and its written

---

113. Ibid., 552; see also E. P. Sanders, *Paul, the Law, and the Jewish People* (Philadelphia: Fortress, 1985), 44. Cf. James D. G. Dunn's comment on Sanders: "The Lutheran Paul has been replaced by an idiosyncratic Paul who in arbitrary and irrational manner turns his face against the glory and greatness of Judaism's covenant theology and abandons Judaism simply because it is not Christianity" ("The New Perspective on Paul," in Dunn, *Jesus, Paul and the Law: Studies in Mark and Galatians* [London: SPCK, 1990], 187).

114. See Campbell, "Divergent Images," 203, 209.

tradition only developed after the first century. Neusner said it was inadequate to construct an image of first-century Judaism from material that in the main emerged only later. In Neusner's opinion, Sanders also was not aware enough of the differences between the different kinds of Jewish literature of this period.[115]

Another aspect of Sanders's work caused Morna D. Hooker to raise questions. In her view, "the pattern of religion" that Sanders depicts in part 1 of his *Paul and Palestinian Judaism* has much similarity to what was commonly believed to be the religion of Paul. It then is a great surprise to discover in part 2 a Paul who is completely different from Palestinian Judaism:

> No doubt many will have thought that they recognized Paul in the pages of the first part of Sanders's book, and will have concluded, as they turned to part 2, "So Paul is thoroughly Jewish after all." Yet it is at this point that Sanders springs his surprise, and argues that the pattern of Paul's religion, also, is quite different from what we had imagined: we end with Paul and Palestinian Judaism as far apart as they have ever been.[116]

Sanders ended his book with a Paul who is breaking with Judaism, although he himself had no intention to do so.[117] He claimed that Paul was setting up a new group, neither Jewish nor Gentile, but a third entity: "Paul's own view was that, with regard to access to membership in the people of God, Jew and Gentile were on equal ground and both had to join what was, in effect, a third entity."[118] It seems rather strange that, according to Sanders, Paul should not have realized what he was doing.[119]

Despite these and other critiques, there is no doubt that Sanders's work is a milestone on the way to overcoming the distorted image of Judaism as a religion of works-righteousness. Stendahl and Sanders radically questioned the foundation pillars of classical Pauline interpretation, which viewed Paul as mainly interested in the salvation of the individual soul and as fighting against Judaism as a religion of works-righteousness. From their insights a variety of new perspectives developed on Paul and his letters, a stream of interpretation that has become known as the New Perspective.[120]

---

115. Bruce Chilton and Jacob Neusner, *Judaism in the New Testament: Practices and Beliefs* (London: Routledge, 1995), 8–18.

116. Morna D. Hooker, "Paul and 'Coventantal Nomism,'" in *Paul and Paulinism: Essays in Honour of C. K. Barrett* (ed. M. D. Hooker and S. G. Wilson; London: SPCK 1982), 47.

117. Sanders, *Paul, the Law and the Jewish People,* 207: "[Paul] seems not to have perceived that his gospel and his missionary activity imply a break with Judaism."

118. Ibid., 192.

119. On this see also Campbell, "Beyond the New Perspective," 11.

120. James D. G. Dunn, "The New Perspective on Paul," *Bulletin of the John Rylands Library* 65 (1983): 95–122.

One of the most prominent representatives of this New Perspective in Pauline studies is James D. G. Dunn. He has followed Sanders in his estimation of first-century Judaism but does not see the break Sanders poses between Paul and contemporary Judaism. Dunn depicts Paul more from within his Jewish background and does not view him as having transferred from one system into another.[121] In Dunn's view this supposed break is completely arbitrary interpretation:

> The most surprising feature of Sanders's writing, however, is that he himself has failed to take the opportunity his own mould-breaking work offered. Instead of trying to explore how far Paul's theology could be explicated in relation to Judaism's "covenantal nomism," he remained more impressed by the *difference* between Paul's pattern of religious thought and that of First-Century Judaism. He quickly, too quickly in my view, concluded that Paul's religion could be understood only as a basically different system from that of his fellow Jews.[122]

Dunn is not convinced that Paul broke with the law simply because it did not lead to salvation in Christ. That explanation is only slightly better than the one it was supposed to replace: "The Lutheran Paul has been replaced by an idiosyncratic Paul who in arbitrary and irrational manner turns his face against the glory and greatness of Judaism's covenant theology and abandons Judaism simply because it is not Christianity."[123]

Dunn's main thesis is that Torah, especially from the time of the Maccabean period onward, served an important function in the definition of the identity of the Jewish people. Its purpose then was to serve as a "boundary marker" for Israel over against other nations, and as an "identity marker" to strengthen their own inner self-understanding. Most important in that context were the commandments in relation to circumcision, food, and the keeping of the Sabbath. They were regarded as proofs of covenantal faithfulness. According to Dunn, it is only in this context that Paul's statements about the law can be understood. The term ἔργα νόμου (works of the law) was thus primarily used in the sense of the social function of the law. What Paul therefore is criticizing is not the law as such, but an understanding of covenantal promise and law as a guarantee and a privilege for Israel. In Dunn's view Paul does not leave Judaism, but he does query Jewish ethnocentrism and pleads for an opening of the covenant for all nations, which had been the intention of the Torah from its beginnings:

---

121. Sanders, *Paul and Palestinian Judaism,* 513, 543.
122. Dunn, "New Perspective," 99.
123. Ibid., 110; cf. 112.

The Jews, proselytes, and God-worshipping Gentiles among his readership would read what Paul says about the law in the light of this close interconnection in Jewish theology of Israel's election, covenant and law. . . . They would recognize that what Paul was endeavouring to do was to free both promise and law for a wider range of recipients, freed from the ethnic constraints which he saw to be narrowing the grace of God and diverting the saving purpose of God out of its main channel—Christ.[124]

The covenant is thus not abandoned but broadened, as in the time of fulfillment it should not be defined by ethnic boundaries and narrowness.

The influence of Dunn's approach is widespread. From a Jewish perspective, Daniel Boyarin in *A Radical Jew* built his interesting image of Paul on Dunn's thesis. Yet, by creating an image of a universalistic Paul, even though from a Jewish perspective, Boyarin echoes the older image of Paul as a representative of universalism, as Baur depicted already in the nineteenth century.[125]

Another scholar who builds on Sanders's work is Lloyd Gaston. He explicitly puts his contribution into the context of the second half of the twentieth century and sees as the agenda of Christian theology the necessity of a radical and irrevocable change after Auschwitz.[126] Like Stendahl, he also has stressed that "justification by faith" is not the central doctrine of Paul. In his view Paul is not opposing Judaism, but he indeed does have some problems with his fellow Jews: they don't follow his view about the status of Gentiles after the Christ event. Since the goal of the Torah is God's righteousness also for Gentiles, "Israel was faithful to Torah as it relates to Israel, but with respect to the goal of that Torah as it relates to the Gentiles, they stumbled and were unfaithful."[127] Israel had not fulfilled her task to be a light to the Gentiles. For the nations, therefore, God had to open another way to salvation, which he did in the Christ event. But this definitely does not mean that the Jews and their special relation to God in the covenant were replaced in favor of Christian Gentiles. In Christ there is a separate covenant for Gentiles.

Gaston picked up a strand of research that earlier had already been represented mainly by Scandinavian scholars such as Johannes Munck, Nils A. Dahl, and Krister Stendahl.[128] Along with them he maintains that the starting point of Paul's doing and writing was his self-understanding derived from his call to be an apostle to the Gentiles. Gaston thus views all of Paul's

---

124. James D. G. Dunn, "The New Perspective on Paul: Paul and the Law," in *The Romans Debate* (ed. Karl P. Donfried; rev., expanded ed.; Peabody, Mass.: Hendrickson, 1991), 307. See also Dunn, *Jesus, Paul and the Law,* 188–200.

125. See the beginning of this chapter.

126. Lloyd Gaston, *Paul and the Torah* (Vancouver: University of British Columbia Press, 1987), 2.

127. Lloyd Gaston, "Israel's Misstep in the Eyes of Paul," in *Romans Debate,* 316.

128. See Campbell, *Paul's Gospel,* 36 n. 4.

converts as Gentiles and mainly also the addressees of his letters. What Paul does, then, is to try to outline what it means particularly for Gentiles to have come to the one God of Israel, who is also the God of all nations. Gaston's approach is not far from Dunn's, and yet there is a different emphasis in their view of what distinguishes Paul from contemporary Judaism. Gaston sees the difference not in particularity and universalism, but in the Jews failing to be the light to the Gentiles, for which they were called. Hence, a debate between Paul and his fellow Jews might not have been about Judaism as such but about what being Jewish means with regard to Gentiles. Gaston's approach leads to the theory of two covenants, one for Jews and one for Gentiles; Dunn maintains that Paul's interpretation of the Christ event implies a broadening of the covenant and the inclusion of Gentiles into Israel.

The debate about understanding Paul and his letters is broad and ongoing, and the literature written in relation to it is immense. Four volumes of *Pauline Theology* emerged from the Society of Biblical Literature seminars on Paul between 1986 and 1996,[129] and these have stimulated further research. In these seminars participants were seriously committed to an exegetical principle that each of the Pauline Letters was formulated in its own specific situation and therefore must be interpreted as such and individually.[130]

These alternative, or new, approaches in Pauline studies have not ceased with the development of what is subsumed under the label the New Perspective. In part 2 of this book, I will deal with more recent strands of research in Paul, labeled Beyond the New Perspective. The relation and networking of different strands of research now leads into aspects of research in feminist approaches on Paul.

Paul and Feminist Theology

The image of Paul in feminist theology is a special issue. In feminist theology and its convincing and established "hermeneutics of suspicion," theologians are increasingly sensitive to avoid the trap of anti-Judaism into which earlier feminist theology had fallen.[131]

---

129. A good overview of this seminar's aims and achievements can be found in J. M. Bassler, ed., *Thessalonians, Philippians, Galatians, Philemon* (vol. 1 of *Pauline Theology;* Minneapolis: Fortress, 1991), preface; and in E. Elizabeth Johnson, ed., *Looking Back, Pressing On* (vol. 4 of *Pauline Theology;* Atlanta: Scholars Press, 1997), preface.

130. William S. Campbell, "Divergent Images," 19: "As far as is humanly possible, we must interpret Paul's mission and Paul himself as they are presented in this specific text, before we resort to harmonization or revision from any other sources, however significant. Within the letter, the same principle applies: we must allow as we are able, each section of the letter to reveal its own peculiar content, before we seek to relate it to a coherent view of the whole."

131. See the overview in chap. 2, above, on "Feminist Hermeneutics," 19ff; Wenschkewitz, ed., *Verdrängte Vergangenheit;* Schottroff and Wacker, eds., *Von der Wurzel getragen.* See further the debate in *Journal of Feminist Studies in Religion* 7.2 (1991).

Especially Jewish feminist scholars[132] have drawn attention to such anti-Jewish tendencies. In some excellent analyses they have demonstrated that in attempting to liberate Christian theology from patriarchal interpretation, feminist theologians often unconsciously had built their views on anti-Jewish images of Judaism drawn from mainstream theologians of whom in other respects they were very critical. Since then, feminists have done much research with respect to the Gospels.[133]

Feminist research on Paul and his letters is gradually increasing. In a wide range of feminist theologies, the image of Paul is rather negative. A first wave of feminist theologians judged Paul mainly from his varied and contradictory statements about women.[134] Certain feminist approaches still regard Paul as the one who, unlike Jesus, could not really see men and women as equal in Christ. They held and still hold Paul responsible for the first step Christianity took back toward patriarchy.[135] In their view, Jesus is the one who initiated a movement of equals, with a liberationist impact also for women; Paul is the one who again asked for their special obedience. Moreover, they depict Paul as arguing from an authoritarian, hierarchical stance, trying to oppress egalitarian voices in the church with his powerful rhetoric.[136]

In this strand of feminist theology there is a tendency to depict Paul as a universalistic Hellenistic thinker whose worldview is influenced by Platonic dualism, and whose rhetoric is entrenched with essential hierarchical dualisms.[137] He had overcome Judaism and its particularity by founding Christianity as a new universalistic religion. Hence, some feminist theologians viewed Paul as the one who began to betray the ethics of the original Jesus movement, which regarded women and men as equals.

Luise Schottroff initiated a different feminist approach. Although she takes seriously the patriarchal structure of first-century societies, she pleads for a careful analysis of Pauline texts, contending that there is more relevance in Paul for feminist theology than might be obvious at a first glance. She also views Paul as arguing much more from within Judaism than from without:

That the feminist critique of sexism and anti-Judaism in Paul applies to Christian Pauline exegesis I am quite certain, . . . but I am doubtful about his

132. Heschel, "Anti-Judaism in Christian Feminist Theology"; Judith Plaskow, "Feminist Anti-Judaism and the Christian God," *Journal of Feminist Studies in Religion* 7.2 (1991): 99–108.
133. E.g., Schüssler Fiorenza, *In Memory of Her;* Luise Schottroff, *Lydias ungeduldige Schwestern: Feministische Sozialgeschichte des frühen Christentums* (Gütersloh: Chr. Kaiser/Gütersloher Verlagshaus, 1994).
134. See, for instance, Schüssler Fiorenza, *In Memory of Her,* 233.
135. Most recently, see Schüssler Fiorenza, *Rhetoric and Ethic,* 149–73, on Gal 3:28.
136. See on this Cynthia Briggs Kittredge, *Community and Authority: The Rhetoric of Obedience in the Pauline Tradition* (Harrisburg, Pa.: Trinity Press International, 1998); Elisabeth Castelli, *Imitating Paul: A Discourse of Power* (Louisville: Westminster/John Knox, 1991); Sandra Hack Polaski, *Paul and the Discourse of Power* (Sheffield: Sheffield Academic Press, 1999).
137. Castelli, "Romans," 285–87.

[Paul's] anti-Judaism. . . . A new reading of the theology of Paul is necessary in a feminist project. Christian feminists, too, have perceived him as an authoritarian, oppressive churchman and professor of theology who had given up his Judaism. I think that we can gain important inspiration through the theology of Paul for feminist theology.[138]

Following Luise Schottroff's approach, a collection of essays on Paul by German-speaking feminist scholars shows an increasing awareness of the need, emphasized in this book, to relate different strands of research to each other, particularly in Pauline studies.[139] Luzia Sutter Rehmann stresses this in her brief overview of different aspects of current feminist research on Paul in German-speaking areas. She declares that the book *Paulus: Umstrittene Traditionen—lebendige Theologie* aims to make "an important contribution to a rereading of Pauline traditions, seeking to relate three discourses: feminist theology, the debate about anti-Judaism, and liberation theology."[140] Moreover, Sutter Rehmann claims:

Much more is involved by now than the "question about women" in Paul, more than a critical deconstruction of androcentric writings, more than the contribution made by the female point of view. Feminist exegesis seeks a fundamentally new perception of the Pauline writings, and thereby a new paradigm to understand Paul and his theology.[141]

The contributors of this book pay special attention to the hermeneutical presuppositions or the "concept" of Paul, which shapes any interpretation of his letters, and also to the issue of anti-Judaism in Pauline exegesis. As an excellent volume of essays, it is an example of the increasing number of feminist theologians doing research on Paul and his letters from this perspective,[142] but wide areas of feminist studies in Paul are still unexplored.

---

138. Luise Schottroff, "'Gesetzesfreies Heidenchristentum'—und die Frauen? Feministische Analysen und Alternativen," in *Von der Wurzel getragen*, 238–40, with my translation of the German: "Dass die[se] feministische Kritik am Sexismus und Antijudaismus des Paulus für die christliche Paulus*exegese* zutreffend ist, bezweifle ich nicht. . . . Ich zweifle aber an seinem [Paulus'] Antijudaismus. . . . Zum feministischen Projekt muss auch eine Neulektüre der Theologie des Paulus gehören. Auch feministische Christinnen haben ihn als autoritären, unterdrückerischen und sein Judentum aufgebenden Kirchenmann und Theologieprofessor verstanden. Ich meine, dass aus der Theologie des Paulus wertvolle Inspirationen für feministische Theologie zu gewinnen sind."

139. Janssen et al., *Paulus;* ET, *JSNT* 79 (2000).

140. "Die aktuelle feministische Exegese der paulinischen Briefe: Ein Überblick," in ibid., 19: "[Der vorliegende Band] versteht sich als wichtiger Beitrag zu einer Re-Lektüre paulinischer Traditionen, der die drei Diskurse feministische Theologie, Antijudaismusdebatte und Befreiungstheologie miteinander verknüpft." ET: "This volume is intended as an important contribution to a rereading of Pauline traditions that relates the discourses of feminist theology, the anti-Judaism debate, and liberation theology to each other."

141. *JSNT* 79 (2000): 5.

142. For example, Pamela Eisenbaum, "Paul as the New Abraham," in *Paul and Politics: Ekklesia, Israel, Imperium, Interpretation* (ed. Richard A. Horsley; Harrisburg, Pa.: Trinity Press International, 2000), 130–45.

Changing perspectives in scholarship have initiated a shift of sometimes radical changes in theological disciplines. From different perspectives scholars have discredited the notion of objective and detached scholarship, and feminists have challenged male domination in academic life generally. In this chapter I have given brief outlines of some of these changes in academic disciplines, particularly on the issues of anti-Judaism, Pauline studies, and feminist theology. Taking seriously the impact of universalizing tendencies leads, among other things, to the recognition of contextuality and diversity in theological thinking. In the next chapter I investigate whether and how this notion of contextuality and diversity impacts on the interpretation of Paul and his letters.

3

Different Perspectives

Contradictions in Paul?

Since New Testament times there has been an ongoing debate on how to understand Paul's letters. As early as the days of the first Christ-believing communities, a follower of Jesus Christ wrote, in 2 Pet 3:16: "There are some things in them [Paul's letters] hard to understand, which the ignorant and unstable twist to their own destruction, as they do the other scriptures." We don't know precisely the problems of understanding they had in those days. Nevertheless, scholars have produced an immense amount of writing, especially since the Reformation, on the core of Paul's theology, the image of Paul, and other issues. This is a clear sign something in Paul's writings has raised questions over the centuries and still is puzzling his readers.

In recent times scholars most frequently deal with issues of contradictory statements within one letter or between different letters. "Traditional" theologians handle such issues in infinitely varied ways. Almost all of them try to find a core or center in Paul's theology, from which his other statements are then evaluated.[1]

Thus, Günther Bornkamm regards Romans as the elevation of themes Paul had dealt with in earlier letters. In Romans he has raised them from particular

---

1. Cf. D. M. Hay, ed., *1 and 2 Corinthians* (vol. 2 of *Pauline Theology;* Minneapolis: Fortress, 1993), chaps. 1–2, 7, 12.

everyday problems to the heights of universal truth.[2] Bornkamm seeks to avoid contradictory interpretations of Paul by regarding him as in the process of developing his theology. Earlier he is still more or less bound to his Jewish past, viewed as a minor stage of faith, and then he develops to an increasingly clear view and understanding of the universal meaning of the Christ event.

Others, such as C. H. Dodd,[3] regard Paul as a man full of contradictions within himself, a fact that emerges in the contradictions of his letters. The contradictions are based, as mentioned above, in Paul's Jewish past, with which he is still struggling:

> The trouble is that the "Jewish objector" is in Paul's own mind. His Pharisaism—shall we say his patriotism?—was too deeply engrained for him to put right out of his mind the idea that somehow the divine covenant with mankind has a "most favoured nation clause."[4]

Paul, though being freed from this past in his "conversion," now and then falls back into his Jewishness, especially when he is worrying about his brothers and sisters in the flesh. Then, according to Dodd, he seems to become overwhelmed by emotion, losing for the moment the clarity of truth in Christ!

E. P. Sanders also sees Paul struggling in coming to terms with his former belief and the new one revealed to him in Christ. Especially in Rom 9–11, according to Sanders, Paul in his confused ideas is expressing his emotions for his own people. W. S. Campbell draws attention to one specific comment by Sanders:

> Paul's solution in chapter 11 is a "somewhat desperate expedient" to meet the problem of "competing convictions which can be better asserted than explained"—of reconciling native convictions with those received by revelation. Paul's anguish is that he seeks desperately for "a formula which would keep God's promises to Israel intact, while insisting on faith in Jesus Christ.[5]

Heikki Räisänen similarly insists that "Paul's thought on the law is full of . . . inconsistencies."[6]

---

2. Günther Bornkamm, "The Letter to the Romans as Paul's Last Will and Testament," *Australian Bible Review* 11 (1963): 2–14; "Der Römerbrief als Testament des Paulus," in vol. 2 of *Geschichte und Glaube* (vol. 4 of *Gesammelte Aufsätze;* Munich: Chr. Kaiser, 1971), 120–39.

3. C. H. Dodd, *The Epistle to the Romans* (London: Hodder & Stoughton, 1932).

4. Ibid., 43.

5. W. S. Campbell, "Divergent Images of Paul and His Mission," in *Reading Israel in Romans: Legitimacy and Plausibility of Divergent Interpretations* (ed. Christina Grenholm and Daniel Patte; Harrisburg, Pa.: Trinity Press International, 2000), 188.

6. Heikki Räisänen, *Paul and the Law* (2d ed.; Tübingen: Mohr, 1987), 264.

All of these attempts to explain or point to the contradictions in Paul must lead to one of two possible conclusions. F. W. Watson states:

> Paul was capable of thinking coherently only for very short periods of time, and if one rejects an artificial harmonizing process, the only possible solution lies in examining afresh the social context and function of Romans in order to make coherent sense of it.[7]

John Gager proposes the other possibility: "We need to establish an entirely new framework for reading Paul."[8] I think both scholars point in a promising direction. Thus, here I look more closely at one specific aspect of this "examining afresh" or "new framework" that they consider necessary: the framework of the thought categories with which we approach the Pauline Letters.

All the above-mentioned approaches that seek to solve the problem of the so-called contradictions in the letters of Paul look at these from a specific perception of life and reality.[9] They regard Paul as a thinker, following a mental track similar to the way of thinking in traditional scholarship, meaning similar to the way of thinking that has been dominant and prevalent in Western culture and society. As a current philosophy, it has its roots in Greek philosophy, and its categories of thinking are Greek.[10]

These traditions have been dominant in various forms from antiquity and throughout the centuries. People interpreted them in a way that supported the hegemonic power claims of the Roman Empire in antiquity. Yet the Renaissance and the Enlightenment period also especially reemphasized these traditions. In this revitalized form emerging from the Enlightenment, these ways of thinking have shaped modern culture and society to a large extent, and philosophical thought in particular. Living, working, and doing research in the Western part of the world, means being influenced and at least partially shaped by this form of reasoning. Theologians are not exempt from this influence.

---

7. Francis B. Watson, *Paul, Judaism and the Gentiles: A Sociological Approach* (Cambridge: Cambridge University Press, 1986), 170. Cf. also Campbell, "Divergent Images," 189.

8. John Gager, "Paul's Contradictions—Can They Be Resolved?" *Bible Review* 14 (Dec. 1998): 35.

9. See Stanley K. Stowers, *A Rereading of Romans: Justice, Jews and Gentiles* (New Haven: Yale University Press, 1994), 6.

10. See, e.g., Jacques Derrida, "Violence and Metaphysics: An Essay on the Thought of Emmanuel Lévinas," in *Writing and Difference* (trans. Alan Bass; Chicago: University of Chicago Press, 1978), 81: "The entirety of philosophy is conceived on the basis of its Greek source. . . . It is simply that the founding concepts of philosophy are primarily Greek, and it would not be possible to philosophise, or to speak philosophically, outside this medium." Or see Martin Heidegger, *What Is Philosophy?* (trans. William Kluback and Jean T. Wilde; London: Vision, 1958), 29–31: "The word *philosophia* tells us that philosophy is something which, first of all, determines the existence of the Greek world. Not only that—*philosophia* also determines the innermost basic feature of our Western-European history."

One aspect of this way of thinking is to try to understand life and reality as closed systems, following a logic that excludes contradictions in the process of recognizing truth.[11] If one cannot achieve conclusions without contradictions, there must be some inconsistency in thinking. Paul is expected to cohere with this form of rationality. Hence, there should be a linear development in his thinking, from a lower to a higher degree of clarification and recognition of truth. If not, some psychologically or otherwise explainable hindrance within himself is confusing his otherwise so-clear thoughts.[12]

All these attempts to understand Paul have their own logic, their reasonable basis in problems and issues in his letters. But in my view they do not sufficiently take into account that Western rationality is just one way to perceive life and reality, one way among others. Claiming that it is the only possible perception means actually to universalize one particular way of thinking, and this in fact renders that type of thinking an ideology. Although the Enlightenment has liberated thinking from church-dominated dogmatics, it has during the course of history been adapted and instrumentalized to serve certain other purposes. These purposes were by no means purely philosophical or spiritual but had rather to do with imperialistic politics intertwined with economic interests.

Thinkers from other parts of the world—areas that for centuries have been dependent upon, and colonialized by, people who had learned to think and perceive the world in the way outlined above—have begun to question the Western perception of reality. Especially theologians from Africa, Latin-America, and Asia have challenged the universalistic claims of Western ways of thinking.[13] Feminist theologians and philosophers have also begun to do the same.[14] Those who were marginalized, even oppressed, by the Western male-dominated culture have begun to show that this culture and this way of thinking is only one way of perceiving life and reality, a way that has led even to the severe alienation and suffering of other people.

---

11. I elaborate on this in sec. "Aspects of Platonic/Aristotelian Ways of Thinking," 53ff. Cf. J. C. Beker, *Paul the Apostle: The Triumph of God in Life and Thought* (Edinburgh: T&T Clark, 1980), 15: "Our habit of systematic denotative thinking in terms of finished structures of thought and restrictive conceptual units has too often suggested false alternatives, as when scholars oppose 'doctrine' and propose 'mysticism' because of their abhorrence of a 'rationalistic' Paul."

12. See Dodd, *Romans,* 43; E. P. Sanders, *Paul, the Law, and the Jewish People* (Philadelphia: Fortress, 1985), 199; Heikki Räisänen, "Paul, God, and Israel: Romans 9–11 in Recent Research," in *The Social World of Formative Christianity and Judaism: Essays in Tribute to Howard Clark Kee* (ed. Jacob Neusner et al.; Philadelphia: Fortress, 1988), 195–96; and Campbell's response to some of these essays in "Divergent Images," 191–200.

13. Elizabeth A. Castelli, *Imitating Paul: A Discourse of Power* (Louisville: Westminster/John Knox, 1991), 126f., gives an overview of this shift of perspective.

14. See Elisabeth Schüssler Fiorenza's classic work *Bread Not Stone: The Challenge of Feminist Biblical Interpretation* (Boston: Beacon, 1984); and Doris Strahm, *Vom Rand in die Mitte: Christologie aus der Sicht von Frauen in Asien, Afrika und Lateinamerika* (Lucerne: Edition Exodus, 1997), 20–36.

Events that have taken place in the midst of civilized Europe in the middle of the twentieth century have raised the most serious questions. In these events we can actually see the Shoah as the breach of civilization—as the Jewish historian Dan Diner[15] has declared. These events of horror question Western culture to its very roots, and Christianity in particular. Thus, the German theologian Dorothee Sölle quotes a Jewish colleague: "I am often asked whether Judaism perished with the Holocaust. My answer is no, but Christianity has perished."[16] Elie Wiesel said, "The sincere Christian knows that what died in Auschwitz was not the Jewish people but Christianity."[17] These events have revealed the implicit potential of violence and oppressive power within the Western way of thinking in its attempt to subsume all that is into one universal system of thought. The Jewish philosopher Emmanuel Lévinas has reflected thoroughly on these connections in his work, maintaining in a talk with François Poirée in 1987: "Even today I have to say that Auschwitz has been committed by the civilization of transcendental idealism."[18]

In this context we have to raise a key question: Is it appropriate to regard Paul as a thinker who fits into the pattern of Graeco-Roman and Enlightenment ways of thinking? As formulated in Pauline scholarship, is Paul a Hellenistic thinker? If so, to what extent? Since the contradictions in his letters remain an ongoing issue, it seems worthwhile to ask whether Paul possibly does not fit into the categories of Western ways of thinking. As W. S. Campbell wrote:

> I note in passing the need to be careful lest we seek anachronistically to judge Paul by our standards of logic and consistency and the need also to maintain an awareness of the fact that Paul was operating in a very different culture to ours where somewhat different standards of consistency—perhaps even of rationality—and methods of argument applied. Paul was after all seeking to convince a first-century audience and we must not judge as if he had targeted us.[19]

---

15. See Dan Diner, ed., *Zivilisationsbruch: Denken nach Auschwitz* (trans. Susanne Hoppmann-Löwenthal, Renate Schumacher, and Angelika Schweikhart; Frankfurt: Fischer Taschenbuch, 1988).

16. Dorothee Sölle, *Träume mich, Gott: Geistliche Texte mit lästigen politischen Fragen* (Wuppertal: P. Hammer, 1994), 125, with my translation of the German: "Ich werde oft gefragt, ob das Judentum mit dem Holocaust zugrunde gegangen sei. Meine Antwort ist: Nein, aber das Christentum."

17. Harry James Cargas, ed., *Responses to Elie Wiesel* (New York: Persea, 1978), 152.

18. François Poirié, *Emmanuel Lévinas* (Lyon: La Manufacture, 1987), 84, with my translation of the German: "Und noch heute sage ich mir, dass Auschwitz von der Zivilisation des transzendentalen Idealismus begangen wurde." On this see also Emmanuel Lévinas in his first main work, *Totalité et infini: Essai sur l'extériorité* (The Hague: M. Nijhoff, 1961); ET, *Totality and Infinity: An Essay on Exteriority* (trans. Alphonso Lingis; Pittsburgh: Duquesne University Press, 1969).

19. Campbell, "Divergent Images," 189.

We need to ask whether what appears as contradictions in terms of Western Graeco-Roman Enlightenment logic, would necessarily be inconsistent in other ways of thinking.[20]

This is not only a question of interest to the scholarly debate. It implies a problem of far-reaching consequences. The debate about the image of Paul, about contradictions in his letters and the question of what kind of thinker he is, is actually a debate about Christian identity.

From the second century onward, Christians have formulated their identity over against Judaism, using the latter as a negative foil: "Not like the Pharisees." The Reformation and liberal Protestant theology intensified this tendency by putting specific emphasis on a supposed contrast in Paul's letters between the law and justification by faith. The contrast implies an irreconcilable opposition between Judaism and Christian faith, making Paul a chief model as he overcomes the particularity of a legalistic Judaism, using the universal truth of a lawfree Christianity.[21] This contrast also implies that Paul had overcome the Jewish way of thinking and of interpreting the Scriptures: he had made his way into the clarity of thinking rationally according to Graeco-Roman philosophical terms. Nevertheless, for centuries this interpretation of Paul and of his way of thinking has, along with other elements, nurtured anti-Judaism, which led to the rise of political anti-Semitism and oppressionist nationalism, with its horrific consequences.

According to the French philosopher Jacques Derrida, those aspects of Greek philosophy that express a desire for "the same" and "the one" and its search for "the essence" *(οὐσί)* are to a vast extent responsible for any kind of oppressionist ideology. He goes as far as to attribute to such philosophy responsibility for oppression in Western thinking and culture generally.[22] In his essay "Violence and Metaphysics,"[23] about the thinking of Emmanuel Lévinas, Derrida says:

> Incapable of respecting the Being and meaning of the other, phenomenology and ontology would be philosophies of violence. Through them the entire

---

20. Wendy Dabourne, *Purpose and Cause in Pauline Exegesis: Romans 1.16–4.25* (SNTS Monograph Series 104; Cambridge: Cambridge University Press, 1999), 17, taking a similar line: "It seems that to accept that the mistakes are Paul's, not ours, is to work in the shadow of historical improbability, and to risk assuming that we know better than Paul what he was trying to do."

21. On this, see W. S. Campbell, "Millennial Optimism for Jewish-Christian Dialogue," in *The Future of Christian-Jewish Dialogue* (ed. Dan Cohn-Sherbok; Lampeter, U.K.: Mellen, 1999), 217–37.

22. Referring to Lévinas, Derrida states, "Ontology as first philosophy is a philosophy of power" ("A Philosophy of the Neutral, the Tyranny of the State as an Anonymous and Inhuman Universality," sec. in "Violence and Metaphysics," in *Writing and Difference,* 97).

23. Ibid., 79–153.

philosophical tradition, in its meaning and at its bottom, would make common cause with oppression and the totalitarianism of the same.[24]

Following Derrida's perception of these philosophical approaches, which have read Paul predominantly through the spectacles of Western rationality, almost inevitably leads to the image of Paul as the one who sought to overcome (and thus oppress) diversity and particularism in favor of uniformity and universalism.

This is not simply to ask the question whether Paul's thinking is rooted in Hebrew ways of thinking rather than in Greek. This is an important issue[25] but only one aspect of even greater changes affecting modern interpretation. Postmodernism has opened the door to a greater variety of approaches that some regard as raising questions about the very basis of Western rationality:

> Far from despairing over modernity's failings, postcritical theologies rediscover resources for renewal and self-correction within the disciplines of academic study themselves. Postcritical theologies open up the possibility of participating once again in the living relationship that binds together God, text, and community of interpretation. . . . These . . . represent a call for new paradigms of reason—a thinking and rationality that is more responsive than originative.[26]

Different Ways of Thinking

Before I look in more detail at Paul's way of thinking, I offer a brief overview of different philosophical and religious paradigms and their impact on the perception and interpretation of life and its meaning. Here I focus on philosophical paradigms relevant for this study. No doubt others could identify different emphases and ways of thinking about and perceiving the world and life than are dealt with here.

---

24. Ibid., 141. Stating this, Derrida does not imply that all of Greek philosophy shows these totalizing tendencies. See Jacques Derrida, *Khôra* (Paris: Galilée, 1993), where he refers to aspects in Plato's thinking through which the categories of being are transcended, implying something "beyond" or "between" the categories of the ideal and actual being. Derrida asks for a *new* Enlightenment, one that resists letting the spirit of the *old* Enlightenment freeze things into dogmatics, an Enlightenment for this century in which the certainties and axioms of the *old* Enlightenment require reconsideration, translation, and transformation. About this aspect of Derrida's thinking, see Elisabeth Weber, ed., *Derrida: Points . . . : Interviews, 1974–94* (Stanford: Stanford University Press, 1995), 428.

25. See the recently published volume of essays on this topic: Troels Engberg-Pedersen, ed., *Paul beyond the Judaism/Hellenism Divide* (Louisville: Westminster John Knox, 2001).

26. Introduction to the series Radical Traditions: Theology in a Postcritical Key, in *Christianity in Jewish Terms* (ed. Tikva Frymer-Kensky et al.; Boulder, Colo.: Westview, 2000), III.

First I give a brief outline of the so-called Western way of thinking, which is mainly based on Greek philosophy and its reception during the different periods of the history of philosophy up to the present. This is the one and main way of thinking that has "exercised huge power in Europe for fully 1600 years."[27] Such thinking was dominant in the Roman Empire during Paul's lifetime. Beginning with nineteenth century German scholarship, it has mostly been labeled as "Hellenism."[28]

The debate about what the term actually means is ongoing. The use of this term and the dichotomy between Judaism and Hellenism is obviously related to ideological issues of nineteenth-century Germany. Some scholars therefore refer to it as something with similarities to what in Germany was called *Bildung* (culture).[29] Others emphasize its relation to the question of universalism and particularity, with the higher valuation of universalism that is found in Hellenism. Meeks notes that "in this discussion 'Jewish' became virtually a code word for 'particular,' 'limited,' 'historically conditioned,' while 'Greek' came to mean 'universal,' 'rational,' and 'ideal.'"[30]

Troels Engberg-Pedersen suggests that "one should constantly bear in mind that the term 'Hellenistic' should be understood in the very broad, almost empty sense."[31] Stating that a term has to be used in an empty sense to be understood properly seems rather anachronistic and almost pointless. The term in itself then becomes meaningless and says nothing at all. Being aware of the ideological background of its use, I nevertheless will continue to use "Hellenism" in the sense of the cultural pattern and way of thinking of the dominant Graeco-Roman power of the first century. Rather than taking it as an "empty" or "neutral" term, Hellenism here refers not to a melting pot of partners who all contribute equally to this pot, but to the cultural pattern imposed on others and supported not exclusively, but in the first instance, by military power. It is almost inconceivable that Hellenism in that sense did not have some influence on Paul's way of thinking.[32]

---

27. George A. F. Knight, *Christ the Centre* (Edinburgh: Handsel, 1999), 3.
28. See Dale B. Martin, "Paul and the Judaism/Hellenism Dichotomy: Toward a Social History of the Question," in Engberg-Pedersen, *Paul beyond the Divide,* 29–62.
29. Martin, "Paul and the Dichotomy," *Paul beyond the Divide* (ed. Engberg-Pedersen), 30.
30. Wayne A. Meeks, ed., *The Writings of St. Paul* (New York: Norton, 1972), 273.
31. Troels Engberg-Pedersen, "Beyond the Judaism/Hellenism Divide," in *Paul beyond the Divide* (ed. Engberg-Pedersen), 4.
32. Richard Horsley and Neil Elliott pay specific attention to the political circumstances and the imperial ideology that impacted on Paul's life and writing. See, e.g., Richard A. Horsley, ed., *Paul and Politics: Ekklesia, Israel, Imperium, Interpretation* (Harrisburg, Pa.: Trinity Press International, 2000). Derrida refers to something similar when he writes of "Latinization" as a process of universalization. See Derrida, "Faith and Knowledge: The Sources of 'Religion' at the Limits of Reason Alone" in *Acts of Religion,* ed. Gil Anidjar (New York: Routledge, 2002), 42–101; original, *La Religion* (Paris: Editions du Seuil, 1996).

Twentieth-century philosophers such as Franz Rosenzweig, Emmanuel Lévinas, and Jacques Derrida referred to the fact that the tradition of Greek philosophy and its influence during the centuries was and is not the only way of thinking that had an impact on Western culture. Jacques Derrida described Hebraism and Hellenism as the two major forces of (Western) culture,[33] and G. A. F. Knight wrote of the "two strands of our heritage."[34]

There is a sharp ongoing scholarly controversy about whether and to what extent there is in fact such a profound difference in these divergent perceptions of life and reality. Even if such a difference is accepted with regard to the Hebrew Bible and Greek philosophy, there are queries when it comes to first-century Judaism and Hellenistic cultures.[35] Different cultures influence each other as soon as contacts among them exist, and cultural purity is rather an ideological construct than existing in reality. Thus, I consider the question of the influence that Hellenism had on Judaism not as a question of "either-or" but as a question of "To what extent?" and "What was the impact of this influence?"

In the discussion of this in *Paul beyond the Judaism/Hellenism Divide*, several writers assert, sometimes without convincing evidence, that the rift between Greek and Hebrew forms of thinking in Paul can now be overcome.[36] They speak of Paul as a typical Mediterranean man or of Hellenism as a "melting pot"[37] of various cultures, Jewish included. However, to acknowledge this does not solve the issue of the sources and influences upon Paul's life and thought. Hegel, Baur, and others in the distant past have stressed Hellenism, and in the twentieth century W. D. Davies has stressed Paul's Jewish heritage; but that does not mean we should give up the question.[38] My

33. Jacques Derrida quotes Matthew Arnold in an introduction to his essay "Violence and Metaphysics: An Essay on the Thought of Emmanuel Lévinas," in Derrida, *Writing and Difference,* 79: "Hebraism and Hellenism—between these two points of influence moves our world." See also Abraham J. Heschel, *God in Search of Man: A Philosophy of Judaism* (New York: Farrar, Strauss & Cudahy, 1955; reprinted, New York: Octagon Books, 1972), 14: "There is more than one way of thinking. Israel and Greece not only developed divergent doctrines; they operated within different categories."

34. Knight, *Christ the Centre,* 3.

35. See Martin Hengel, *Judaism and Hellenism: Studies in Their Encounter in Palestine during the Early Hellenistic Period* (2 vols.; trans. John Bowden; Philadelphia: Fortress, 1981).

36. See, e.g., Engberg-Pedersen, "Introduction," in *Paul beyond the Divide* (ed. Engberg-Pedersen), 3. The history and the definition of the term *Hellenism* are complex issues. Articles in the same volume analyze the ideological and historical use of the term: Dale B. Martin, "Paul and the Dichotomy," 29–62; Wayne A. Meeks, "Judaism, Hellenism, and the Birth of Christianity," 17–28; and Philip S. Alexander, "Hellenism and Hellenization as Problematic Historiographical Categories," 63–80. Alexander states: "Hellenism is also a highly charged and value-laden concept in the discourse of post-Enlightenment European thought" (67). Martin draws attention to the fact that "up until nineteenth-century Germany, in fact, no one ever posited a dichotomy between Hellenic and Judaic culture or 'mentalities'" (31).

37. Engberg-Pedersen, *Paul beyond the Divide,* 2.

38. I deal with this question with reference to Paul and his way of thinking in more detail in the sec. "Paul and the Judaism/Hellenism Debate," in chap. 4, 125ff.

theory is that although Hellenism influenced Judaism in different ways, significant differences between Jewish and Graeco-Roman ways of thinking persisted during the first century as well as later.[39]

After giving a brief overview of aspects of Graeco-Roman philosophical categories that have predominantly influenced the Western tradition of interpretation, I look at aspects of the Hebrew way of thinking in the Hebrew Scriptures and its development, especially in first-century Judaism. That was Paul's native tradition as a Jew of the first century, who lived with and interpreted his Scriptures, the Hebrew Bible. Since the Greek way of thinking has had a dominant and formative influence in the Western part of the world over the centuries, looking at biblical Hebrew thought means looking at a way of thinking that developed, shaped, and perceived life and reality from the margins. In relation to mainstream thinking, this is a view from the outside.

To the investigation of these two strands of our heritage, I add a third. It would be enough to look at these two strands on their own if, over the centuries up to our time, they had both—in different ways and to different degrees—not largely excluded the life, experience, and thinking of half of humankind: women's life, experience, and thinking from their own perspective.

Feminist theories of knowledge have emerged during the last fifty years, approximately starting with Simone de Beauvoir's pioneering work of nine hundred pages *The Second Sex,* published in French in 1949.[40] Over the centuries women had been excluded from main/malestream ways of thinking. Only men had access to education, and therefore the academic discourses in philosophy and theology were predominantly and almost exclusively male discourses. Women had no way to raise their voices officially and in public and to share in the discourses that tried to understand and find meaning in reality and life. Thus, when women now formulate and interpret reality and life from their own experiences and in their own ways, they also work in ways similar to those of Jewish thinkers in the first century as well as later. They are doing this from the margins, somehow from outside, although not completely, since no one in Western society can remain completely outside the main framework. Especially since the Enlightenment, the domination of mainstream ways of thinking has been all-inclusive, pervading general and academic education. Hence, there is at least some influence of it on all who

---

39. See sec. "First-Century Jewish Interpretation of Scriptures," 65ff.
40. Simone de Beauvoir, *Le deuxième sexe* (Paris: Gallimard, 1949); ET, *The Second Sex* (trans. and ed. H. M. Parshley; London: Cape, 1953; reprinted, London: Pan, 1988).

have gone through the form of education that is shaped by Western-Enlightenment rationality.[41]

Nevertheless, feminist approaches provide philosophical paradigms that differ radically from traditional Western discourse as they are formulated from a different—that is, women's—perspective. This development is one contemporary example of the diversity of perceptions of life and reality, the diversity of different ways of thinking. Although we must clearly distinguish between modern society and society in the Roman Empire of the first century, we may well find analogies in patterns of thinking from a dominant perspective, as well as from a perspective arising in the margins of society.

As a Jew Paul belonged to a minority in the Roman Empire, not only in terms of politics but also in terms of religion, culture, and status. I investigate whether and how and to what extent the above-mentioned different perceptions of life and reality of antiquity might have influenced Paul and his way of thinking, and what their implications could be for a hermeneutics of Paul's letters.

Then I outline aspects of feminist theories and theologies as one alternative to the contemporary dominant discourse and ask what the relevance of such alternative discourses could be for Pauline studies and a feminist perspective on Paul.

Aspects of Platonic/Aristotelian Ways of Thinking and Their Legacy

The Western tradition of thinking, including the Christian tradition, is deeply rooted in classical Greek metaphysics, depending on Platonic/Aristotelian concepts of language and truth. We can find these basic concepts throughout Western philosophy, from Plato and Aristotle to Descartes, Rousseau, Kant, Hegel, and beyond. There was general agreement with what Hans-Georg Gadamer has described: "Greek philosophy more or less begins with the insight that a word is only a name, i.e., that it does not represent true being."[42]

---

41. This is valid not only for feminist theories in particular but also for critical theory in general, as declared by R. Barry Matlock, *Unveiling the Apocalyptic Paul: Paul's Interpreters and the Rhetoric of Criticism* (Sheffield: Sheffield Academic Press, 1996), 336: "For indeed the Enlightenment tradition itself is not something we can simply step out of, but something we must work through to the other side (if there is another side)." Paul Feyerabend says: "A society that is based on a set of well-defined and restrictive rules, *forces the dissenter into a no-man's land of no rules at all and thus robs him of his reason and his humanity*" (quotation from ibid., 336). On the difficulties of finding their own language and self-definition in a feminist perspective, see Adriana Cavarero, "Ansätze zu einer Theorie der Geschlechterdifferenz," in *Der Mensch ist Zwei: Das Denken der Geschlechterdifferenz* (by Diotima, Philosophinnengruppe aus Verona; Vienna: Wiener Frauenverlag, 1989), 66–102.

42. Hans-Georg Gadamer, *Truth and Method* (translation revised by Joel Weinsheimer and Donald G. Marshall; 2d, rev. ed.; New York: Crossroad, 1989), 366.

According to these concepts, we can only find truth beyond language and sensual apprehension, in a transcendent realm of "true, essential being," in silent ontology. Language and words are nothing but pointers, referring to the "essential" truth. According to Plato, language is not truth but only an imitative sound.[43] There remains a unbridgeable gap between the signifier and the thing itself. "The essential *what* of a thing is the subject of discourse; the formulations of discourse are not themselves *what is (οὐσία)*."[44] The formulations of a discourse are not the essence of what the discourse is about. It is impossible to make any kind of statements about the thing as such, Kant's *"Ding an sich."* As Socrates says in the dialogue *Cratylus:*

> He who follows names in search after things, and analyzes their meanings is in great danger of being deceived. . . . How real existence is to be discovered is, I suspect, beyond you and me—we must rest content with the admission that the knowledge of things is not to be derived from names. (436a, 439)

Truth and ultimate meaning reside only in the unchanging realm of ideas, in immutable forms. Thus people cannot attain real knowledge *(Erkenntnis)* through language but only in the realm of ideas that they cannot approach through anything other than the mind *(νοῦς)*, the human intellectual capacity, which is able to transcend particularity and "attain direct intellectual vision of things as they are."[45]

Intrinsic to this perception of reality is a dualistic ontology. There is the contingent, imperfect realm of the visible, material world, and there is the real, essential realm of pure and immutable ideas. This dualism is definitely not based on equality; it is hierarchical in its roots. As David Rutledge put it:

> The idea that there is a sphere beyond linguistic exchange where things simply *exist* in a purely pre-verbal state means that the philosophical ideal is to conceptualise, to think in the abstract, and not to get bogged down in the distracting particularities of words.[46]

Implicit to this valuation of the two spheres is devaluating the concrete and particular aspects of life.

---

43. Plato, *Cratylus* 423b: "A name is . . . a vocal imitation of any object, and a man is said to name an object when he imitates it with the voice."

44. Susan Handelman, *The Slayers of Moses: The Emergence of Rabbinic Interpretation in Modern Literary Theory* (Albany: State University of New York Press, 1982), 8.

45. David Rutledge, *Reading Marginally: Feminism, Deconstruction, and the Bible* (Leiden: Brill, 1996), 8.

46. Ibid., 60.

Aristotle differs from Plato in that he sees the essence of a thing not as residing in an eternal realm of ideas, but within the thing itself. Nevertheless, he perceives the knowledge of truth as attainable only beyond language and the senses.

Most important and of far-reaching consequences were Aristotle's elaborations on how people could attain knowledge of "things as such" or of "the nature of things." Since words and language are regarded as mere signs of "things as such," this knowledge of "things as such" could only emerge in the realm of the mind *(νοῦς)*. True science has nothing to do with verbal discourse but only with thoughts of the soul, intellectual visions that reflect things. Knowledge of truth can be attained only in the realm of thought. This implies that things as they exist in the material reality are not part of this logical, scientific search for truth or the nature of "the things as such." Consequently, Aristotle separated the spheres of poetics and rhetoric, where the relation of words and things is intrinsic, from the sphere of "true science."

He based science on an instrumental theory of language, and separated language and the realm of thinking. According to this, one can find truth only in "science." This implies that poetics, rhetoric, and so on, dealing with concrete, material things, are inferior and as such are excluded from the possibility of serving as means and ways to find truth and ultimate meaning in life. This separation, and the methodology and logic of science that developed from it, dominated Western culture throughout the centuries. Truth, it was claimed, could only be attained through *this* logic of science in the realm of thoughts, not in the realm of words and things.

The Law of Contradiction

At the beginning of his work *De interpretatione,* Aristotle stated that only in the combination of words as a declarative sentence could there be truth or falsity:

> Every sentence is significant (not as a tool but, as we said, by convention), but not every sentence is a statement-making sentence, but only those in which there is truth or falsity. There is neither truth nor falsity in all sentences: a prayer is neither true nor false. The present investigation deals with the statement-making sentence; others we can dismiss, since consideration of them belongs rather to the study of rhetoric or poetry.[47]

Truth or falsity can only be found in statement-making sentences, and the words of a statement-making sentence have to have one univocal meaning—

---

47. Aristotle, *De interpretatione* 16b33–17a5.

ambiguous or equivocal terms have nothing to do with science, that is, truth: "To say that what is is and what is not is not is the true definition of truth and falsehood conversely."[48] In consequence, Aristotle formulates the law of contradiction, which he declares to be the firmest of all principles: "It is impossible for the same thing to belong and not belong to the same thing in the same respect."[49] Self-contradiction and inconsistency in meaning are cardinal sins in the realm of true science and logic.

Although there have been other traditions (explored in more detail below) and realms that claimed to interpret life and reality according to patterns different from Aristotelian logic, its claim of being "the true method" of interpreting reality gained almost universal official acceptance in Western culture.[50] Suppose that the Platonic/Aristotelian perception had remained one perception and interpretation of reality among others, and/or for a limited part of reality only. Rather than claiming universal applicability, it might not have had the oppressive effects on so many aspects of life and people as it actually had. As one tool to investigate certain aspects of reality under certain limited conditions, Platonic/Aristotelian methods lead to useful results, as demonstrated by certain developments in science in the contemporary world. But as soon as it claims to be the only true way to interpret life and reality, we are right to question and criticize it from different perspectives.[51]

Impacts of Platonism/Aristotelianism on Biblical interpretation

Intertwined with the influence of Plato and Aristotle on the philosophical tradition of the West generally was their influence on Christian theology and biblical interpretation in particular. I cannot here elaborate on this in detail. Yet a brief look at some aspects of this influence is useful for our purpose.

The dualistic perception of the world resulted in a general devaluation of the concrete, material world in Christianity, with its devastating impacts, not exclusively but particularly on women and Jews, who as such were associated

---

48. Aristotle, *Metaphysica* (book 4) 1011b.
49. Ibid., (book 4) 1005b.
50. On this also see Walter Brueggemann, *Theology of the Old Testament: Testimony, Dispute, Advocacy* (Minneapolis: Fortress, 1997), 82: "The methods of classical Western theological discourse, want to overcome all ambiguity and give closure in the interest of certitude. I am not sure why the Western Christian tradition has tended to such closure that tilts toward reductionism. It may be because classical Western Christianity has been committed, from early on, to Aristotelian logic that could not countenance the existence of opposites at the same time."
51. Derrida, "Violence and Metaphysics," in *Writing and Difference*, 91, states with reference to Lévinas: "Such a formulation shows clearly that within this experience of the other the logic of noncontradiction, that is, everything which Lévinas designates as 'formal logic,' is contested in its root. This root would be not only the root of our language, but the root of all Western philosophy, particularly phenomenology and ontology."

with this concrete, material, and "fallen" world.[52] One of the central Christian interpretive axioms was based on this perception, the letter/spirit distinction, which contended that truth and ultimate meaning can only be found in the realm of the Spirit and never in the particularity of the letter of the biblical text. It implied that the church claimed to exclusively interpret biblical texts truly in the "spirit." Christians used this dualistic pattern to affirm dogmas and to extract universal statements from biblical texts. They perceived the Jewish interpretation, on the other hand, as adhering to the "letter," the written text with its multiple and sometimes contradictory readings, which they discarded as a merely literal and thus wrong understanding.

Since in accordance with Aristotelian principles there could be only one true univocal reality behind the text, the true reading of a biblical text had to be unambiguous and without any kind of contradictions. How then could interpretation be anything else than univocal since its purpose was to find this true unambiguous reality? In consequence, there could be only one true orthodox reading, the reading the one church claimed to possess. The church enforced this claim with power, oppressing divergent readings once it became affiliated with the imperialistic state. The claim had oppressive effects on those who disagreed with the church or were regarded as less or even incapable of climbing to the heights of true, rational, logical thinking.[53] Throughout history church leaders have frequently and consistently used the ideal of the one true, univocal meaning of a biblical text as an instrument of domination against, e.g., Anabaptists and feminists.

Patterns of Thinking in the Hebrew Scriptures

The way of thinking we encounter in the Scriptures written in Hebrew is different from the Greek perception of the world and life, different from Western philosophy, which developed according to Greek principles.[54]

Aspects of Language

Differences in languages are more than differences in systems of signs to name a thing or express thoughts. Language is more than just something formal. Language is a way to perceive reality and human experience. Indeed,

---

52. More detailed analyses can be found in Rosemary Radford Ruether, *Gaia and God: An Ecofeminist Theology of Earth Healing* (London: SCM, 1993), 27–32, 115–201; and Mary Grey, *Redeeming the Dream: Feminism, Redemption and Christian Tradition* (London: SPCK, 1989).

53. Rutledge, *Reading Marginally,* 60–63, elaborates on this especially with regard to patriarchy.

54. On this see Heschel, *God in Search of Man,* 12–14.

it is in itself experiencing the world and life, since the way we experience and perceive the world and life is very much shaped and expressed by language. We cannot think without language, and since language shapes our experiences and perceptions, it also shapes our ways of thinking. Likewise, our ways of thinking in turn shape our language.[55] Thus it is not just a mere difference of signs in which Greek and related languages differ from Hebrew.[56] The fact that they differ fundamentally in their grammatical structure points to the fundamental difference between Greek (and related languages) and Hebrew ways of thinking. The Jewish philosopher Abraham J. Heschel emphasized:

> There is more than one way of thinking. Israel and Greece not only developed divergent doctrines; they operated within different categories. . . . Hebrew thinking operates with categories different from those of Plato or Aristotle, and the disagreements between their respective teachings are not merely a matter of different ways of expression but of different ways of thinking. . . . Speculation starts with *concepts,* Biblical religion starts with *events.* The life of religion is given not in the mental preservation of ideas but in events and insights, in something that happens in time.[57]

In itself the Hebrew Bible is not a mere unity. Since it encompasses texts of different kinds, love poems as well as legal texts, narrations as well as wisdom texts, hymns as well as prophetic warnings, we can find great variations in style and language. These texts emerged over a long period, leading to variations in the language in the Hebrew Bible. Although we cannot give precise dates for the writing down of the different texts that together eventually became the Hebrew canon, we can recognize that they encompass written traditions from a period of around eight hundred years. Yet in spite

---

55. See, e.g., Friedrich-Wilhelm Marquardt, *Das christliche Bekenntnis zu Jesus, dem Juden* (vol. 1 of *Eine Christologie;* Munich: Chr. Kaiser, 1990), 141: "What is crucial in this respect can hardly be understood by Western Europeans, who are embedded in their own culture: the 'style' of language is more than mere form. 'Language' is a world: our world as we communicate; as long as we do not communicate our world through language, it is not ours. In this respect it could be said that language is *prior to* reality: it is the 'house of being' (Martin Heidegger)." This is my translation of the German: "Worauf es ankommt, können wir westlichen Europäer mit unserer Kultur schwer verstehen: 'Stil' von Sprache ist mehr als Form. 'Sprache' ist eine Welt: unsere Welt, wie wir sie kommunizieren; kommunizieren wir unsere Welt nicht sprachlich, ist sie nicht die 'unsere.' Insofern kann man sagen: Sprache ist *vor* aller Wirklichkeit, ist 'Haus des Seins' (Martin Heidegger)."

56. Ibid., 299: "Language is . . . a form of noninterchangeable participation in the world; how someone finds oneself in this world is expressed also in one's language"; my translation of the German: "Sprache ist . . . eine Form unverwechselbarer Teilnahme an der Welt; wie einer sich in der Welt bewegt, drückt er und drückt sich auch in seiner Sprache aus."

57. Heschel, *God in Search of Man,* 15–16. Cf. also Martin Buber and Franz Rosenzweig's project of the "Verdeutschung der Schrift," to which Martin Buber refers in "Die Schrift und ihre Verdeutschung," in *Schriften zur Bibel* (vol. 2 of *Werke;* Munich: Kösel, 1964), 1111–82.

of these inherent differences in language and style, there are some basic commonalities in these variations of the Hebrew texts, expressing some basic commonalities in Hebrew ways of thinking and in the specific discourse of the Hebrew Scriptures. We want to look closer at some of these.

It is striking, for instance, that biblical Hebrew does not know abstract nouns as such. Entities such as *spirit, reason, emotion,* and so on are expressed in concrete terms: *ruaḥ, lēb, reḥem,* and so on. Thus, the text can express something in the world or experience in life only in a concrete way, connected to something concrete and earthly. Everything is bound to concrete experience; there is no such thing as abstract thinking in the sense of thinking entirely freed from concrete and earthbound life.[58]

In consequence, the Hebrew Scripture does not perceive human beings as divided into different parts—such as body, soul, and spirit—as they are in Greek philosophy. People of the Hebrew Bible could not think of such a thing as a soul or a spirit that could be independent of a body! *Nephes̆,* the noun translated in the Septuagint as ψυχή and in English versions as "soul," first of all means "throat" in Hebrew. Using this word, the Israelites expressed what a throat does: it cries, croaks, gasps for breath, devours food and water when hungry and thirsty. This part of the human body also symbolizes an aspect of human life: human beings as in need of something and somebody, human beings as longing for life. Being in need of something/somebody and dependent makes them vulnerable. The people of Israel knew this from their own experience of dependence and of being strangers in Egypt: "You shall not oppress a resident alien; you know the heart [throat, *nephes̆,*] of an alien, for you were aliens in the land of Egypt" (Exod 23:9). In the relationship between God and human beings, *nephes̆,* this power of life and of longing for life, is of prime importance. In the *Shema Israel,* Jews even today recite: "You shall love the LORD your God with all your heart, and with all your soul [*nephes̆,*], and with all your might" (Deut 6:5).

These examples show that the Hebrew *nephes̆* is something different from the Greek ψυχή or the Western idea of the soul. In the Greek tradition and the Western way of thinking, the soul is something beyond body and visibility, belonging to an eternal sphere. The soul, the more valuable part of a human being, has to gain control over the inferior body. The Hebrew Bible does not know of such essentialist, hierarchical divisions, and there is no dualistic perception of life and human experience as in Greek perceptions.

---

58. See Silvia Schroer, "Auf dem Weg zu einer feministischen Rekonstruktion der Geschichte Israels," in *Feministische Exegese: Forschungsbeiträge zur Bibel aus der Perspektive von Frauen* (ed. Luise Schottroff, Silvia Schroer, and Marie-Theres Wacker; Darmstadt: Wissenschaftliche Buchgesellschaft, 1995; Darmstadt: Primus, 1997), 168; ET, *Feminist Interpretation: The Bible in Women's Perspective* (trans. Barbara and Martin Rumscheidt; Minneapolis: Fortress, 1998).

There is no classification of higher spiritual values and lower concrete and corporeal things. People do not need to overcome earthbound life, body, and concrete experiences as things that (supposedly) prevent human beings from living according to their higher vocation. They perceive earth, body, and concrete life as gifts of the one God, Creator of heaven and earth. Thus the community of faith and the human body are, as Paul has formulated in accordance with his Hebrew tradition, God's temple (1 Cor 6:19).[59]

Apart from the fact that biblical Hebrew does not know separate terms for abstract nouns, nouns generally are of much less importance than verbs. In Hebrew, verbs grammatically determine a sentence to a much greater extent than in English or German.[60] To do something, to act, is of much greater importance than to describe how things or life are. In Hebrew, there is no precise equivalent to the English verb *to be* or the German *sein;* hence, there is no *being* or *essence (Sein, Wesen)* apart from doing or acting. Thus, when Moses asks God to reveal his name at the burning bush, God says: *"'ehyeh 'ǎšer 'ehyeh"* (Exod 3:14). This reply does not say anything about the essence of God, nor does it express an eternal being of God, but instead means, as in verse 12, "I will be with you *('ehyeh 'immāk).*" The verb *'ehyeh* here expresses a relationship and what it means for God to be in this relationship, to accompany his people on their way.[61] When speaking about God, the Hebrew Bible describes him as acting. God "is" not without acting, and in acting he "is."[62] The German theologian Dietrich Bonhoeffer said with reference to this: "A God who exists does not exist (Einen Gott, den es gibt, gibt es nicht)."[63] God does not reveal himself in an abstract way, but he is the God "who brought us up out of slavery in Egypt into the Promised Land."[64]

Thus also *dābār* is not just equivalent to *word* as such but implies thing, action, event, matter, process. *Dābār* does not have the connotation of any kind of essence or οὐσία behind it, but implies that reality is something that happens, as an event.[65] Thus, when God is speaking, he is acting; and when he is acting, he is speaking. As the LORD says in Isaiah:

---

59. Ibid., 168.
60. On this see Brueggemann, *Theology,* 145: "At the core of Israel's theological grammar are sentences governed by strong verbs of transformation. . . . This focus on sentences signifies that Israel is characteristically concerned with the action of God—the concrete, specific action of God—and not with God's character, nature, being, or attributes, except as those are evidenced in concrete actions."
61. On this, see Rolf Rendtorff, *Theologie des Alten Testaments: Ein kanonischer Entwurf* (vol. 1 of *Kanonische Grundlegung;* Neukirchen-Vluyn: Neukirchener Verlag, 1999), 37.
62. Marquardt, *Das christliche Bekenntnis,* 143.
63. Dietrich Bonhoeffer, *Letters and Papers from Prison* (ed. Bethge Eberhard; enlarged ed.; London: SCM, 1971).
64. See also Brueggemann, *Theology,* 145: "This focus on verb, moreover, commits us in profound ways to a *narrative* portrayal of Yahweh, in which Yahweh is the one who is said to have done these deeds."
65. Rendtorff, *Theologie,* 1:6, states: "God is always present, immediately acting. Even when God is speaking, he does so primarily in acting: in creation, in the giving of the covenant with humanity and all

For as the rain and the snow come down from heaven, and do not return there until they have watered the earth, making it bring forth and sprout, giving seed to the sower and bread to the eater, so shall my word be that goes out from my mouth; it shall not return to me empty, but it shall accomplish that which I purpose, and succeed in the thing for which I sent it. (Isa 55:10–11)

God manifests himself through words, and words are aspects "of the continuous divine creative force itself."[66] Indeed, the world was created through divine speech: "And God said, 'Let there be . . .'" (Gen 1:3). From this the German philosopher Hans Jonas concluded:

There was an anti-metaphysical agent in the very nature of the Biblical position that led to the erosion of classical metaphysics, and changed the whole character of philosophy. . . . The Biblical doctrine pitted contingency against necessity, particularity against universality, will against intellect. It secured a place for the contingent within philosophy, against the latter's original bias.[67]

Grammar and structure of language shape and are shaped by the perception of the world and life. It is not due to insufficiency, or because the Israelites did not know any better, that a description of God's essence (as traditionally understood) cannot be found in the Hebrew Bible. This was simply not a question for the people of Israel: it was irrelevant for their life and their relationship to him. Characteristically, the text states what is said about him and this relationship not in terms but in sentences. We can understand the individual words that constitute a sentence only in relation to, and from within, the context of other words. Grammatical peculiarities indicate that the characteristics of thinking and arguing as expressed in the texts of the Hebrew Bible are contextual and relational.

Moreover, the text of the Hebrew Bible/Old Testament is the text of, with, and for the Jewish community. It is the text of the story of Israel and God, the story of one particular community and its relationship with God. Here we need to notice two important implications:

---

creation, in the election of Abraham, in the gift of the Torah at Sinai, and in guiding Israel to the borders of the promised land." Translating: "Gott ist als unmittelbar Handelnder ständig gegenwärtig. Auch wenn Gott spricht, ist dies in erster Linie ein Handeln: in der Schöpfung, in der Setzung des Bundes mit der Menschheit und allem Geschaffenen, in der Erwählung Abrahams, in der Gabe der Tora am Sinai und schliesslich in der Führung Israels bis an die Grenze des verheissenen Landes."

66. Handelman, *Slayers of Moses,* 32.

67. Hans Jonas, *Philosophical Essays: From Ancient Creed to Technological Man* (Englewood Cliffs, N.J.: Prentice-Hall, 1974), 29. See also Brueggemann, *Theology,* 148: "Israel attests that Yahweh creates the world by speech—by royal utterance, a powerful decree that in its very utterance is eagerly and dutifully enacted. This 'theology of the word' is exceedingly influential in subsequent theological reflection."

1. These texts deal with human beings as parts of a community rather than as individuals and their inner life. They reflect on life as a network of relationships—within this particular community, between this community and the world (the Gentile nations), between this community and creation, and between this community and God.

2. The discourse of the Hebrew Scriptures thus reflects on the specific particularity of the life of this community, a particularity that opposes universalization. Its issues are mainly the concreteness of everyday life, and people can only find meaning in the here-and-now lived reality of life.

Israel lives its life in relation to God, and the way Israel expresses this relationship is far from a discourse of reason in a philosophical sense. Encountering and relating to God practically excludes the option of so-called "reasoned" speech, as Paul Ricoeur has said:

> The prophet through whom the word is expressed . . . does not "think" in the Hellenistic sense of the word; he cries out, he threatens, he orders, he groans, he exults. His "oracle" . . . possesses the breadth and the depth of the primordial word that constitutes the dialogical situation at the heart of which sin breaks forth.[68]

In short, the Hebrew Bible is about the relationship between God and human beings, and of human beings with each other and with creation. We can find the form of these relationships in the structures of the Hebrew language of the Bible and the expressed ways of thinking. In this mental mode, it is almost impossible to separate form from content, body from soul and spirit. George A. Knight has thus emphasized:

> Man is a union of flesh and spirit in his *nephesh*. . . . His *nephesh* is consequently a parable of the *nephesh* of God. This belief, or, if you like, awareness of the relationship between God and humans, comes to mind when we remember that the human *nephesh* is not complete in itself, but is in reality a "whole person" only when it is in full and fruitful relations with the *nepheshes* of others. In other words we are meant to be social beings. If that needful social relationship breaks down, then it means that we are not perfectly good, but sinners. But since the "whole" God . . . is holy, . . . he may extend his *nephesh* to his chosen and covenant people in order to empower them through his loving concern for them, to enter into true and creative relations with others in their turn.[69]

---

68. Paul Ricoeur, *The Symbolism of Evil* (Boston: Beacon, 1969), 53.
69. Knight, *Christ the Centre*, 27.

Martin Buber and Franz Rosenzweig recognized and stressed the significance of these basic differences in the structure of biblical Hebrew. In their project of translating the Hebrew Scriptures, they followed as closely as possible these characteristics of the biblical Hebrew, maintaining its distinctive structure and rhythm in German translation.[70]

The Composition of the Text

There is a further aspect indicating that the Hebrew Bible originates from a way of thinking that differs from the mainstream tradition of the Western world. Christian Old Testament scholars have tried to show a center or a principle of the Hebrew Bible/Old Testament as a whole. A huge diversity of "centers" have emerged from these approaches,[71] thus showing that the texts of the Hebrew Bible do not fit easily into systems one tries to impose on them.

Over against such "centralizing" approaches, scholars such as Walter Brueggemann, Rolf Rendtorff, and Erich Zenger have convincingly shown that the Hebrew Bible is in itself polyphonic. According to them, this is not so just by mere accident, or because this work developed over such a long period, or because the "redactors" had not been aware of tensions and contradictions, but because for the greater part this is what is explicitly intended. Differences within these Scriptures—repetitions, variations, even contradictions—are no signs of incompleteness but an intended symphony for theological reasons. There is a plurality of traditions to be found, not an imagined unity. Brueggemann accordingly notes:

> The discourse, moreover, refuses to generalize or to systematize. It characteristically presents one text at a time, and is not at all vexed about juxtaposing texts that explicitly contradict each other. Most often, the editorial process seems to exhibit no great need to overcome such contradictions. At a cognitive or ideational level, the text taken as a whole, seems to have no sustained interest in sorting matters out or bringing to resolution many of the contradictions.[72]

Thus, the Hebrew Bible pleads for the pluriformity of theology. It is characteristically dialogical. It does not aim at formulating transcendental truths. The richness of these narrative witnesses cannot be pressed into coherent systems according to Western logic. There is only one consensus to be found: all these different and differing traditions are related to the one God of Israel.

---

70. See Buber "Die Schrift und ihre Verdeutschung," 1111–82.
71. On this see Erich Zenger, *Am Fusse des Sinai: Gottesbilder im Ersten Testament* (Düsseldorf: Patmos, 1993), 56.
72. Brueggemann, *Theology*, 82.

They are narratives of a relationship that is concrete, incidental, and particular. Those who listen to these traditions must do constructive or interpretive work. This creates not unity but intercoherence, which means that dispute and discussion are not excluded. Being in dispute and discussion about something and with somebody means you are related to, and interested in, this issue and also related to the people involved in the discussion.[73]

In the Hebrew Bible the search for God and the meaning of his will is regarded as an open process that calls for controversy and discussion and does not necessarily lead to final or eternal conclusions. Walter Brueggemann has pointedly formulated this understanding:

> There may be momentary or provisional resolution, but both parties are intensely engaged and are so relentlessly verbal, we are always sure that there will be another speech, another challenge, another invitation, another petition, another argument, which will reopen the matter and expend the provisional settlement. Thus Israel's religious rhetoric does not intend to reach resolution or to achieve closure. This rhetoric, rather, is for the very long run, endlessly open-ended, sure to be taken up again for another episode to adjudication, which this time around may have a different—but again provisional—outcome.[74]

Brueggemann goes on to state:

> There is in Israel's God-talk a remarkable restlessness and openness, as if each new voice in each new circumstance must undertake the entire process anew. Remarkably, the God of Israel, perhaps so characteristically Jewish, is willing to participate yet again and again in such an exchange that must be extraordinarily demanding. For Israel and Israel's God there is no deeper joy, no more serious requirement, no more inescapable burden, than to be reengaged in the process of exchange that never arrives but is always on the way.[75]

The Jewish people did not develop these characteristics of thinking on an island and in splendid isolation, but through a vivid process of interaction with the surrounding cultures of the Near East. This process also did not come to an end with the arrival of Greek and (later) Roman power and culture in the region. But compared to earlier centuries, the situation had

---

73. On this see E.-J. Waschke, "Die Einheit der Theologie heute als Anfrage an das Alte Testament—ein Plädoyer für die Vielfalt," in *Alttestamentlicher Glaube und biblische Theologie: Festschrift für Horst Dietrich Preuss zum 65. Geburtstag* (ed. Jutta Hausmann and Hans-Jürgen Zobel; Stuttgart: Kohlhammer, 1992), 339–41.

74. Brueggemann, *Theology*, 83, 206.

75. Ibid., 84.

changed by the first century in that the Scriptures (although not in their final form) had been attributed a status similar to what later was called canonical authority. Interpretation thus began to replace the process of creating new "Scriptures." The emerging patterns of interpretation of these Scriptures are indications of Jewish ways of thinking of the first century and later, as explored in the next section.

First-Century Jewish Interpretation of Scriptures

It is beyond any doubt that the Scriptures were the basis of Jewish ways of thinking in the first century. Despite the contradictions and differing traditions we find in the Hebrew Bible, we read the story of Israel, "unfolded in the Torah, appealed to in the Prophets, and celebrated and rehearsed in the Psalms," according to van Buren. He continues: "Even for as Hellenized a Jew as the philosopher Philo, this story was the foundation of his thought. Even Israel's Wisdom tradition, which often sounds so Hellenistic, was molded by it."[76] The Scriptures were shaping the Jews' ways of thinking and perceiving the world, their understanding of the political, economic, and cultural situation in which they lived. In turn, their situation—being ruled by Roman power in a cultural atmosphere interwoven with what is labeled as "Hellenism"[77]—was not without significant influence on their way of looking at the Scriptures.[78] The question in debate is how and to what extent this outside influence occurred.

The Beginning of Interpretation

Ezra is credited with establishing "the Book," the written Torah as the center of life for the Jews. The Book of Ezra depicts him as "a scribe skilled in the Law of Moses that the LORD the God of Israel had given" (7:6). The Book of Nehemiah reports: "They read from the book, from the law of God, with interpretation. They gave the sense, so that the people understood the reading" (8:8). These passages are often quoted as indicating the beginning of the tradition of what later was called midrash: the interpretation of a specific biblical text in contemporary circumstances.[79]

This text shows that interpretation of Scripture did not suddenly appear on the scene in postbiblical times. Several passages in the Scriptures are actu-

---

76. Paul van Buren, *According to the Scriptures: The Origins of the Church's Old Testament* (Grand Rapids: Eerdmans, 1998), 26.
77. See the debate on defining the term in sec. "Different Ways of Thinking," 49ff.
78. See Peter J. Tomson, *"If This Be from Heaven . . .": Jesus and the New Testament Authors in their Relationship to Judaism* (Sheffield: Sheffield Academic Press, 2001), 28.
79. Handelmann, *Slayers of Moses,* 43–44, gives more details on this.

ally exegetical, and some writings (e.g., Ps 1:2) stress meditating on the Torah. It thus is no surprise to find Chronicles interpreting Samuel and Kings, or some of the historical psalms retelling the story of Israel. Hence, Geza Vermes has concluded: "Post-biblical midrash is to be distinguished from the biblical only by an external factor, canonisation."[80]

Different Traditions and Communities of Interpretation

Precisely because the canonization of Scriptures had not come to completion by Jesus' day, there was an ongoing debate about what actually could be regarded as Scriptures, the Word of God. Was it the written Torah, as the Sadducees apparently saw it, or did it include the Oral Torah (cf. Mark 7:3), as the Pharisees conceived it? Depending on which perception one adhered to, turning to the Scriptures meant either turning only to the written words of Torah, Prophets, and Writings, or also consulting its interpretation in earlier forms of halakah, haggadah, midrashim, and relatively free scriptural translations, as well as in some apocalyptic and wisdom traditions.

However first-century Jews answered this question, they regarded the Scriptures in their three parts as "a collection of God's words for the benefit of his people Israel and, through Israel, for the whole world. The words were given by God himself, as inspired by the Holy Spirit; they were the complete revelation (Deut 30:11ff.)."[81] First-century Jews thus did not look at these texts as if they were merely telling them something about past events; instead, they "saw reality lying directly in the text itself."[82]

E. P. Sanders in his *Paul and Palestinian Judaism*[83] has convincingly demonstrated that first-century Judaism was not what traditional New Testament scholarship had depicted it to be (a religion of works-righteousness), and that it was not a uniform unity; instead, it consisted in a variety of different and differing movements and groups. James Charlesworth has thus stated:

> Early Judaism was not a philosophy, a theology or a doctrinal system; it rather reflected myriad faithful (and unfaithful) responses to a Creator, to a dynamically active God, who was confessed in one universally binding prayerful

---

80. Geza Vermes, "Bible and Midrash," in his *Post-Biblical Jewish Studies* (Leiden: Brill, 1975), 59–62; also Hermann L. Strack and Günter Stemberger, *Einleitung in Talmud und Midrasch* (8th ed.; Munich: C. H. Beck, 1992), 233; ET, *Introduction to the Talmud and Midrash* (Edinburgh: T&T Clark, 1991).

81. Van Buren, *According to the Scriptures*, 31.

82. Ibid., 30. On this see also Luke T. Johnson, *The Writings of the New Testament: An Interpretation* (Philadelphia: Fortress, 1986), 42: "Within Torah as text, Jews in every nation and every generation discovered their identity as a people, a sense given to those who share a common story."

83. E. P. Sanders, *Paul and Palestinian Judaism: A Comparison of Patterns of Religion* (Philadelphia: Fortress, 1977).

affirmation, the *Shema,* which was recited by religious Jews at least twice daily on the week days *('arebhîth weshaharîth).* Liturgy, based upon shared traditions and history, memories and hope, kept the differences, so essential to a lively faithfulness, from exploding apart the living reality we call Judaism.[84]

Whether one agrees with Sanders's thesis that the underlying pattern of religion of all of these different forms of Judaism was "covenantal nomism" or not, a broad scholarly agreement holds that there actually was a great variety of different forms of Judaisms in the first century.[85]

Taking into account that Jews lived in different geographical, social, political, and religious settings, it is not difficult to understand that they had developed different forms of Judaism, and that specific ways of interpreting the Scriptures shaped them. These interpretations led Jews to different conclusions about how to understand and come to terms with the situations in which they lived.[86] Interpretation of the Scriptures played a significant role in the forming of a community or its division. Thus Roy E. Ciampa states: "To understand early Jewish or Christian perceptions of what Scripture said and taught, that is, to understand what constitutes 'scriptural' discourse *for them,* we must familiarize ourselves with the variety of interpretive traditions that may have shaped those perceptions."[87]

Already as early as 1975, Geza Vermes spoke even more decisively of the need for New Testament scholars to study Jewish Scripture interpretation:

> Scripture interpretation turns out to be the most basic and vital expression of post-biblical mind. . . . Since the Christian *kerygma* was first formulated by Jews for Jews, using Jewish arguments and methods of exposition, it goes without saying that a thorough knowledge of contemporary Jewish exegesis is

---

84. James H. Charlesworth, *The Old Testament Pseudepigrapha and the New Testament: Prolegomena for the Study of Christian Origins* (Cambridge: Cambridge University Press, 1985), 56.

85. Sanders's depiction of first-century Judaism is challenged from several perspectives; cf. Charles H. Talbert, "Paul, Judaism, and the Revisionists," *Catholic Biblical Quarterly* 63.1 (2001): 1–22. But even if Sanders is not right in detail, he has demonstrated that Judaism certainly was not and is not a religion of works-righteousness.

86. Geza Vermes, *Post-Biblical Jewish Studies,* 38: "By the middle of the second century B.C., however, shortly after national unity had been achieved against the lethal threat of Hellenism, Palestinian Judaism disintegrated into the separate and rival groups of Pharisees, Sadducees and Essenes, to which were added in the first century of the Christian era Zealots and Judeo-Christians. Each of these religious parties was convinced that its particular teachings and customs were perfectly in accord with divine revelation. From the one body of sacred writings, that is to say, and employing the same methods of interpretation, each evolved a distinct religious outlook and way of life in conflict, very often, with those of the others."

87. Roy E. Ciampa, *The Presence and Function of Scripture in Galatians 1 and 2* (Tübingen: Mohr/Siebeck, 1998), 284. On this see also Anthony T. Hanson, *The Living Utterances of God: The New Testament Exegesis of the Old* (London: Darton, Longman & Todd, 1983), 2: "The New Testament writers inherited the various exegetic traditions current in Judaism. . . . We cannot hope to understand the thought of the New Testament writers unless we take account of their interpretation of Scripture."

essential to the understanding (and not just better understanding) of the message of the New Testament and, even more, of Jesus.[88]

This applies not only to the understanding of the Gospels and of Jesus but also to the understanding of Paul and his letters. Paul's interpretation of the Christ event must be seen as part of, and in the context of, first-century Judaism.

Looking at some characteristics of different forms of first-century Judaism and their patterns of interpreting the Scriptures might provide us with clues of where to locate Paul and his way of thinking in this spectrum and how to understand his letters.

First I turn to Pharisaic patterns of interpretation, forerunners of later rabbinic exegesis,[89] and then give an overview of types of interpretation found in the Qumran writings. These sources are contemporaries of Paul's letters. After looking at apocalyptic literature, which expresses a general atmosphere in first-century Judaism generally, I examine some interpretations explicitly influenced by Hellenism.

Pharisaic—Pre-Rabbinical Interpretation

There is historical evidence for the significance of the Pharisaic movement during the Second Temple period and for the incorporation of Pharisaic traditions into later rabbinic literature.[90] Because rabbinic literature in its written form only emerged at the beginning of the third century, it is difficult to retrace and date older traditions included in it. I basically rely on research results of scholars such as Geza Vermes,[91] Daniel Patte,[92] Hermann L. Strack and Günter Stemberger,[93] and Peter Tomson.[94] They all have argued for the antiquity of interpretive traditions in rabbinic literature.

Tomson sees evidence for the inclusion of traditions antedating the destruction of the Second Temple in the fact that rabbinic literature identifies explicitly with teachers such as Hillel, Gamaliel, and Yohanan ben Zakkai.[95] Rabbinic literature hardly mentions the term Pharisees. Apparently it had some negative connotations; therefore, outsiders used it, but the Pharisees themselves did not use it as a self-designation. It occurs together

---

88. Vermes, "Bible and Midrash," 88.
89. On this see Tomson, *"If This Be from Heaven,"* 50–55, 81–86.
90. Ibid., 50–55.
91. Vermes, *Post-Biblical Jewish Studies.*
92. Daniel Patte, *Early Jewish Hermeneutic in Palestine* (Missoula: Scholars Press, 1975), 17.
93. Herman L. Strack and Günther Stemberger, *Einleitung in Talmud und Midrash,* 8th ed. (Munich, C. H. Beck, 1992), 14–15.
94. See Peter Tomson, *Paul and the Jewish Law: Halakha in the Letters of the Apostle to the Gentiles* (Minneapolis: Fortress, 1990); and idem, *"If This Be from Heaven."*
95. Tomson, "If This Be from Heaven," 51.

with the term Sadducees in a report about a debate between different groups (m.Yad4.6–7). The use of the term Sadducees in Rabbinic literature is, according to Tomson, a strong indication for a pre-70 tradition. After the destruction of the temple, the Sadducees are no longer mentioned.[96]

The use of rabbinic literature for historical reconstruction is appropriate if we keep in mind the difficulties implicit in their use. The writings of Josephus and of the New Testament are further sources of information about the Pharisees.

Through Josephus we learn that one characteristic position of the Pharisees was their conviction that the oral tradition, Oral Torah, had authority similar to the written Torah. This obviously had been a fundamental difference between them and the Sadducees.

The Pharisees had passed on to the people certain regulations handed down by former generations and not recorded in the Law of Moses, for which reason they are rejected by the Sadducean group, who hold that only those regulations should be considered valid which were written down [in Scripture], and that those which had been handed down by former generations need not be observed.[97]

If the polemics of Qumran against the *dōršê ha-ʿalaqot,* "the seekers of smooth things," in a distorted way did mean the Pharisees and their belief in the authority of the Oral Torah, this would support Josephus's record.[98] Their appreciation of the oral tradition for legal matters as well as for other beliefs (resurrection, angels, apocalyptic influences) means that the Pharisees were a reform movement. In new situations not foreseen by the written Torah, they sought to find answers according to what was understood as the full divine message to Israel. This seems to have caused some irritation among other groups of first-century Judaism.[99]

As noted above, creative interpretation of the Scriptures had already begun before the completion of the canon, within the Bible itself. New situations and new questions called for new answers. If one is convinced that the Scriptures reveal the entire will of God and that everything is meaningful in the Scriptures, it is almost impossible not to be challenged to search for new

---

96. The Sadducees historically disappear after 70—thus when they are mentioned in Rabbinic literature this is taken by Tomson as an indication of a pre-70 tradition. Ibid., 51.

97. Josephus, *Antiquitates Judaicae* 13.10.6.

98. *Thanksgiving Hymns* II, 32; Ekkehard W. Stegemann and Wolfgang Stegemann, *The Jesus Movement: A Social History of Its First Century* (Edinburgh: T&T Clark, 1999), 142.

99. There is a scholarly debate on whether this meant that the Pharisees regarded any written interpretation of the Torah as inappropriate, or whether this referred just to the contrast—written in the Scriptures or not written in the Scriptures—as emphasized by Jacob Neusner, *The Rabbinic Traditions about the Pharisees before 70* (3 vols.; Leiden: Brill,1971), 3:143–79. In contrast, Tomson, *"If This Be from Heaven,"* 54, interprets "oral" literally as "oral": in his view the Pharisees renounced any form of writing of the "oral tradition."

ways of understanding. The Scriptures had to be meaningful for the actual Jewish community, which sought to live according to this divine revelation. The Torah had to be adjusted to life.[100] But since the text is a revelation of God, how is it possible that it is not plain and clear enough so that it can be understood beyond doubt?

Human eyes see and human minds understand the things they encounter in life in different ways. Regarding written words as divinely revealed consequently confronts people inevitably with the problem of hermeneutics and authority. Which interpretation can claim to understand the divine message properly? Each of the different groups at the end of the Second Temple period developed "its interpretative system to justify the biblical authenticity of its beliefs and way of life."[101]

When the church became associated with imperial power, the problem was solved by means of dogmatic decrees and imperial military force. In rabbinic Judaism, different positions on the nature of the Oral Torah emerged, as David Weiss Halivni writes:

> The *maximalist* position claims that God revealed to Moses on Mount Sinai the entire Oral Torah consisting of all the legitimate arguments for, and all the legitimate solutions to, every issue that may arise, including "the comments that an astute student will someday make in the presence of his teacher." Humanity merely needs to uncover them. . . . The *intermediary* position claims that God revealed to Moses on Mount Sinai all the legitimate arguments of every issue that may arise but not their solutions. The solutions were left for human beings to offer, and whatever they offer becomes part of "the words of the living God." . . . Contradictions are thus built into revelation. Revelation was formulated within the framework of contradiction in the form of argumentation pro and con. . . . The *minimalistic* position claims that God revealed to Moses on Mount Sinai directions for humanity to follow and principles to implement, but not detailed stipulations. . . . [It] presents humanity with the opportunity, and authority, for the fleshing out of halakic arguments and details from directorial principles.[102]

However later centuries dealt with the problem of interpretation and authority, the Pharisees stood for the need of interpretation, for the need to

---

100. Patte, *Early Jewish Hermeneutic*, 76, 89.

101. Vermes, "Bible and Midrash," 62.

102. David Weiss Halivni, "Plain Sense and Applied Meaning in Rabbinic Exegesis," in *The Return to Scripture in Judaism and Christianity: Essays in Postcritical Scriptural Interpretation* (ed. Peter Ochs; New York: Paulist, 1993), 120–21.

understand sacred texts in and for contemporary life. As far as we know, they did not separate themselves from society as did the people from Qumran, but they intended to be present in society and to gain influence in it. One aim of their ways of interpretation was to live everyday life according to the Scriptures and within contemporary Jewish society.[103]

Though rabbinic interpretation is not identical with first-century Pharisaic interpretation of Scriptures, there is strong scholarly support for the view that rabbinic patterns and techniques of interpretation can be retraced back to the Pharisaic movement. The expression "explanation, study of the Torah *(midrash ha-Torah)*" can be found in Qumran (1QS VIII, 15); and Ben Sira includes the term "house of learning/instruction (beth midrash)" (51:23). Since Paul himself was part of the Pharisaic movement (Acts 23:6; Phil 3:5), it is most likely that he was familiar with its patterns and techniques of interpretation. It therefore is no surprise to find such patterns and techniques throughout his letters. Others have dealt with this aspect of Paul's letters at length.[104] Here it is sufficient to outline briefly some characteristics of Pharisaic/rabbinic patterns of interpretation as they shed light on Paul's way of arguing and thinking.

Targumim

By the first century A.D. many Jewish people had some trouble understanding the Hebrew text of the Scriptures. Aramaic translations of biblical texts were among the writings from Qumran. Such Targumim survived from the later rabbinic period, but with the translations of Job and Leviticus as well as the Genesis *Apocryphon* (1Qap Gen) found at Qumran, there is no doubt that Targumim already were in use in the late Second Temple period.[105]

From their beginning the purpose of the Targumim was twofold: "They were used as a way of offering an interpretation of Scripture for the Bible student, and bridging the gap between his vernacular and the original Hebrew."[106] Thus, a Targum was more than a mere translation of a text from one language to another. The sense of the word *Targum* itself is close to the Latin word *interpretatio,* indicating that a plain translation in itself is something

---

103. See E. Stegemann and W. Stegemann, *The Jesus Movement,* 143.
104. On this see W. D. Davies, *Paul and Rabbinic Judaism: Some Elements in Pauline Theology* (50th anniversary ed.; Mifflintown, Pa.: Sigler, 1998); Tomson, *Paul and the Jewish Law;* Dan Cohn-Sherbok, *Rabbinic Perspectives on the New Testament* (Lampeter, U.K.: Mellen, 1990).
105. See Philip S. Alexander, "Jewish Aramaic Translations of Hebrew Scriptures," in *Mikra, Text, Translation, Reading, and Interpretation of the Hebrew Bible in Ancient Judaism and Early Christianity* (ed. Martin J. Mulder; Assen: Van Gorcum, 1988), 247.
106. Ibid., 248.

almost impossible.[107] In the Targumim, translation and commentary were both present.[108] We can with little doubt regard the Targumim as the origin of the Midrashim of later rabbinic literature: "The Targum contains already all the structure and all the themes of the Midrash."[109]

According to Philip Alexander,[110] there is a basic distinction between "paraphrastic" and "literal" Targumim, depending on the length of the Targum compared to the original. Alexander further distinguishes two main types of paraphrastic Targumim: "In type A, a viable one-to-one translation of the Hebrew can be extracted from the paraphrase by bracketing out the additions. In type B, a base translation cannot be recovered: the translation is dissolved in the paraphrase."[111] Yet both types aim to interpret every element of the text in the order given, and they do not leave out any word of the original. Both types used methods of interpretation. Some methods are directly related to linguistic issues, such as applying a differing vocalization of the consonants to interpret a word in its textual context, or playing with a homonymous root or a different meaning of the same word. Also, a Targum could change meaning by separating words in a sentence or sentences in a text in different ways.[112] Such techniques are similar to the thirty-two *middoth* (hermeneutical rules) of Rabbi Eliezer ben Jose ha-Gelili.[113] Much later, rabbis compiled techniques that were already in use in the Targum type of interpretation before appearing in the Midrash.[114]

Behind this early use of different techniques of interpretation, we can trace a common attitude toward the Scriptures. Since Jews were convinced that everything is meaningful in the Scripture, it had to be meaningful to the contemporary community, therefore implying also an actualization of Scripture. Further, there is the rule that Scripture has to be explained by Scripture, which included the Oral Torah.

Interpretation of Scripture by Scripture presupposes a perception of time that is different from a linear historical one. The last of the thirty-two middoth of Rabbi Eliezer ben Jose ha-Gelili expresses this outlook: "There is no before and after in Scripture." Historical chronology can therefore be

---

107. On the difficulties of translation, Derrida wrote: "[A] translation, however excellent it may be, necessarily remains a translation—that is to say an always possible but always imperfect compromise between two idioms." "Force of Law: The 'Mystical Foundation of Authority,'" in *Acts of Religion*, Gil Anidjar, ed. (New York, London: Routledge, 2002), 230–300 (232).

108. Alexander, "Jewish Aramaic Translations," 239.

109. Patte, *Early Jewish Hermeneutic*, 50–52, who follows Renée Bloch, "Moïse dans la tradition rabbinique," *Cahiers Sioniens* 8 (1954): 214–15.

110. As referred to by Patte, *Early Jewish Hermeneutic*, 228–37.

111. As referred to by ibid., 234.

112. Ibid., 56.

113. For details see Strack and Stemberger, *Introduction to the Talmud and Midrash*, 25–34.

114. Patte, *Early Jewish Hermeneutic*, 57–58.

ignored.[115] This perception opens up the possibility to view different events that happened at different times in different places and count them as closely interrelated. Such a perspective creates a unity expressed in the basic belief that all the different events recorded in the Scriptures are *dābār*, the act or word of the one God of Israel.[116]

These characteristics indicate that in the Targumim the pattern of interpretation is not based on a theological system, as in "systematic theology." Apart from the Scriptures, there is no overall system within which students could take the insights or understandings gained through different techniques and methods and set them into a specific order. One could rather see these interpretations as expressions of an "atomistic theology."[117] They closely follow the biblical text, investigating it in detail and raising questions from actual life in order to extract guidelines from it. Thus, it seems that interpreters were in a constant dialogue with the biblical text and with each other in order to understand God's revelation in contemporary life. Moreover, they were not only in dialogue with the biblical text and with each other, but also with both in relation to contemporary events.[118] Daniel Patte summarizes this:

> In other words what is essential is not a correct (orthodox) theological doctrine but an openness to Scripture, a "listening to Scripture" in the context of actual life. This in fact results in "a multiplicity of theological conceptions" not necessarily fitting with each other.[119]

Midrashim

What has been said about interpretation methods in the Targumim applies

---

115. For a detailed discussion see ibid., 67–74.

116. Patte, in ibid., 70–71, refers to an illustrating example of this he found in Roger Le Déaut, *La Nuit Pascale: Essai sur la signification de la Pâque juive à partir du Targum de Exode XII 42* (Rome: Institute Biblique Pontifical, 1963): "Let us take the example that Le Déaut found in *Targum Neofiti I* on Ex 12:42, which brings together the four important nights of the history of the world, *viz.,* the night of the creation, the night of Abraham (either the night of the covenant, Gen 15:13, or that of the *Aqueda,* i.e., 'binding' of Isaac on the altar), the night of the Passover, and the eschatological night of the Messianic salvation. The identity of these nights is expressed first by ascribing them to the same calendar day. Thus the Covenant of Abraham with God is put on Nissan 15, that is, the Passover night. The same thing is done with the *Aqueda,* the night of the creation and that of the *Eschaton*. Furthermore, the identification of these four nights allows the interpreter to understand each of them in terms of the other. The Exodus is understood in terms of the Creation, and the Creation is understood in terms of the Exodus. . . . In the same way the *Eschaton* is interpreted in terms of the Exodus (*viz.,* as an Exodus from this world to the world to come), as well as in the terms of Creation (a re-creation and not a renovation). The *Aqueda* is interpreted in terms of, and helps to interpret, the Passover. In the same way Gen 15 (the covenant with Abraham) is interpreted in terms of the Exodus and of the Eschaton." See esp. 65 and 70ff.

117. See Patte, *Early Jewish Hermeneutic,* 75.

118. See W. S. Campbell, "Paul's Application of Scripture to Contemporary Events," paper presented at the British New Testament Studies seminar on "Use of the Old Testament in the New," Hawarden, U.K., 1988.

119. Patte, *Early Jewish Hermeneutic,* 75.

also to the explicit type of interpretation, the midrash. The two genres cannot be clearly separated. Their origin is often seen in Neh 8:8: "So they read from the book, from the law of God, with interpretation. They gave the sense, so that the people understood the reading." As we have seen above, Targumim were more than mere translations. The close relation of both types of interpretation has also to do with their common *Sitz im Leben,* the synagogue and the school.

The word *midrash* is derived from *dārash,* which means "to seek, to interpret." The Bible already uses this verb in a specifically theological meaning, as in Ezra 7:10: "For Ezra had set his heart to *study* the law of the LORD," and in Isa 34:16: "*Seek* and read from the book of the LORD." As we have noted above, an explicit use of the term appears in the Hebrew text of Sir 51:23: "*bet ha-midrash* (the house of learning/instruction)." There is hardly any precise definition of the midrashim; one can describe them as "a type of literature, oral or written, which stands in a direct relationship to a fixed, canonical text, considered to be authoritative and the revealed word of God by the midrashist and his audience, and in which this canonical text is explicitly cited or clearly alluded to."[120]

Geza Vermes gives a detailed description of the different types of midrash.[121] He distinguishes between "pure" and "applied" exegesis. In a more specific way these are the main distinctions already in use in the Targumim. The first category takes as its starting point for interpretation a problem arising from within the text; this might be a word whose exact meaning cannot be discovered from the context, a lack of details, contradictions to another biblical passage, or an unacceptable meaning.[122] The purpose of the "pure" exegesis type of midrash was, as Vermes writes, "to render every word and verse of Scripture intelligible, the whole of it coherent, and its message acceptable and meaningful to the interpreter's contemporaries. 'Pure' exegesis is organically bound to the Bible. Its spirit and method are of biblical origin."[123]

In the case of applied exegesis, the starting point is problems and queries that arose from everyday life, or contemporary customs and practices that the interpreter sought to connect with Scripture. This type seems to have attained importance primarily among the Pharisees. Whenever their interpretation departed from what was perceived to be the norm, they had to find solid arguments for binding it to the Scriptures in order to convince others. Especially for legal interpretation (halakah), which had to be relevant in practical life, some kind of verifiable method had to be found to establish the

---

120. Gary Porton, "Defining Midrash," in *The Study of Ancient Judaism* (ed. Jacob Neusner; New York: Ktav, 1981), 62.
121. Vermes, *Post-Biblical Jewish Studies,* 59–91.
122. Ibid., 63.
123. Ibid., 80.

validity of an interpretation. Thus, according to tradition, Hillel compiled the seven rules (middoth) of interpretation, which later were subdivided into thirteen by Rabbi Ishmael and increased to thirty-two by Rabbi Eliezer ben Jose ha-Gelili.[124]

These middoth were particularly important for legal exegesis, but rabbis also used them in haggadic interpretation, although the latter was more open to creative elements.

A central issue of scholarly debate is the question of Hellenistic influence on these Jewish methods of interpretation. There is little doubt that there must have been some kind of influence. The question is how much and how deep this influence actually was, and what this actually meant. David Daube has demonstrated that the seven hermeneutical rules ascribed to Hillel are all deeply influenced by Hellenistic rhetorical teaching.[125] But what precisely does this mean? Does it imply that only with the use of these Hellenistic categories could rabbis apply sound and logically traceable methods? Did it mean that they also introduced Graeco-Roman categories of arguing and thinking into the interpretation of the Hebrew Scripture? In debate with Daube, Saul Lieberman made a pointed statement on the issue:

> The early Jewish interpreters of Scripture did not have to embark for Alexandria in order to learn there the rudimentary methods of linguistic research. To make them travel to Egypt for this purpose would mean to do a cruel injustice to the intelligence and acumen of the Palestinian sages. Although they were not philologists in the modern sense of the word, they nevertheless often adopted sound philological methods.[126]

I tend to agree with Lieberman's and others' arguments for a moderate influence of Hellenism on Jewish ways of interpretation for several reasons: We have seen (above) that interpretation of Scripture already occurs within Scripture. This demonstrates that an interpretive tradition already existed before there was any Hellenistic influence on Palestine. If we hold that the rabbis could have introduced proper linguistic and interpretive methods only under Graeco-Roman influence, we have undervalued the cultural and

---

124. For more detail, see, e.g., Strack and Stemberger, *Introduction to the Talmud and Midrash*, 17–34.

125. Daube states: "The famous seven norms of hermeneutics he [Hillel] proclaimed, the seven norms in accordance with which Scripture was to be interpreted, hitherto looked upon as the most typical product of Rabbinism, all of them betray the influence of the rhetorical teaching of his age." From David Daube, "Rabbinic Methods of Interpretation and Hellenistic Rhetoric," *Hebrew Union College Annual* 22 (1949): 239–64; reprinted, in *Collected Works of David Daube* (vol. 1; ed. Calum M. Carmichael; Berkeley: University of California, 1992), 344, 333–355.

126. Saul Lieberman, *Hellenism in Jewish Palestine* (2d ed.; New York: Jewish Theological Seminary of America, 1962), 53.

specifically exegetical skills and achievements of those Jewish people involved in the task of interpretation. Moreover, we should keep in mind that the writing and compilation of the Scriptures already is in itself a cultural achievement on a high level.

It is no surprise that even within the Scriptures we can find traces of influences of the surrounding Mediterranean cultures.[127] Nobody and no people are real islands; human beings live related to each other. There is not only an exchange of material goods between people and cultures but also an exchange on the level of ideas, customs, and so on. A "pure" culture or a "pure" people would be an ideological construct. Cultures and people are always mixtures to some extent.[128]

Thus, the Hellenistic influence was just one added to previous ones, such as Egyptian, Babylonian, and Persian. But through and with all these different influences at different times and places, Jews developed their own ways of dealing with such influences and integrating them into their perception of life and the world. Their perception was based on the belief in the one God, who had led them out of slavery and into freedom. Thus, wherever interpretative methods might have had their origins—and in the first century the culturally dominant Graeco-Roman surroundings obviously influenced them—the main purpose these had to serve was to help Jews understand and live according to the relationship/covenant with the one God. Thus, Hellenism influenced the rules of Hillel (and others). But they Hebraized whatever they borrowed in forming the middoth, these in turn being organized in accordance with Jewish life and thus integrated into the Jewish "symbolic universe."[129]

The Scriptures expressed the history of the relationship between God and his people. There was no interpretation or religious ruling separate from the Scriptures. Hence, the Jews had to relate each and every idea or view to the Word of God if it was to gain any kind of acceptance in the community. The Word of God was expressed in Hebrew, and the sages emphasized the distinction of sacred (Hebrew) text from any translation.[130] Since Hebrew is a language and a way of thinking closely related to concrete life, this way of thinking influences any interpretation of the text.

---

127. See, e.g., Silvia Schroer, *Die Weisheit hat ihr Haus gebaut: Studien zur Gestalt der Sophia in den biblischen Schriften* (Mainz: Matthias-Grünewald, 1996).

128. Cf. also sec. "Aspects of Platonic/Aristotelian Ways of Thinking," 53–57.

129. This is also acknowledged by Daube, "Rabbinic Methods," in *Collected Works,* 1:334: "That is to say that the borrowing took place in the best period of Talmudic jurisprudence, when the Rabbis were masters, not slaves, of the new influences. The methods taken over were thoroughly Hebraized in spirit as well as form, adapted to the native material, worked out so as to assist the natural progress of Jewish law." See more details about this also with reference to Philo in sec. "Paul and the Judaism/Hellenism Debate," in chap. 4, 153ff.

130. Alexander, "Jewish Aramaic Translations," 238: "Every effort had to be made to avoid confusing the targum with the written text of Scripture."

The Targumim and the midrashim closely relate interpretation to the original Hebrew text, often taking its starting point in a linguistic problem. They continue this concrete way of thinking precisely through the close relationship with the text. As they build on the concreteness of the given text, contradictions or gaps are no reason to abandon the text (since "everything in Scripture is meaningful"). Because the Jews closely adhered to and followed the order of the text rather than starting an interpretation from a specific theme, this type of exegesis might give us the impression of being inconsistent, contradictory, even chaotic.

We could count such exegesis as chaotic if we continue thinking in, and arguing from, our usual perspective, influenced primarily by Graeco-Roman philosophical categories used to legitimate hegemonic power claims and also, in its wake, the Enlightenment tradition. But there could be another approach to this type of interpretation. We could see it as deriving from the other way of thinking, outlined in the section on the Hebrew Scriptures (above).

Rooted in the Scriptures, it is no great surprise that the very same way of thinking primarily influences biblical interpretation. Looking at it from this different perspective, there is no inconsistency in contradictions and no chaos in following the order of Scripture itself. Instead, all of this is an expression and a consequence of the commitment to the one God, an expression and a consequence of the living and lively relationship between God and his people Israel. A system cannot grasp a relationship; one cannot understand a relationship in terms of traditional logic or in a final way. A relationship must by its nature remain as open as life itself, in order to continue and stay alive. "Atomistic" theology and the never-ending way of *dārash* seems to be quite an appropriate method of interpreting this relationship. The "inconsistencies" that traditional scholarship has found in Paul's letters could have something to do with such a way of thinking and arguing theologically. I will come back to this in more detail in part 2, especially in the section "The Jewish Texture of Paul's Way of Thinking," in chapter 4.

Qumran's Interpretation of Scriptures

The only identifiable group of first-century Judaism that we know from their own writings, except for early Christ-believing groups, is the community of Qumran. Since the other known writings of that period are either anonymous or pseudepigraphic, or represent the views and ideas of one particular writer,[131] we can only hypothesize about the people behind these writings or the historical background from which they emerged.

---

131. As is the case with Philo and Josephus.

The Qumran texts give us significant information about the group from which they originated and its self-understanding, thus providing us with unique and original insights into the way of thinking of one particular Jewish group of the Second Temple period. Moreover, those texts that are not exclusively sectarian share significant information about patterns and methods of interpretation of the Scriptures, patterns widespread among different groups of Judaism of that time. They thus also could shed light on patterns and methods Paul applied in his scriptural interpretation.

Whether the covenanters of Qumran and the Essenes were in fact identical groups is a matter of scholarly debate, and there are well-argued reasons for both options. There is nothing to add to this debate, nor am I able to decide whose arguments are the most reliable ones. Since the focus here is on patterns of interpretation and ways of thinking, we need not pursue this debate further.[132]

There is probably no first-century Jewish group other than the Qumran community that defined itself and its identity as clearly on its distinct and differing interpretation of Scripture. As Michael Fishbane says: "It was, in fact, precisely in the special way that the old laws were reinterpreted or extended, the old predictions reapplied or decoded, and the institutions of ancient Israel restructured or regenerated, that the covenanteers of Qumran saw themselves as distinct from other contemporary Jewish groups."[133] We cannot find the basis of this distinct interpretation so much in specific methods and techniques as in the history of the origin of the Qumran community and the self-understanding it derived and developed from that origin.

The Qumran covenanters had separated from mainstream Jewish society and developed their own social structures, religious literature, and rules of everyday life, most likely as a group who had split from the priestly hierarchy at the Jerusalem temple. After the successful Maccabean revolt against Hellenistic and pagan influence, the Maccabees had replaced the Zadokite high priest with their own candidate, and thus had reduced the influence of the Zadokites as long as they were ruling the country. It seems most likely that the origins of the Qumran community can be found in the unwillingness of at least some of the Sadducees to accept this replacement.

From the famous *Halakic Letter* (4QMMT), which seems to have been composed at the beginning of the schism, we learn of twenty-two halakic

---

132. On this see Lawrence H. Schiffman, *Reclaiming the Dead Sea Scrolls: The History of Judaism, the Background of Christianity, the Lost Library of Qumran* (Philadelphia: Jewish Publication Society, 1994); Hartmut Stegemann, *Die Essener, Qumran, Johannes der Täufer und Jesus* (Freiburg: Herder, 1993); Shemaryahu Talmon, "Bilanz und Ausblick nach 50 Jahren Qumranforschung," in *Die Schriftrollen von Qumran: Zur aufregenden Geschichte ihrer Erforschung und Deutung* (ed. S. Talmon; Regensburg: F. Pustet, 1998), 137–58; Geza Vermes, *The Complete Dead Sea Scrolls in English* (New York: Penguin, 1997).

133. Michael Fishbane, "Use, Authority and Interpretation of Mikra at Qumran," in Mulder, *Mikra*, 360.

disputes over the interpretation of the Jewish law, disagreements between the schismatics and those in control of the temple in Hasmonean Jerusalem. By this letter those who later became the Qumran covenanters had sought to reconcile with their opponents. After they failed and the "Teacher of Righteousness" had gained significant influence as their leader, the group definitively separated and began to shape itself as a sect. Thereafter they developed an "intensely apocalyptic, sectarian mentality"[134] and probably decided to move to the desert at Qumran.[135] Their apocalyptic, sectarian mentality derived from this specific historical background and thus shaped the interpretation of Scripture characteristic of the Qumran covenanters.

Nevertheless, from the content of the scrolls found in the caves around Qumran, we can see that most of the methods and techniques with which the covenanters interpreted Scripture were

> forerunners and parallels to all the types of interpretation we find in the later Jewish tradition as transmitted by the rabbinic sources: Targum, the Aramaic translation of the Bible; direct, simple interpretation of the sense of Scripture; haggadic expansion; and the halakic midrash. All these techniques were available when Pharisees were competing with the various sectarians to dominate the religious scene in Hasmonaean Palestine.[136]

Only in one specific system of interpretation known as *pesher* (discussed below) did they differ from others. They also claimed that only in the interpretation guided by the Teacher of Righteousness or those authorized by him to interpret, could they know the true divine intent of the Torah and the words of the prophets.

The Qumran covenanters were committed to Scripture and its proper understanding. Almost every book of the Hebrew Bible was found in the caves. In the Qumran community Scripture was the basis for their life and hope; they aimed to live and act as strictly as possible on this basis. "The covenanters of Qumran thus lived the Law of Moses and longed for the day of the Lord in resolute confidence that their interpretations of the Scripture were true and certain."[137]

After the definitive split from their opponents at the temple in Jerusalem, they regarded themselves as the only true Israel. They regarded only their own interpretation of the Law as being in accordance with God's will. Only

---

134. Schiffman, *Reclaiming the Dead Sea Scrolls*, 95.
135. For more details on this, see ibid., 83–95.
136. Ibid., 222.
137. Fishbane, "Use, Authority and Interpretation," 340.

those who accepted their interpretations and lived according to them could be saved in "the end of the days," which they saw as very near or even as having dawned in their own time.

Apart from different interpretations in matters of purity, the different calendars in use at Qumran and at the temple in Jerusalem were a main cause of harassment. The Qumran community rejected the lunar calendar introduced by the Hasmonean rulers and instead continued to count days and weeks and months according to the solar calendar that was earlier in use. Hence, the beginning and end of *Shabbat* became a matter of dispute, as well as the dates for celebrating the Jewish festivals. Also, the Qumran community did not think that the sacrifices in the temple were being performed at the proper times.

They therefore viewed the majority of the Jews as following the wrong law or as breaking the law of God: for example, they did not begin and end the Sabbath at its proper time. One condition for being a member of "the covenant" was accepting the right times: "They shall not depart from any command of God concerning their times; they shall be neither early nor late for any of their appointed times. They shall stray neither to right nor to left of any of his true precepts" (1QS I, 13–15). Those who did not follow these "true precepts" could "neither be purified by atonement, nor cleansed by purifying water, nor sanctified by seas and river, nor washed clean with any ablution" (1QS III, 4–5)

In non-Christian Jewish interpretations of Scripture, one technique has been found exclusively in the Qumran texts. The Qumran people interpreted biblical texts as directly and uniquely referring to events in the history of the community or, as we can see from other *pesharim,* to historical events generally.[138] Scholars find it interesting to consider to what extent Paul and his contemporaries were influenced by, or made use of, this connection between Scripture and contemporary events.

In quoting a biblical passage and then interpreting it, introduced by the words "*pesher ha-dābār* (the interpretation of the matter is)" or "*pishro* (its interpretation is)," the *pesher* type of interpretation in its different forms became a most important tool for the Qumran community to define its own self-understanding.[139]

Although the people of Qumran claimed to be the only true remnant of Israel and although they had separated sharply from the majority of the Jews, they never conceived of themselves as being anything other than Jewish. They based their self-understanding on the Holy Scriptures of the Jewish

---

138. For a more detailed analysis see Schiffman, *Reclaiming the Dead Sea Scrolls,* 223–41.
139. Ibid., 224.

people and its interpretation. The ideas concerning, and the perception of, contemporary events, as specifically Qumranic as they were, could never have developed from anything other than from this basis.

Apocalypticism and the Interpretation of Scripture

"And then the earth brought an accusation against the oppressors. . . . And there were many wicked ones and they committed adultery and erred, and all their conduct became corrupt." This passage from *1 Enoch* 7:6; 8:2 could serve as a general description of the mood of apocalyptic literature and the traces of apocalypticism that can be found in other literary genres of the Second Temple period.[140] Although my concern in the previous section was to present the Qumranic interpretation in its own distinctiveness, I am aware that apocalyptic is part of the Qumran literature and that some of what is said here applies also to Qumran.

The advent of Hellenism in the Near East provoked a variety of reactions. Among others, one was the emergence of apocalypticism. It perceived the changes, initiated by military and cultural Hellenization, as something scandalous.

Traces of apocalypticism can be found in many writings of the Second Temple period, including Paul's letters. Yet a cluster of apocalyptic writings had already emerged around the time of the Maccabean revolt, and then later after the destruction of the temple in 70. This is a hint directing us to view apocalypticism largely as a negative reaction to catastrophic events, leading to a sense that "the world is out of joint." The world as it is seemed to contradict entirely the promises of God for his people and the hope for life and justice. These visionaries looked to another world, either in heaven or in the eschatological future, because this world was unsatisfactory.[141] This is not to say that apocalypticism is the literature of only the oppressed and marginalized. Although experiences of oppression and marginalization have contributed to its emergence, we must also take into account the complexity of the reasons for, and possible social contexts of, apocalyptic ideas.[142]

There is an ongoing debate about the origins of apocalypticism, as to whether they may be found in prophecy or in wisdom circles, and to what

---

140. The Pseudepigrapha is quoted from James H. Charlesworth, ed., *The Old Testament Pseudepigrapha* (2 vols.; Garden City, N.Y.: 1983–85), loc. cit. I will not give an overview of the broad discussion about apocalyptic literature and apocalypticism. For a detailed discussion see John J. Collins, ed., *The Encyclopedia of Apocalypticism* (vol. 1; New York: Continuum, 1999); Karlheinz Müller, *Studien zur frühjüdischen Apokalyptik* (Stuttgart: Katholisches Bibelwerk GmbH, 1991).

141. Collins, *Encyclopedia of Apocalypticism,* 1:158.

142. On this see W. S. Campbell, "The Sociological Study of the New Testament: Promise and Problems," *Journal of Beliefs and Values* 14.1 (1990): 4.

extent perceptions of other Near Eastern religions influenced the emergence of this phenomenon.[143] John J. Collins gives a convincing description of the issue:

> But this whole debate about the origins of apocalypticism is misplaced. . . . We are dealing with a new phenomenon in the history of Judaism, which was very much a product of the way in which "the world was changed" by the impact of Hellenism on the Near East. The apocalyptic visionaries drew on materials from many sources: ancient myths, biblical prophecies, Greek and Persian traditions. But what they produced was a new kind of literature that had its own coherence and should not be seen as a child or adaptation of something else.[144]

The question is, however, whether this "new phenomenon," this "new kind of literature," was new in its distinct way of combining material from different traditions only, or whether this "new" also meant a breach with the previous faith tradition and its interpretations.

Compared to previous prophetic perceptions of salvation that expected God's intervention within history, the expectation of another world in another time seems to be a radical breach. In apocalypticism, the faithful community no longer expects salvation within time and history but beyond these.[145] We cannot find such ideas explicitly declared in prophecy or earlier traditions. On the other hand, apocalyptic writings are still expressing the same hope the prophets had already proclaimed: through and after these evil contemporary events, God will act for the salvation of his people. The difference between apocalypticism and earlier traditions of biblical faith is a difference in timing. Apocalypticism no longer directly identifies historical events with salvation. But it does maintain the hope that God will eventually act on behalf of his people and that he will keep his promises.

The starting point of ever so many visionary experiences is the Scriptures. The study of the Scriptures often was the occasion or reason for a revelation or vision. Revelations or visions rarely deal with textual problems, but they interpret present historical or existential problems in the light of the Scriptures, the transcendent world, and the eschatological future. This particular way of interpretation was the content of the heavenly journey or revelation. The visionary perceived his own interpretation as authoritative since it was understood as a revelation from heaven.

---

143. On this see Collins, *Encyclopedia of Apocalypticism,* 1:146–48; Müller, *Studien zur frühjüdischen Apokalyptik,* 19–34.
144. Collins, *Encyclopedia of Apocalypticism,* 146.
145. On this see also E. Stegemann and W. Stegemann, *The Jesus Movement,* 134; Müller, *Studien zur frühjüdischen Apokalyptik,* 53.

Similarly, on the basis of earlier revelations and traditions, prophets had already interpreted contemporary events. There is even a "remarkable systematic formal relationship"[146] between Ezekiel's vision of the new Jerusalem and later apocalyptic visions, as well as in the use of extended metaphors in both Ezekiel and apocalyptic literature. But we can find not only analogies in form in late prophecy and apocalypticism; there are also analogies in content, as for instance in Isa 24–27, which declares prophecies of God's vengeance as well as prophecies of future joy.[147]

We also have to take into account the fact that the authors of apocalyptic literature choose biblical heroes as pseudonyms. The analogies with prophecy indicate clearly that apocalyptic writers sought to formulate messages closely related to the scriptural tradition of Israel. This means that the relation to the Scriptures served as the basis of authority for apocalyptic revelations; authority did not derive merely from the new revelation itself. Thus, apocalypticism remained within the tacit agreement that since prophecy had come to an end, it was by means of interpreting the Scriptures (written or oral) that one could learn about God's will in the present.

Nevertheless, this general relation to the Scriptures did not lead to an extensive use of scriptural texts as such in direct quotations or as proof texts. We do find the reinterpretation of Jeremiah's seventy years, or the dependence of *4 Ezra* (2 Esd) 13 on Dan 7, or of *2 (Syriac Apocalypse of) Baruch* on Jeremiah generally; but these are not typical examples for the way the apocalyptists interpret the Scriptures.

One rather gathers the impression that apocalyptic visionaries lived with the Scriptures in a more general sense. These texts served as the basis or the pattern behind the visions and revelations, without being quoted and often even without being explicitly mentioned. In visions and revelations the visionaries claim to have learned about the true and hidden meaning of Scripture and its significance for the contemporary world. The visions and revelations serve as a means for understanding contemporary events in the light of Scripture, according to the general apocalyptic perception of the world.[148]

Hellenistic Influences on the Interpretation of Scriptures

Since Hellenism was the prevailing culture of the Mediterranean world, it

---

146. Michael Stone, ed., *Jewish Writings of the Second Temple Period* (Assen: Van Gorcum, 1984), 387.
147. For a more detailed description and further material, see ibid., 385–88.
148. The understanding of this general apocalyptic mood sheds light on aspects of Paul's interpretation of the Christ event as well as his living within, and in association with, Scriptures without always consciously and explicitly referring to them. I deal with the relevance of the mystical-apocalyptic background for the interpretation of Paul and his letters in more detail in the section "The Jewish Texture of Paul's Way of Thinking," chapter 4, 142ff.

could hardly be ignored, nor can its influence on Judaism in the Diaspora as well as in Palestine be dismissed.[149] I have already referred to the fact that there is an ongoing debate about the definition of the term *Hellenism* and its ambiguity.[150] But however we perceive the degree of Hellenistic influence and its significance, there exists a kind of literature by some Jewish authors of that time that is explicitly influenced by Hellenism. In the strands of first-century Judaism and their interpreting methods that I have discussed thus far, this influence was rather implicit; now I turn to some of these explicitly Hellenistic Jewish interpretations of Scriptures, which indicate their way of thinking.

The authors of this kind of literature often clearly link their utterances to Greek cultural heritage. Since there are numerous literary evidences of explicitly Hellenistic Judaism, I limit my overview to the writings and authors I consider most relevant for understanding Paul in his context.

The apostle Paul is most frequently compared to Philo of Alexandria, the Jewish philosopher who was his contemporary. Then there also is Josephus, who was brought up in Palestine but lived in the Diaspora for the second half of his life. He thus experienced life as a Jew in both parts of that world, as did Paul. Both Philo and Josephus related and expressed their religious tradition in Hellenistic terms, appreciating especially the achievements and claims of Graeco-Roman culture and even politics. Other writings, such as Wisdom of Solomon or 4 Maccabees, were obviously familiar with Hellenistic literature, thought patterns, and rhetorical skills, but nevertheless used these rather to express an antagonistic attitude toward their environment. I also look at the Wisdom of Solomon since there is a scholarly debate on whether Paul might have known Wisdom or whether both authors were using similar traditions.[151]

Philo

The most prominent of those Jewish authors who were deeply acculturated to Hellenism is the Alexandrian philosopher Philo. Many of his writings have survived, possibly giving him more significance than he deserves. Yet, as John Barclay declares, "in Philo we have one fully documented example of an

---

149. See Erich S. Gruen, *Heritage and Hellenism: The Reinvention of Jewish Tradition* (Berkeley: University of California Press, 1998), xv.

150. Cf. ibid., 60ff. and 92ff.; also the historical analyses by Shaye J. D. Cohen, *From the Maccabees to the Mishnah* (Philadelphia: Westminster, 1987), 35; and Gruen, *Heritage and Hellenism*, xiv.

151. John M. G. Barclay, *Jews in the Mediterranean Diaspora: From Alexander to Trajan (323 BCE–117 CE)* (Edinburgh: T&T Clark, 1996), 159.

upper-class and educated Jew, explaining his tradition and his continuing allegiance to it in carefully framed accommodation with the Hellenistic world."[152]

Philo belonged to the most wealthy class of first-century Alexandria, at a time when the Jewish community enjoyed its final period of peace and prosperity there. His family position allowed him to live the life of a contemplating philosopher, educated in all the skills highly valued by the Hellenistic upper class throughout the Roman Empire, enjoying literature, mathematics, astronomy, rhetoric, and music. Thus he was part of the elite cultural and social life of Alexandria. Philo was a typical philosopher, whose greatest delight was to contemplate in solitude and peace while searching for eternal truth. He was most thankful when he could escape having to deal with political and economic affairs.[153]

Philo's perception of the world as well as his interpretation of the Scriptures was based on Plato's dualism of the visible and the invisible world, the invisible being the only realm where people can find truth. Thus, for Philo allegorical exposition of the Scriptures is the method of interpretation through which the hidden meaning, as the only true one, can be discovered.

Sometimes Philo can read the Scriptures on a literal level, counting Abraham as a supremely wise man, for example.[154] Yet, he considers "the surface meaning of the text" to be for the masses, while he is among the few who look at the hidden meaning, to discover truths about the soul, not just the body.[155] Philo was convinced that almost all—or at least most—of the law book is allegorical.[156] He reads the Bible as a philosophical book, which analyzes the human condition and gives guidelines for human well-being. In his opinion, the Scriptures are of universal significance. "In principle, *anyone* could read the Pentateuch as their 'story,' *anyone* could identify with Abraham in his progression from 'encyclical studies' to philosophy, *anyone* could learn to escape the pleasures of the body and cultivate the fruits of the soul."[157]

It is surprising that a man so deeply acculturated to Hellenistic culture and life was at the same time deeply committed to the faith of his ancestors. Even though Philo knew Greek philosophy thoroughly, the basis of his thought was and remained the Jewish Bible.[158] Although he seems to have had access to it only in its Greek translation, the Septuagint, he regarded its translated text as

---

152. Ibid., 451.
153. See ibid., 162.
154. Philo, *De Abrahamo* 68.
155. Barclay, *Jews in the Mediterranean,* 166.
156. Philo, *De Iosepho* 28.
157. Barclay, *Jews in the Mediterranean,* 171.
158. Philo is thus an articulate example of the possibility of having a dual identity. On this aspect, see sec. "Paul and the Judaism/Hellenism Debate," in chap. 4, 125ff.

inspired and no word in it as superfluous. Each and every word must have made sense in one way or another. This attitude is similar to that of the later sages and rabbis who conceived each and every word, even letter, as being revealed at Mount Sinai and containing a divinely inspired message.[159]

Philo's philosophical interpretation is based on this scriptural principle. Moses and the Scriptures are the main authorities, and Philo would not accept any evaluating distinction between text and text.[160] In this sense, as Barclay characterizes him in modern terminology, he is "not a literalist" but "a textual fundamentalist."[161] He applies Hellenistic methods of interpretation to endorse the original truth of the sacred texts, which in Philo's view was identical with the norms and values of Greek philosophy such as education, a life of piety, and the pursuit of virtue. Philo depicts Jewish theology as being equal with the best philosophy, and the Jewish community, constituted according to the Mosaic law, as somehow the ideally organized *politeia* (state).[162] Thus Philonic allegory, rather than being a means of suppressing Jewish distinctiveness, "is an effort to make Greek culture Jewish rather than to dissolve Jewish identity into Greek culture."[163]

Philo perceived himself as a philosopher in a very Greek sense, but he obviously never had any doubts about his real and primary commitment. As a philosopher, he longed for a life of contemplation; yet as a Jew, he felt his responsibility for the Jewish community and therefore became involved in practical and political issues. Moreover, despite his emphasis on the allegorical meaning of the law, he insisted that Jews should by no means abandon its literal observance: "We should think of the literal observance as like the body, and the allegorical meaning as the soul: just as we ought to take care of the body, since it is the home of the soul, so we ought to pay heed to the letter of the Law."[164] Philo turned sharply against interpreters who perceived the allegorical sense as the only and exclusively true meaning of the law, rendering its literal observance unnecessary.[165]

However highly he valued the spiritual aspects of life, Philo knew that soul and body are bound together, and that the one cannot exist without the other. As a Jewish philosopher he was still aware of the need to be embedded in the social and political context of his community. His commitment

---

159. On this see, e.g., Handelman, *Slayers of Moses*, 37–39.

160. There seems to have been an inner-Jewish theological debate about certain aspects of Scripture, as we can see in Philo, *De plantatione* 69–72.

161. Barclay, *Jews in the Mediterranean*, 169.

162. On this see H. A. Wolfson, *Philo: Foundations of Religious Philosophy in Judaism, Christianity, and Islam* (2 vols.; Cambridge: Harvard University Press, 1948), 2:374–95.

163. D. Dawson, *Allegorical Readers and Cultural Revision in Ancient Alexandria* (Berkeley: University of California Press, 1992), 74.

164. Philo, *De migratione Abrahami* 93.

165. Ibid., 90.

obviously destined him to be the leader of the Jewish delegation sent to the Roman emperor after the Alexandrian pogrom in 38. Those horrible events provoked his deep suspicion against Alexandrian society and strengthened his sense of responsibility for all Jews everywhere.[166]

Philo, deeply acculturated to the Hellenistic world in which he lived, was educated and trained according to Hellenistic standards. He had acquired all the skills perceived as crucial for interpreting and understanding texts, and he had no problems in applying them to the interpretation of the Scriptures. Philo was a Platonic philosopher, adhering to a universalistic worldview, but he was a Jewish Platonist: he never lost touch with real earthbound life and the wisdom that human beings cannot exist apart from their social context. The basis of his way of thinking, as Hellenistically educated as he might have been, thus remained Jewish, relying on the text of the Scriptures, whose thought pattern was Hebrew even in its Greek translation. The application of Hellenistic methods and the evaluation of Greek philosophy apparently did not alienate Philo from his Jewish community and faith in any explicit way.

Josephus

Another major literary oeuvre from the Diaspora is that of Josephus. Although he too belonged to the upper class of his people, his life and acculturation differed from that of Philo in many ways, and so does his interpretation of the Scriptures. He lived in the Diaspora only for the second half of his life, and this not by his own choice. He came to Rome as a protégé of the Roman emperor in the aftermath of the Judean War, in which his role had been anything but glorious.

According to his own account, he was educated in the Jewish traditions and was proud of them. He claimed that the Jewish people "give credit for wisdom only to those who have accurate knowledge of the law and are able to interpret the meaning of the Holy Scriptures."[167] He acquainted himself with Hellenistic literature, rhetoric, and philosophy only after he had arrived in Rome. Nevertheless, he wrote his works mainly for non-Jews, trying to make Jewish history and tradition attractive and intelligible to his Hellenistic contemporaries.

His major work dealing with the Scriptures is the *Antiquitates Iudaicae*. In retelling the biblical stories, Josephus emphasizes his perception of the history of his people as a process of divine reward and punishment, thus showing his dependence on the Deuteronomistic concept of history. It is a perception not

---

166. See Philo, *In Flaccum* 62, 73–77, 84–85, 95–96; and *Legatio ad Gaium* 184–94, 281–84, 330.
167. Josephus, *Antiquitates Iudaicae* 20.264.

unknown to Greek traditions, which could also view history as a field of moral instruction.

Josephus uses Hellenistic vocabulary to retell biblical stories, and he shapes them according to Hellenistic narrative patterns: persons give long speeches, and the writer analyzes their emotions and motivations. But Josephus hardly ever uses allegory to explain difficult biblical passages. Although he seems to know something about Greek philosophy and ethics, his purpose is obviously not to express Jewish traditions in these terms. From what he is retelling and what he is omitting from the biblical stories, we conclude that his motivation was primarily apologetic. He omits embarrassing events of Israel's history such as the golden calf, he presents the "forefathers" (Abraham, Joseph, Moses, et al.) as heroes without any faults, and he avoids any reference to Israel's national sovereignty and promises of the land. From this we can gather that Josephus tried to portray the Jewish traditions mainly as a matter of "law and constitution," thus opening a possibility for Jewish life in the Diaspora.[168]

Josephus appreciated the favorable treatment of the Romans and depicted them—in accordance with their own imperialistic ideology—as the guarantors for a tolerant pluralism throughout the Roman Empire. His purpose in acquainting himself with Hellenistic education and writing for a non-Jewish public was to gain goodwill from the Hellenistic society in which he and his fellow Jews lived. With this perspective he adopted the claims of Hellenistic universalism as the ideology of the Roman emperors. Josephus was indebted to Hellenistic culture and the political system of the Roman Empire in a way that differed from Philo's experience. To some extent he submitted to the force majeure and involuntarily to the ideology of his benefactors. But Josephus rarely refers to the Greek tradition as such with appreciation.[169] His basis for retelling the history of Israel was solely the Scriptures, and his purpose for interpreting biblical stories in Hellenistic terms remained the wellbeing of his people.

According to Erich S. Gruen, Josephus is a typical Jewish-Hellenistic writer, although the primary audience he seems to be writing for is different from the one usually addressed by such writings. Gruen emphasizes that other Jewish-Hellenistic writings in Greek addressed primarily Jews:

> The retelling of biblical stories for those who dwelled in Greek-speaking communities proved to be an especially lively enterprise. But it was more than mere self-indulgence or entertainment. The writers . . . addressed themselves to devout

---

168. See Barclay, *Jews in the Mediterranean*, 356–61.
169. See ibid., 360 n. 54.

Jews who knew their Scriptures, at least in Greek translation. None evoked any distrust in the authority of the text. . . . The interpreters of Scripture honored their tradition while making it speak to their contemporaries.[170]

Josephus certainly did the same and also made Scripture speak to contemporary non-Jews. The next text also honored scriptural tradition, but while addressing Jews rather than non-Jews.

Wisdom of Solomon

It is uncertain precisely when this piece of Hellenistic Jewish literature was written and what is its historical context. The assumptions vary from 150 B.C. to A.D. 50. There are rare indications of awareness of political or social circumstances, but it is quite obvious that Wisdom expresses a sense of opposition and oppression. Barclay therefore relates Wisdom to the last decades of Ptolemaic rule and the first decades of the Roman era in the Egyptian Diaspora.[171]

The book is a praise of (sometimes personified) wisdom and an invitation to let one's own life be guided through her. It depicts wisdom as a savior of those who suffer from injustice and oppression. The book mentions some biblical forefathers as examples of righteousness who are saved by wisdom, but its main emphasis is on retelling the story of the exodus. Scholars generally value it as one of the most profound expressions of Hellenization of Diaspora Jews. Its vocabulary and its use of rhetorical features betray hints of a complete Greek education. Greek philosophy has influenced aspects of theology in Wisdom such as the belief in immortality (yet here as God's gift to the righteous rather than from the nature of the soul; 1:12–15). One can also find strong universalistic attitudes. God is caring for the whole creation; his providence and mercy are universal. The author hardly mentions any names of biblical heroes and does not refer to the people of God as Jewish. Several scholars interpret this as a universalistic typological use of biblical figures.[172] The author also knows the Greek argument from analogy, as can be seen in his narrative of the exodus. He attacks the worshipers of idols—especially of the elements fire, wind air, sun, and so on—because idolaters could have acquired the knowledge of the true God from the beauty and power of the world. "Not even they are to be excused; for if they had the ability to know so much that they could investigate the world, how did they fail to find sooner the Lord of these things?" (13:8–9).

---

170. Gruen, *Heritage and Hellenism,* 135–36.
171. Barclay, *Jews in the Mediterranean,* 451.
172. So by John J. Collins, *Between Athens and Jerusalem: Jewish Identity in the Hellenistic Diaspora* (New York: Crossroad, 1986), 185.

There is clear evidence that the author of the Wisdom of Solomon was deeply acculturated in Hellenism. However, statements such as the one just quoted indicate that we have to observe and analyze carefully how the author of this book uses his skills and what purpose they actually serve. Taking into account that 1:1–6:11 includes the opening framework of the praise of wisdom and the following account of the exodus, Barclay's interpretation seems convincing. These opening chapters emphasize the high value of wisdom, but they are also full of sharp warnings of judgment against the ungodly, who oppress the righteous. Barclay states: "His chief purpose is to give comfort and encouragement to the oppressed. Immortality is promised as the just reward to those thus persecuted (2:21–3:4), and their vindication before God is described at length (3:1–9; 5:15–16)."[173] This can be observed also through the account of the exodus, where the author can state: "The worship of idols not to be named is the beginning and cause and end of every evil" (14:27).

On the other hand there are statements about the Jews' true knowledge of God (15:1–4), and their status as "a holy people and blameless race" (10:15), "your [God's] people" (12:19; 16:2, 20; et al.). The Book of Wisdom divides the social world into oppositions. As Barclay states: "The author identifies himself and his readers/hearers with a persecuted people, a nation delivered from implacable enemies by divine powers. The conflictual tone of the Exodus stories both matches and shapes his perception of social relations between Jews and Gentiles."[174]

Wisdom of Solomon shows that Jews could be deeply acculturated to Hellenism, but at the same time be even more indebted to their native religious and cultural bonds. In times of conflict between Jews and their Gentile neighbors, the Jews could use their Hellenistic skills to strengthen and defend the Jewish community and its identity.

The Book of Wisdom demonstrates that even the most learned application of Hellenistic skills cannot be taken as a straightforward indication of a cultural, religious, or political identification with the majority culture, and certainly not as a sign of obliterating one's own distinct identity.

Judaism or Hellenism—Is This the Question?

Philo, Josephus, and Wisdom of Solomon are just three samples of the convergence of Judaism and Hellenism, and there are more. What we derive from the three examples outlined above as well as from the overview of first-century

---

173. Barclay, *Jews in the Mediterranean,* 185.
174. Ibid., 189.

Jewish interpretation of Scripture is that Hellenism undoubtedly had an influence on Jews of the Diaspora as well as in Palestine.[175]

However, David Daube and various scholars, most recently in a volume of essays published by Troels Engberg-Pedersen, have challenged the notion that there actually exists any fundamental dichotomy between Hebrew/rabbinic and Greek/Platonic ways of thinking. Daube sees the middoth of Hillel, which developed as the framework for all subsequent halakah, as originating entirely from Graeco-Roman systems of rhetoric. The common Hellenistic background had an irresistible impact on the development of Jewish interpretive methods, as Daube asserts.[176] Moreover, Philip Alexander sees rabbinic hermeneutics as having arisen from, and having been shaped most prominently by, the dominant Hellenistic society, and thus as "thoroughly of its time and place."[177]

As stated above, there is sufficient evidence of such influence on first-century Judaism to make this plausible. In fact, there must have been cultural influences from any majority society in which Judaism lived as a minority (as in Spain, Germany, and so on). But the mere fact of this influence does not say anything about the extent of acculturation, in this case the Hellenization of Judaism, and what purposes it served. For instance, we need to ask: What actually are the implications of the use of technical tools derived from the majority culture? Does this show a complete acculturation to the majority society, or is it the mere technical outward use of a tool with otherwise little influence on the ways of thinking and cultural, social, and religious identifications of the minority group? In his illuminating study Erich S. Gruen assumes that

> [the Jews] did not confront daily decision on the degree of assimilation. They had long since become part of a Hellenic environment that they could take as given. But their Judaism remained intact. What they required was a means of defining and expressing their singularity within that milieu, the special characteristics that made them both integral to the community and true to their heritage.[178]

---

175. See Gruen, *Heritage and Hellenism,* xiv–xv.
176. See Daube, "Rabbinic Methods," *HUCA* 22 (1949): 257.
177. Philip Alexander, "Quid Athenis et Hierosolymis? Rabbinic Midrash and Hermeneutics in the Graeco-Roman World," in *A Tribute to Geza Vermes* (ed. R. R. Davies and R. T. White; Sheffield: JSOT Press, 1990), 103.
178. Gruen, *Heritage and Hellenism,* xv, 188: "The tales might embellish the feats of ancient Israelite figures, thus to underscore a powerful legacy that stretched through the ages, or to claim a Hebraic contribution to the origins of a common Mediterranean culture. The self-esteem of Hellenistic Jews certainly provided stimulus for such creations. But it does not suffice to see this activity as a polemical engagement, a competitive battle to gain an edge on Gentiles. . . . They have wider significance. They display a strong sense of identity and national self-consciousness rather than a scramble to fabricate it."

The overview I have given shows that although Hellenism is the given cultural context of Judaism in the Diaspora as well as in Palestine, its influence did not annul the basic Jewish shaping of, and commitment in, Jewish literature of that period and Jewish biblical interpretation in particular. I deal with this question and the possibility of a dual identity in chapter 4 because it has decisive impact on the Judaism/Hellenism debate in Pauline studies as well.

In the (foregoing) sections on first-century Jewish interpretation of Scripture, we have seen that people can interpret life and reality as well as texts from different perspectives. In different and divergent ways the two strands of our heritage, Hebrew and Greek, have shaped the perception and interpretation of reality as well as of texts in antiquity, following different kinds of logic. We have also found that, due to cultural interaction and exchange, we cannot make clear-cut distinctions between one pattern and another. Nevertheless, we recognize that people can preserve certain basic patterns of hermeneutical presuppositions and thinking even where acculturation has progressed to a high level.

I have demonstrated that divergent perspectives existed in the first-century, and now I turn to a contemporary perspective that is "divergent" from the mainstream perspective of traditional scholarship: feminism.

Contemporary Ways of Thinking: Feminist Perspectives

From different perspectives and for diverse reasons, alternative approaches to Western philosophical discourse have developed in the twentieth century. The most shocking events of this century, the two World Wars, also affected traditional Western perceptions of the world that people till then had mostly regarded as objectively true depictions of reality. Thinkers—especially those from different backgrounds, such as Emmanuel Lévinas and Jacques Derrida, or from viewpoints from the margins of mainstream society, such as women—began to question accepted presuppositions of thinking and of the resulting ethical implications, examining the roots of mainstream society.[179] A wide range of discourses deserve to be mentioned, but there is no room in this study to elaborate on them at length.[180] I limit my overview to some aspects of feminist theory that are particularly significant for the purpose of this study.

---

179. See sections "Hermeneutical Presuppositions," 9ff; and "Hermeneutical Consequences," 16ff, in chap. 2.
180. The impact of Derrida's thinking on Pauline studies would be a worthwhile topic for further research.

Roots of Feminist Perspectives

The world of thought in the dominant culture of the West has been the domain of men, not just for centuries but even for thousands of years, at least as far as the written history of philosophy and theology reports. Elisabeth Schüssler Fiorenza has stated:

> The prohibition of all wo/men from public speaking and the restriction of politics and rhetoric to elite freeborn males has constructed academic scholarship and biblical studies as a masculine-gendered discipline and rhetorical culture. It has also defined the parameters of Western thought and Christian theology in elite white malestream terms. Since throughout the centuries all wo/men were excluded both from speaking in public and from authoritatively shaping cultural, academic, and religious discourses, theology and religious studies have become defined by elite males only.[181]

This applies not only to theology and religious studies but also to philosophy. Women did not exist in the history of academic discourses except as objects defined by men. These definitions, seldom to the advantage of women, served as reasons for excluding them from the discourse of thinking, public life, and political power.[182] Aristotle, for instance, contended that men are the better part of humanity and therefore destined to rule, since women are nothing but somewhat "crippled men."[183] Kant viewed women as being incapable of doing any scholarly studies, and Schopenhauer stated: "Being without understanding does not harm women; but rather overwhelming rational power or genius could have a negative effect as an abnormality."[184]

Ever since Plato's perception of the priority of principles and ideas over against the material and empirical world, philosophers on his trail have viewed that visible world as inferior, as something that has to be overcome in order to obtain real knowledge of truth.

Since the average woman has less brute strength than the average man, philosophers perceived them as weaker in thinking and reasoning. Moreover,

181. Elisabeth Schüssler Fiorenza, *Rhetoric and Ethic: The Politics of Biblical Studies* (Minneapolis: Fortress, 1999), 8.

182. On this see Sandra Harding, "Is Gender a Variable in Conceptions of Rationality? A Survey of Issues," in *Beyond Domination: New Perspectives on Women and Philosophy* (ed. C. C. Gould; Totowa: Rowman & Allanheld, 1983), 43–63.

183. Aristotle, *Politica* 1254b.12.

184. Immanuel Kant: "Unverstand schadet bei Weibern nicht: eher noch könnte überwiegende Geisteskraft oder gar Genie als eine Abnormität ungünstig wirken." Schopenhauer Arthur, *Die Welt als Wille und Vorstellung*. Erster Band (Sämtliche Werke, Bd 2) Darmstadt (1968), 696.

they regarded women as enslaved by their emotions, which hindered their ability to think rationally and clearly. The Christian doctrine of the fall (Gen 3) added to this the image of women as seducers, who used their sexuality to draw men down from the heights of rational thought and spiritual life to the inferior and dirty grounds of the empirical world. Women, apart from some rare exceptions, had hardly any chance to gain access to the discourses of philosophical and theological thinking.[185]

Men have shaped the patterns of thought in the official and dominant discourse. They viewed rationality and binary logic (which can think of differences only in terms of exclusive contrasts) as the highest developed abilities of human beings, the only means by which people could acquire true knowledge. Philosophers perceived emotions and affections as well as social ties as unscholarly attitudes, to be kept outside any serious scholarly debate. They regarded only men to be capable of such emotionless and pure rational thinking. And since only men were involved in this discourse and its social development, the construction of this theory involves a circular argument.

Alongside these mainstream ways of thinking were a few other voices. Among them were philosophers such as Blaise Pascal (1623–62), who recognized the limits of pure rationality. Pascal himself valued rational thinking, as emphasized by his friend Descartes, but he also clearly saw its limits, especially where existential or moral aspects of human life were concerned.[186] We could mention others,[187] but none of the philosophers who in those earlier centuries recognized the limits of pure rationality gained much importance in mainstream ways of thinking.

The patterns of mainstream ways of thinking are dominant not only in educational systems but also generally in Western culture. Hence, it is hard to overcome or escape them even when we realize that they are just one particular perspective from which to see and interpret life and the world in which we live. When I say "we," I mean women as well as men, since this dominant perspective has socialized and enculturated both.

Theories critical of these mainstream and universalizing thought patterns have developed not just from a feminist perspective. But now I turn to feminist philosophical theories as one stream of specific contemporary alternatives to mainstream/malestream patterns of thinking. After examining several issues of primary significance in feminist theories, I investigate similar issues in feminist theology. I do not intend to give a coherent and comprehensive overview of feminist theories generally but will concentrate only on

---

185. Among these rare exceptions we can find women such as Hypathia (a Hellenistic philosopher around A.D. 400), Hildegard of Bingen, Catharine of Siena, and others, but they were all "neutral" in that they were either visionaries, muses, wise old women, or nuns, who had "overcome" their bodily existence.

186. Cf. Carola Meier-Seethaler, *Gefühl und Urteilskraft* (Munich: C. H. Beck, 1997), 36f.

187. For more information see ibid., 34–111.

issues I perceive as relevant in relation to this study, issues central both in feminist theology and in the study of Paul's letters.

The Emergence of Feminist Theory

Feminist theory as a philosophical discipline emerged with the original publication of Simone de Beauvoir's *The Second Sex*, in 1949. Yet not till the early 1970s did feminist theorizing begin to be established at the university level.[188] Rather than being a specific and limited academic discipline, we should see it as a basic issue that impacts on almost all academic disciplines.

Feminist theory emerged out of the struggles of women for their liberation from oppression and for their empowerment. It is therefore grounded not in abstract thinking but in political movements that actively sought to change the situation of women in society. Soon it became apparent that it is one thing to protest against oppression and seek for new ways of living without such oppressive structures. But it is another task to analyze the complex structures of life that are influenced by many layers of systems of inequality. Even patterns and processes of thinking are shaped by specific presuppositions that are far from being value-free and objective, as claimed by traditional Western discourse. Feminist theory thus emerged as a tool to analyze these deeply rooted patterns of thought and practice, and to develop new visions of differing patterns of living and thinking. It has thus challenged the traditional so-called objective academic discourse in establishing itself as a distinct perception of reality that has taken as its starting point the particular perspective of women's experience.[189]

Since the beginnings of feminist theorizing, wider theoretical shifts in intellectual disciplines have taken place, termed generally as postmodernism or postcritical approaches. Feminist theory developed and became more diverse in the process of its short history. Through these new approaches, it became apparent that the starting points (such as women's experience) for thinking and perceiving life from a feminist perspective were actually (though not so intended) universalizing particular perspectives in ways structurally similar to the universalization of the white male perspective of traditional scholarship. Linda Nicholson has pointed this out:

> In large part the problem was a consequence of the methodological legacies which feminist scholars inadvertently took over from their teachers. . . . But,

---

188. This has to be seen in the context of the intellectual milieu in which mainstream academic claims of neutral objectivism were generally questioned. See also sec. "Different Ways of Thinking," in chap. 3, 49ff.

189. On this see Serene Jones, *Feminist Theory and Christian Theology: Cartographies of Grace* (Minneapolis: Fortress, 2000), esp. 2–10.

while the specific manifestations of such universalising tendencies in feminist theory might have been diverse, the underlying problem was the same. It was the failure, common to many forms of academic scholarship, to recognize the embeddedness of its own assumptions within a specific historical context. These problems generally have to do with the trends which dominated modern scholarship and ways of thinking in the aftermath of the Enlightenment and their claims of neutral objectivity.[190]

The critical shift against this alleged neutrality in the intellectual disciplines was not initiated by feminist scholars alone, but they certainly were among the pioneers.[191] The initiated process of diversification and the growing awareness of their own presuppositions resulted in a wide-ranging variety of different strands of feminist theories in different disciplines.[192] This process implied the recognition that we can no longer regard theoretical reflections and the frameworks through which they are formulated as grand schemes with universalistic claims. Sheila G. Davaney has given an excellent definition of theorizing from a feminist perspective:

> Theory has come to be interpreted as a heuristic device that clarifies presuppositions, gives a better grasp of the issues involved in feminist debates, locates feminist thought in relation to other theoretical proposals, and explores the repercussions of varying feminist frameworks. Theories and the assumptions that underlie them are thus contingent hypotheses, constructed not found, that need to be tested and continually revised.[193]

A variety of different theoretical approaches have developed, such as essentialist, deconstructivist/constructivist, new historicist, and so on.[194] They all give evidence of the ongoing and vivid process of exploring and clarifying issues arising from feminist debates in contemporary society.

Some of the issues, dealt with as of central importance in feminist debates, surprisingly seem to show structural analogies to issues raised in Pauline studies. Later in this book I investigate and analyze some of these analogical aspects. Now I turn to these issues as they are raised from within the context of feminist theories: the issues of "Identity and the Question of Women's Nature," of "Diversity and Difference," and "Relationality and Mutuality."

---

190. In Linda Nicholson, ed., *Feminism/Postmodernism* (New York: Routledge, 1990), 1ff.

191. In the sec. "Different Ways of Thinking," in chap. 2 (above), see references to the Frankfurter school, Lévinas, and Derrida.

192. For an overview see Linda Nicholson and Maggie Humm, eds., *Modern Feminisms: Political, Literary, Cultural* (New York: Columbia University Press, 1992).

193. "Introduction," in Rebecca S. Chopp and Sheila Greeve Davaney, eds., *Horizons in Feminist Theology: Identity, Tradition, and Norms* (Minneapolis: Fortress, 1997), 3.

194. For an overview see, e.g., Linda Nicholson, ed., *The Second Wave: A Reader in Feminist Theory* (New York: Routledge, 1997).

Identity and the Question of Women's Nature

It was not just since Simone de Beauvoir's famous statement, "One is not born, but becomes, a woman,"[195] that the question of women's identity has been a matter of debate in philosophical and theological discourse. But ever since then feminists have certainly taken it as an issue of primary importance and focused on it from their perspective.

Before that, men had almost exclusively defined what woman was or ought to be. From this male perspective, women are those who are different, or "the other" as such. They are what man is not.

The traditional essentialist assumptions about woman are deeply rooted in Graeco-Roman philosophical thought patterns, which classified things according to inherent essences; philosophers regarded these as universal and unchangeable. Since they viewed these essentials as inborn, innate, and native, they also regarded them as not learned and thus having nothing to do with social and cultural training. They regarded these female essentials as naturally given and therefore closely related to sexual differences perceived from a male perspective. Men related these essentials to the bodily experiences of women insofar as they differ from men's experiences, such as menstruation, pregnancy, childbirth, and nurturing.

These natural, biological givens produced emotional and other attributes, such as passivity, instability, emotionality, caring, close relationship to body and nature, and so on. Such natural, universal essences constitute inherently the true and real woman; the only choice women have is either to reject or acknowledge them, to become the authentic women they are meant to be, or fail to be that.[196] Such definitions of woman corresponded with definitions of man in similar essentialist terms with a slight but major difference: what men defined as male essences were not just male, but essences attributed to the ideal human being as such. As the ideal essences of human beings, they were the normative criteria from which all other essences were evaluated. Thus, being active, autonomous, rational, stable, independent, mind-oriented, and so on, is to be authentically male as well as truly human. Men evaluated "woman's nature" according to the standard of "man's/human nature." They derived man's nature from men's experience of life according to traditional role patterns, which they again took as given by nature, with the male part as the ideal for human life generally.

Challenging this traditional pattern of defining women's identity means unscrambling an entire pattern of thought. Scholars raised and educated within this tradition find it hard to avoid thinking in these patterns or to

---

195. Beauvoir, *Second Sex* (1953).
196. See Jones, *Feminist Theory,* 27.

leave them completely behind. Seeking for new ways of thinking and speaking about women's identity involves seeking for new patterns of thought, and actually seeking for a completely new language. In her instructive classical article "Cultural Feminism versus Post-Structuralism: The Identity Crisis in Feminist Theory," Linda Alcoff has said:

> No matter where we turn—to historical documents, philosophical constructions, social scientific statistics, introspection, or daily practices—the mediation of female bodies into constructions of woman is dominated by misogynist discourse. For feminists, who must transcend this discourse, it must appear we have nowhere to turn.[197]

The dilemma of women's self-definition, the definition of their own identity, is that while we take the concept of woman as we know it (the starting point for any kind of feminism) and must at the same time deconstruct and de-essentialize it because it is a man-defined concept. Alcoff argues that since the late 1970s two primary responses to this challenge have emerged in feminist theory, which she labels as "cultural feminism" and "poststructuralist feminism." Linell Elizabeth Cady, however, identifies categories of responses that she labels as "essentialism" and "postmodernism," adding to them "liberal feminism" and a "historicist alternative."[198] Leaving aside the category of liberal feminism, I basically follow Cady's outline, which builds on Alcoff's analysis, to give an overview of different approaches to the question of women's identity.

Cultural or Essentialist Definitions of Women's Identity

"Cultural feminism is the ideology of a female nature or female essence reappropriated by feminists themselves in an effort to revalidate undervalued female attributes."[199] This definition by Alcoff (labeled "essentialism" by Cady) points to the fact that in this approach toward a feminist definition of women's identity, women revalidate and do not abandon the traditional thought patterns and characteristics. What society has previously perceived negatively and as a weakness, women now appreciate and appraise as highly valuable from a feminist perspective.

Thus, one can praise woman's passivity as her peacefulness, her emotionality as her strength in nurturing, her subjectiveness as her advanced self-awareness. Such feminists retrace distinctively female moral developments and women's

---

197. In Nicholson, *Second Wave,* 330.
198. "Identity, Feminist Theory, and Theology," in Chopp, ed., *Horizons in Feminist Theology,* 17–32.
199. Linda Alcoff, "Cultural Feminism versus Post-Structuralism," in Nicholson, *Second Wave,* 332.

ways of knowing.[200] This approach did not really create a new definition of women's identity but was rather a revalidation of traditional characteristics and values attributed to women. The response of essentialist feminists to misogyny and sexism was to adopt a homogeneous, unproblematized, and ahistorical concept of woman. The earliest to raise critical questions against essentialist feminism were women from "the margins," women of different cultural, religious, and racial backgrounds and origins. They challenged the assumptions on which essentialist feminism was based, such as a common homogeneous female identity and a common experience of oppression, irrespective of context.

There are nevertheless quite a few positive effects of essentialist feminism in its insistence on viewing traditional feminine characteristics from a different perspective. It does make a difference to argue that not only so-called male values are of importance in the public realm, but also that the traditional world of women is full of virtues and values for which we can give credit and from which we can learn. But as Alcoff has said:

> To the extent that it reinforces essentialist explanations of these attributes, it is in danger of solidifying an important bulwark for sexist oppression: the belief in an innate "womanhood" to which we must all adhere lest we be deemed either inferior or not "true" women. For many feminists the problem with the cultural feminist response to sexism is that it does not criticize the fundamental mechanism of oppressive power used to perpetuate sexism and, in fact, reinvokes that mechanism in its supposed solution.[201]

It seems, in fact, to be nothing else than "turning upside down" the traditional male definitions that it opposes. Thus, it is no surprise that Cady sees inherent in essentialist feminism some sort of ethnocentrist and imperialist tendency, whose basis is shaken by the rapid development of cross-cultural and interreligious gender studies.[202]

---

200. See, e.g., Carol Gilligan, *In a Different Voice: Psychological Theory and Women's Development* (Cambridge: Harvard University Press, 1982); and Sara Ruddick, *Maternal Thinking: Toward a Politics of Peace* (Boston: Beacon, 1989).

201. Alcoff, "Cultural Feminism," 336.

202. Chopp and Davaney, *Horizons in Feminist Theology,* 22. Scholars such as Susan Bordo in turn criticize such a critique of essentialism, pointing to limits of poststructuralist critiques of essentialism. Among other things, Bordo emphasizes: "We also *should* have learned that while it is imperative to struggle continually against racism and ethnocentrism in all its forms, it is impossible to be 'politically correct.' For the dynamics of inclusion and exclusion (as history had just taught us) are played out on multiple and shifting fronts, and all ideas (no matter how 'liberatory' in some contexts or for some purposes) are condemned to be haunted by a voice from the margins . . . awakening us to what has been excluded, effaced, damaged" ("Feminism, Postmodernism, and Gender-Skepticism," in Nicholson, *Feminism/Postmodernism,* 138, 133–56).

Identity—Postmodernist Feminist Approaches

The postmodern and poststructuralist[203] response to Simone de Beauvoir's question "Are there women?" would be "no" since this perspective challenges the category and the concept of woman in much the same way as it problematizes subjectivity itself. According to postmodern theories, there is no essential, natural core to a subject. Social discourses that are beyond individual control construct and mediate the experience of subjectivity. Such theorists thus do not view identity as a stable and homogeneous entity but as a site of multiple and conflicting discourses and practices. If applied to feminism, this results in the view that the category "woman" is a construct, even a fiction, and the aim of feminism then is to unveil this constructed fiction. Derrida's interest is in deconstructing traditional Western discourses of thinking, with its implied essentialism and binary hierarchies. For him, the fact that women have been excluded from these discourses as "the other" might provide them with the ability to contribute to the fundamental resistance to these traditional Western discourses (logocentrism, in Derrrida's terms). As those who were always labeled as the "subjugated difference" within a system of binary oppositions, according to him, women can only break out of this structure by subverting this structure in itself, in asserting total difference. Identity then cannot be described save in an exclusively negative way for what it is not. Consequently, the French poststructuralist Julia Kristeva says, "A woman cannot be; it is something which does not even belong in the order of being."[204]

The postmodern critique of subjectivity contributed greatly to the understanding of the construction and mechanisms of oppression as well as of specific gender categories related to social discourse. It also supports a free play of possibilities for women's self-definition without letting gender definitions be a hindrance. But the dilemma with this response to the feminist identity question is that in the end it might lead to the extinction of feminism itself. Alcoff asks: "What can we demand in the name of women if 'women' do not exist and demands in their name simply reinforce the myth that they do? How can we speak out against sexism as detrimental to the interests of women if the category is a fiction?"[205]

---

203. On the interchangeable use of these terms *postmodern* and *poststructuralist,* I follow the pattern of Judith Evans, *Feminist Theory Today: An Introduction to Second-Wave Feminism* (London: SAGE Publications, 1995), 140 n. 1, in chap. 9, "The Postmodernist Challenge."

204. Julia Kristeva, "Woman Can Never Be Defined," in *New French Feminisms* (ed. Elaine Marks and Isabelle de Courtivron; New York: Schocken, 1981), 137.

205. Alcoff, "Cultural Feminism," 340.

Since self-understanding and autonomy are just what women are seeking, the reduction of female agency to a "doing without a doer" seems directly to undermine feminists' own goals.[206] More serious, according to Alcoff, is even the fact that the rejection of subjectivity shows certain analogies with the universal human being and the denial of differences in traditional Western philosophy. Such philosophers perceive particularities of individuals and groups as being irrelevant since they are nothing but social constructs. Thus, implicitly, the rejection of subjectivity is similar to traditional Western concepts of sameness.[207]

With women's identity being as fragmented as it is in most postmodern feminist approaches, feminist critiques ask whether this might not lead to a weakening of the political and social aims of feminist approaches as well as to ethical relativism.[208]

Positional/Historicist Alternative

Taking into account weaknesses as well as strengths of essentialist and poststructuralist theories of women's identity, a number of feminists—such as Linda Alcoff, Teresa de Lauretis, Jane Flax, and others—have developed alternative theories of women's identity diversely labeled as "positionality,"[209] "historicism,"[210] or "strategic essentialism."[211]

All these approaches underscore that identity is not a given. It is what a woman perceives and understands as her own identity, as she negotiates and achieves it in a continuing process of interaction and engagement with the practices, discourses, and institutions that lend significance to life and the world in which we live. Teresa de Lauretis states that identity is neither determined by biology nor by free rational intentions but by experience. People thus construct identity in and through a process of reflected practical experience. De Lauretis has developed this approach further through focusing on the crucial role of historical consciousness in constructing individual and

---

206. On this see Seyla Benhabib, *Situating the Self: Gender, Community, and Postmodernism in Contemporary Ethics* (New York: Routledge, 1992), 215; also Rosi Braidotti: "Dismissing the notion of the subject at the very historical moment when women begin to have access to it, while at the same time advocating the 'devenir femme' . . . of philosophical discourse itself, can at least be described as a paradox." In "Patterns of Dissonance: Women and/in Philosophy," in *Feministische Philosophie*, ed. Herta Nagl-Docekal (Vienna: Oldenbourg, 1990), 108–23 (119–20).

207. Alcoff, "Cultural Feminism," 340.

208. See Jones's discussion in *Feminist Theory*, 40–42.

209. Alcoff, "Cultural Feminism," 346–52.

210. Elizabeth Linell Cady, "Identity, Feminist Theory, and Theology," in *Horizons in Feminist Theology* (ed. Chopp and Davaney), 23–26.

211. Jones, *Feminist Theory*, 42–48.

collective identity. She states that one's history "is interpreted or reconstructed by each of us within the horizon of meanings and knowledges avail-
able in the culture at given historical moments. . . . Consciousness, therefore,
is never fixed, never attained once and for all, because diverse boundaries
change with historical conditions."[212]

Gender is a starting point in this process, not in the sense of a biological
or psychological given but as a construct that we can form through patterns
of habits, practices, and discourses in the continuing process. Historically
bound, it nevertheless is open to interpretation in particular historical, cultural, and social contexts. As men and women, we are both subjects of, and
subjected to, such social constructions in history.[213]

It is obvious that individual identities can never develop or stand isolated
from collective identities; they are contextual not just in terms of history and
culture but also in a social sense. Any self is first of all located in a social
group that shapes individual identity in a basic way. While it is important to
underscore the shifting and provisional nature of identity, we should not
underestimate the integrating and stabilizing contribution of collective identities for the individual.

Nevertheless, neither the individual nor the collective identity can ever be
static or homogeneous. Individual and collective identities are a continuous
telling and retelling of narratives that are responding to, and interacting
with, the changing historical and social contexts in which one lives. From
different perspectives and disciplines, scholars have written about the construction of identity. In an excellent study the Jewish historian Yosef Hayim
Yerushalmi has elaborated on the construction of Jewish identity through the
Jewish narrative of history.[214] Similarly, George Lipsitz has stated: "What *we*
choose to remember about the past, where we begin and end our retrospec-
tive accounts, and who we include and exclude from them—these do a lot
to determine how we live and what decisions we make in the present."[215]

According to this perspective, identity is not predetermined or static, nor
is it something that we can only describe negatively as having no identifiable
core at any time. Instead, we continuously and selectively negotiate identity
in relation to a specific historical, cultural, and social context. Thus, women
can only formulate and reformulate their identity in an ongoing process of
interaction and relation to respective contexts.

---

212. Teresa de Lauretis, ed., *Feminist Studies/Critical Studies* (Bloomington: Indiana University Press,
1986), 8.
213. See Alcoff, "Cultural Feminism," 347.
214. Yosef Hayim Yerushalmi, *Ein Feld in Anatot: Versuche über jüdische Geschichte* (Berlin:
Wagenbach, 1993).
215. George Lipsitz, *Time Passages: Collective Memory and American Popular Culture* (Minneapolis:
University of Minnesota Press, 1990), 34.

Diversity and Difference

The "vive la différence" of essentialist appraisals of female characteristics undoubtedly has its merits, as shown above. But this emphasis on gender difference has produced a basic problem: it tends to erase differences and diversity among women themselves. The issue is complex.

Most feminist approaches now acknowledge differences, especially since women of color, of different cultural and religious backgrounds, and lesbians raised their critical voices against the assumptions of sameness of women in feminist approaches. The early appreciation of differences nevertheless presupposed commonality in gender, as described mostly by women in privileged social positions, primarily from white, middle-class feminists. In her excellent article "'What Has Happened Here': The Politics of Difference in Women's History and Feminist Politics,"[216] Elsa Barkley Brown deals with this fact:

> Although many woman's historians and political activists understand the intellectual and political necessity, dare I say moral, intellectual, and political correctness, of recognizing the diversity of women's experiences, this recognition is often accompanied with the sad (or angry) lament that too much attention to differences disrupts the relatively successful struggle to produce and defend women's history and women's politics, necessary corollaries of a women's movement.[217]

Only in the late 1980s and early 1990s did scholars come to realize how deeply differences of culture, race, sexual orientation, social context, and religion shape the experiences of women as women. These aspects are not merely added to the otherwise common category of gender but basically codetermine how women experience gender itself. Brown strongly argues that in order to achieve a real and thorough appreciation of diversity and differences, women have to overcome the fear of ending in a vacuum or in chaos while so achieving. Instead, she emphasizes that taking into account, and reflecting on, particular historical and cultural experiences in fact provides us with the possibilities of a variety of new and refreshing insights. For example, these experiences could provide us with new options to rethink and reshape traditionally Western-oriented thinking processes as such.

---

216. Elsa Barkley Brown, "'What Has Happened Here': The Politics of Difference in Women's History and Feminist Politics," revised and expanded version of a paper presented at the Historical Association in New York in December 1990, published as "Polyrhythms and Improvisation: Lessons for Women's History," *History Workshop Journal* 31 (Spring 1991): 85–90; reprinted in *Second Wave* (ed. Nicholson), 272–287.

217. Brown, *Second Wave* (ed. Nicholson), 273.

Brown draws from her own African-American cultural background and shows how, from this particular background, ways of thinking about difference evolve that are fundamentally different from traditional Western thought systems. We cannot consider history and politics only in linear symmetrical ways, as in Western tradition, but also in a way that Brown explains with the example of jazz music. Multiple rhythms are played simultaneously and in dialogue with each other; each member of the group has to listen to the others in order to respond and at the same time concentrate on one's own improvisation. Similarly, events in this world happen simultaneously and are ongoing in a variety of rhythms at the same time. Not all but some (and more than we usually think or are aware of) are related to each other in a sort of living dialogue. Looking at events from this perspective requires a different way of writing history.

The point Brown stresses here is that although it is necessary to recognize differences, this actually is not enough. As long as we do not see these differences among women in their relations to each other, there is an inherent danger of silencing again those we regard as different. Moreover, we could silence the implications that differences might have had and still have, when they are not registered in our minds in conjunction with the experience to which they are related. Brown states:

> Middle-class white women's lives are not just different from working-class white, Black and Latina women's lives. It is important to recognize that middle-class women live the lives they do precisely because working-class women live the lives they do. White women and women of color not only live different lives but white women live the lives they do in large part because women of color live the ones they do.[218]

To come to an appropriate appreciation of these differences, it is crucial and effective to look at diversity and differences specifically and in depth, as well as to pay attention to how they relate to each other. Women cannot really find a common basis as long as they avoid looking at and naming aspects that are painful and that separate them deeply; this is part of a history of oppression and inequality.

Previously, feminists had not been serious enough in taking into account the problems of commonality and difference. From this insight, and in a vein similar to their response to the identity quest, postmodern feminists have elaborated on the related issue of difference. According to Iris M. Young, it is particularly the desire for community, the desire to identify with one

---

218. Ibid., 275.

another and what is common and the same, which prevents us from appreciating differences and allows us rather to perceive them as threatening. An oppressive tendency on one side and a universalizing tendency on the other inhere in the project of building a feminist approach on a common ground that all women share, irrespective of their differences. Both are structurally similar and somehow analogical to the traditional Western tradition.

To overcome these tendencies, Young builds on Derrida and also relates to some extent to Lévinas's approach in emphasizing what we need to acknowledge:

> Difference means the irreducible particularity of entities, which makes it impossible to reduce them to commonness or bring them into unity without remainder. Such particularity derives from the contextuality of existence; the being of a thing and what is said about it is a function of its contextual relation to other things.[219]

Thus, we have to overcome the illusion that as subjects we could really understand one another. Each human being is "the other" for another human being; nobody has ever taken any step with my feet nor seen anything with my eyes. And I can never walk with somebody else's feet.[220] Although some mutual understanding is possible, it can never be complete, and it always remains fragile because misunderstanding is always at the doorstep. According to poststructuralist theory, a subject is not a unity but a confluence of influences. Hence, it cannot serve as the starting point for understanding and knowing another's needs and desires because a subject cannot even really know and understand oneself. As Young has explained, "If each subject escapes its own comprehension and for that reason cannot express to another its needs and desires, then necessarily each subject also escapes sympathetic comprehension by others."[221]

According to this theory, there is no basis for any commonality between women. Therefore, commonality cannot serve as the means by which differences are held together. Any attempt to construct commonality in order to create community is problematic. Young develops a model of "city life" in which people appreciate differences as differences rather than something to be overcome. There people peacefully relate to each other, not because they

---

219. Iris Marion Young, "The Ideal of Community and the Politics of Difference," in *Feminism/Postmodernism* (ed. Nicholson), 304, 300–23.

220. See Iris Marion Young, *Justice and the Politics of Difference* (Princeton: Princeton University Press, 1990), 105.

221. Young, "Ideal of Community," 310–11.

are similar and understand each other, but despite the fact that they remain strangers and understanding is fragile and difficult.[222]

Several feminist perspectives challenge such a radical poststructuralist approach to the issue of diversity and difference. I have already mentioned Susan Bordo's critique of the fragmented identity of feminist poststructuralism; she also makes some useful remarks about difference and diversity still worth taking into account. For example, Bordo hints that if it had not been for those who had revalidated women's difference from a feminist perspective (such as Gilligan and Chodorow), no critical discourse on gender difference would be possible. She also shows that, in practice, it still does make a difference whether universalizing and totalizing assumptions are made from a position of power, as in the case of mainstream Western discourse, or from a position from the margins. Bordo thus stresses the obligation to identify the political purpose of denying any common ground to feminist approaches. The argument against totalizing and universalizing tendencies in certain "essentialist" feminist approaches could also serve as a means to diminish the voice of feminism.[223]

Relationality and Mutuality

The emphasis on diversity and difference within feminist discourse has demonstrated the inherent problems of assumptions about commonalities among women. There remains the question of how human beings generally, and in this case women in particular, as "irreducibly particular entities"[224] can relate to each other and form social groups or communities beyond provisional, accidental, and punctual encounter.[225]

Those feminist approaches that revalidated characteristics and values traditionally attributed to women as essentially female, have drawn attention especially to social and relational skills. Despite the critique raised against essentialist feminism, one should recognize that feminist relationalism marked a resistance to, and a moving beyond, early feminism, which was based on the assumption of the basic equality of men and women and had claimed equal rights for women.

Nancy Chodorow and Carol Gilligan paid attention to gender difference from a psychological perspective. They analyzed children's development according to gender-specific ways without attributing to those differences

---

222. Ibid., 317–20.
223. See Bordo, "Feminism, Postmodernism," 141, 151–53, with her illuminating hint at developments in the feminist movement of the 1920s and 1930s.
224. Young, *Justice and Politics*, 304.
225. As suggested in Young's description of the "unoppressive city life," in *Justice and Politics*, 317–20.

any natural essence. Chodorow attributes differences between male and female personalities to the fact that women, almost universally, are responsible for early child care. This impacts deeply on the development of girls and boys because they experience the same social environment differently: they either identify with, or differentiate themselves from, the earliest person they relate to, which usually is a woman. For Chodorow, this means that "girls emerge from this period with a basis for 'empathy' built into their primary definition of self in a way that boys do not." She notes further: "Girls emerge with a stronger basis for experiencing another's needs or feelings as one's own (or of thinking that one is so experiencing another's needs and feelings)."[226] From this insight, she draws the conclusion that women and men experience relationships, dependency, and separation differently, not because this is naturally inherent to them, but because of their different social conditioning. According to this theory, social interactions and personal relationships characterize women's lives, whereas separation and individuation characterize men's lives.[227]

This revalidation of characteristics, valued negatively and as inadequate when measured over against the liberal ideal of the rational independent human being, initiated a rethinking of values. This reassessment revealed that it is a matter of perspective, in this case of gender perspective, how certain characteristics are viewed and valued.

From different perspectives, however, feminists reacted strongly against what they called "reinscription" of feminine characteristics into women's lives. They argued that although this revalidation had its merits, it nevertheless tied women down to what they were traditionally tied down to anyway, and reduced them to what they were viewed as being experts in, also in traditional perspectives. Politically, this could serve as a basis for reactionary arguments to reinforce gender roles in society. The debate evolved into the fundamental discussion between essentialist and poststructuralist feminist approaches. I have given an overview of this debate while dealing with the identity issue.[228]

The issue of relationality is one specific aspect of this debate. Apart from the objection that attributing relationality to women had reactionary and regressive implications, scholars raised other critiques.

In her differentiated analysis of communitarianism, Iris M. Young draws attention to the dangers of homogenization in the ideal of community,

---

226. Nancy Chodorow, *The Reproduction of Mothering* (Berkeley: University of California Press, 1978), 167.
227. See Carol Gilligan, "Woman's Place in a Man's Life Cycle," in *Second Wave* (ed. Nicholson), 200–201.
228. See above, 97–102.

which can develop a tendency toward totalitarianism. According to her, the basis of the ideal of community is "the logic of identity,"[229] which implies that people have to think things together into one unity and unify things into universal categories, using principles that again are ideally reduced to one first principle. Through the "logic of identity," they deny differences and bring the particularities of concrete experiences, with all their ambiguities, into stable concepts of thought. Inherent in such a concept is a totalizing tendency: in its unifying tendency it seeks control over everything.[230] Young thus sees the ideal of community as repressing difference and being exclusive over against those who do not identify with the group or with whom the group does not identify.[231]

Moreover, the ideal of community presupposes some common ground between the subjects who form the community. They may find this common ground in the autonomous self of the rational subject. Such subjects are able to relate to each other and form a community because they share a common consciousness, or because they can empathically understand the distinctiveness of the other and react to the other's needs and capacities so that the other feels recognized.[232] In such a process of mutual reciprocity, communal life is possible. Young criticizes this concept, referring to Derrida, but she does not, as Keller contends, deny the validity of mutual reciprocity and the possibility of mutual intersubjective transcendence as such. She rather asks whether this is an adequate theory to serve as a basis for a vision of communal life.[233] To make face-to-face relations the basis and ideal for community life tends to make sameness and understanding the basis of political life. This is a dangerous enterprise, according to Young, because it actually has to deny difference as difference, and to deny the asymmetry of subjects. As such, Young sees a totalizing tendency in relationalism.[234]

Catherine Keller gives an even more extreme example of a critique of feminist relationalism,[235] quoting a statement made by Julia Kristeva in an interview: "I think that all *global* problematics are archaic; that one should not formulate global problematics because that is part of a totalitarian and totalizing conception of history."[236] Keller interprets this as an expression of

229. Young, *Justice and Politics*, 98–99.
230. Ibid., 98.
231. Ibid., 227.
232. Ibid., 231.
233. Ibid., 230: "Whether expressed as shared subjectivity or common consciousness, on the one hand, or as relations of mutuality and reciprocity, the ideal of community denies, devalues, or represses the ontological difference of subjects, and seeks to dissolve social exhaustibility into the comfort of a self-enclosed whole."
234. Ibid., 233.
235. See Catherine Keller, "Seeking and Sucking: On Relation and Essence in Feminist Theology," in *Horizons in Feminist Theology* (ed. Chopp and Davaney), 64ff., 54–78.
236. Ibid., 64.

a tendency of postmodernism generally, and feminist postmodernism in particular. According to this tendency, it seems necessary to abandon any form of generalization in order to concentrate exclusively on the local discourse or even on the individual discourse. Keller describes this: "No longer universally accountable, 'the individual' is now the unaccountable one, the one whose virtue will be defined by the quality of his or her 'discourses.'"[237] Statements such as Kristeva's seem to reinstate the ideal of the independent individual; they are similar to the Enlightenment ideal of man as an autonomous, separate self.

Over against such radical antirelationalist strands and their influence on certain feminist theologies, Catherine Keller emphasizes relationalism from a nonessentialist perspective. She stresses that relationalism is based on theories holding that humans as well as other living beings have to rely on relations. Adolf Portmann, for example, has stated: "Man is a socially premature human being." Thereby he implied that human beings, in order to survive and grow, need to relate to, and be protected by, other human beings. All human beings, not just women, are formed and dependent on relations to others. Hence, one cannot assume that women are essentially or naturally more connective or relational. They are likely to be more aware of these qualities due to traditional role and gender models. Thus, Keller states:

> Women, in other words, do not carry the burden of relations because of some relational essence, some necessarily more nurturant nature. . . . Rather, we have been socially and discursively molded to perform the intimately and consciously relational tasks which men of power could always abdicate. There is no intrinsic virtue in such performances.[238]

Keller continues: "To outgrow the androcentric discourse of separation and independence, we need to understand that connectivity cannot be equated with femininity or dependency. Relationalist insight needs maturation through constructive criticism, not abandonment."[239]

Catherine Keller further emphasizes that any of our actions are in fact interactions, and even such an individual human activity as knowing is always an act of knowing together, a reciprocal or mutual interaction of subjects. To recognize that we are mutually dependent upon, and related to, each other is the beginning of ethics.[240] There is broad agreement among feminists from a theoretical as well as from a theological perspective that

---

237. Ibid., 65.
238. Ibid., 76.
239. Ibid., 78.
240. Ibid., 74.

feminist analysis is never a means in itself but has, theologically speaking, an eschatological dimension. Feminist analysis and the theoretical assumptions about its own presuppositions and underlying assumptions serve the goal of overcoming oppression and injustice, and of nurturing the belief that things can become better.[241] Thus, ethical questions about justice and injustice, liberation and oppression, right and wrong—which are actually questions about relationships—are not a mere appendix to an otherwise disengaged exercise in abstract thinking; instead, they are actually the very purpose of feminist theory.[242]

In this section we have seen that feminist theory initiated a radical change in perspective on topics directly concerning women, and also on other philosophical and ethical questions. I have demonstrated that the dominant malestream perspective on women's identity, for example, is very limited. Here I have questioned methods of research as well as the pattern or systems by which a topic is analyzed; these are already part of a dominant discourse. E. B. Brown has demonstrated that the hermeneutical system shaping our perception of the discourses of history and politics, determines and shapes these disciplines.[243]

Feminist theories likewise demonstrate that there is more than one way of thinking, more than the Western malestream perception of life and reality, and that, similar to antiquity, there are various perceptions even within feminist theoretical approaches themselves. In the next section I consider whether and how feminist theologies address the changes in perspectives—as feminist theories reflect on them, especially on the issues discussed above (identity, difference and diversity, relationality and mutuality)—and whether and how these changing perspectives are related to, and interact with, developments in feminist theories.

The Issues of Identity, Diversity, and Mutuality in Feminist Theologies

Sometimes intertwined, but mostly without any direct reference to each other, feminist theologians have developed their own feminist approaches to theology in parallel with feminist theorists in the realm of philosophy. Whether it is relevant for feminist theologians to engage with feminist theory has been, and to some extent still is, a matter of debate. With feminist theologians such as Rebecca Chopp, Sheila Greeve Davaney, and Serene Jones, I consider it a necessity for feminist theologies to engage in theoretical reflection.

---

241. See Jones, *Feminist Theory*, 9; and Davaney in *Horizons in Feminist Theology* (ed. Chopp and Davaney), 3ff.
242. Jones, *Feminist Theory*, 9–10.
243. See sec. "Diversity and Difference," 103ff.

It now is time to clarify the implicit presuppositions and often-unconscious assumptions that also shape feminist approaches. This process has nothing to do with escaping into abstract traits of thinking, disengaged from any practical consequences. Instead, it means actually taking into account and acknowledging the responsibility for the possible effects of even the most hidden assumptions. Later in this book I deal with this aspect of theoretical reflection while analyzing certain presuppositions in some feminist commentaries on Romans.[244]

The focus of this chapter, however, is on aspects of feminist theologies closely related to issues emphasized in feminist theories, as discussed above. Both disciplines address the same or similar issues, although with somewhat different emphases; after all, they both emerged from the same concerns for women's liberation from any kind of oppression. Like feminist theorists, feminist theologians seek ways to do their work from a feminist perspective, beyond the traditional male-dominated thought patterns, yet while struggling with the same or similar problems.

Elisabeth Schüssler Fiorenza most prominently addresses these problems, beginning with *Bread Not Stone* and continued in *Jesus: Miriam's Child, Sophia's Prophet* and other writings.[245] She asserts:

> I seek to create a "women"-defined feminist theoretical space that makes it possible to dislodge christological discourses from their malestream frame of reference. The hermeneutical-rhetorical creation of such a space intends to decenter hegemonic malestream christological discourses and to frame them in terms of critical feminist theology of liberation.[246]

Hence, we need to be aware of the problems of a complete separation of feminist from traditional discourses.[247] This need to create a "women-defined feminist theoretical space" applies to all theological issues.

We thus find feminist theologians addressing the question of women's identity in the context of creation and redemption,[248] for instance, or more specifically in the question of the *imago Dei*.[249] Womanist theologians specifically raise the question of difference and diversity, and we can see an emphasis on

---

244. See chap. 5, 161ff.
245. Elisabeth Schüssler Fiorenza, *Jesus: Miriam's Child, Sophia's Prophet: Critical Issues in Feminist Christology* (New York: Continuum, 1995).
246. Ibid., 3.
247. See subsec. "Roots of Feminist Perspectives," in sec. "Contemporary Ways of Thinking," 93f.
248. Rosemary Radford Ruether, *Women and Redemption* (Minneapolis: Fortress, 1998); idem, *God and Gaia;* and Elisabeth Moltmann-Wendel, *I Am My Body: New Ways of Embodiment* (London: SCM, 1994).
249. See Elisabeth Gössmann, "The Image of God and the Human Being in Women's Counter Tradition," in *Is There a Future for Feminist Theology?* (ed. Deborah F. Sawyer and Diane M. Collier; Sheffield: Sheffield Academic Press 1999), 26–56.

relationality and mutuality as a key or, as Schüssler Fiorenza notes, almost a "canonical"[250] topic in most feminist theological approaches.

Identity or the *Imago Dei* Question

From a feminist theological perspective, the identity question is a double issue. As in feminist theories, there is first the question of women's identity or of how to formulate women's identity without falling into dominant malestream frameworks of thinking. Second, it is also the question of how to formulate Christian identity from a feminist perspective. This includes the first issue because it implies the question of how to formulate Christian identity without misogyny. This second aspect has parallels with the question of how to formulate Christian identity without anti-Judaism.

I concentrate on the first aspect of the issue since it is parallel to the issue dealt with in feminist theories. But I do address the second aspect briefly because it is related to the issue raised at the beginning of this study—the question of how Christian identity can be formulated without misogyny and anti-Judaism. I again take up this matter later.[251]

Like feminist theorists, feminist theologians are well aware of the difficulties in formulating women's identity. Schüssler Fiorenza sees the sex/gender system along with male/female distinctions as one reason for the traditional definition of women as being all that men are not. Thus, before any new definitions can be found, one has to rid oneself of this dualistic perception of human reality. It is not enough just to define oneself as a woman from a women's perspective, since even so, one is still adhering to dualistic ways of thinking. Hence, as our starting point it is crucial for us to analyze and carefully take into account "the diverse cultural-religious contexts, the historically shaped subjectivity, and the diverse voices of wo/men."[252] Schüssler Fiorenza proposes that rather than conceptualizing reality in terms of gender dualism, we should see it as "a socially constructed web of interactive structures."[253] She thinks this will lead us to see that the categories of man and woman are constructs determined not only by biological sex but also by race, class, and culture. Rather than just being natural givens, maleness and femaleness are cultural norms backed by social sanctions. As such, in Schüssler Fiorenza's view, society constructs them as relations of domination and subordination. The theological implication of this "negative" identity description is that careful analysis of any position and any statement about

---

250. Schüssler Fiorenza, *Jesus*, 54.
251. See chaps. 6 and 7, 177ff, 195ff.
252. Schüssler Fiorenza, *Jesus*, 188–89.
253. Ibid., 36.

male/female is necessary in order to avoid any backsliding into patterns of domination/subordination. We root the presupposition of this position in the assumption that all human beings have basic equality, irrespective of sex and gender.

In her approach Mary McClintock Fulkerson draws attention to the references to the *imago Dei* metaphor in feminist theologies.[254] Similar to Schüssler Fiorenza's position, Fulkerson's concern is to avoid hegemonic claims in feminisms that define themselves as alleviating women's oppression. Fulkerson refers to poststructuralism as a helpful theory for a feminist theological reformulation of feminist identity.

In referring to the *imago Dei* in women, feminist theologians are emphasizing that not only men but *also* women are of value; *they* too are created as *imago Dei*. Such a feminist appeal to the *imago Dei* affirms the division of the world into two categories of people, gender criticism thus becoming a kind of "me too" theory.[255] For Fulkerson, the *imago Dei* metaphor is helpful when we seek to formulate gender identity beyond traditional hegemonic definitions: it entails no essential definition of human beings. We can only name human beings as subjects of God's saving care, characterized by finitude and God-dependence.[256] Thus, one can conclude that whatever in the reigning discursive system is meant by "man," it is not the *imago Dei*. This does not imply what woman is in essence, nor even what both are in essence. It only says what is not.

Fulkerson views this recognition as the starting point of a feminist theological exploration to find women's identity, as the starting point of "a good feminist theological story."[257] It can only be formulated again and again as a particular incomplete story that is part of the story of the God-loved creation, "a creation for which the only requisite features of imaging God are finitude and dependence. . . . It must sponsor the capacity for total self-criticism, for commitment to the goodness of the partial, and for the possibility that all is redeemable."[258] Thus, defining women's identity from a feminist theological

---

254. Mary McClintock Fulkerson, "Contesting the Gendered Subject: A Feminist Account of the *Imago Dei*," in *Horizons in Feminist Theology* (ed. Chopp and Davaney), 99–115.

255. Ibid., 109.

256. Ibid., 108.

257. Ibid., 114.

258. Ibid., 114. This eschatological aspect is also emphasized by Manuela Kalsky in her doctoral thesis *Christaphanien: Die Re-Vision der Christologie aus der Sicht von Frauen in unterschiedlichen Kulturen* (Gütersloh: Chr. Kaiser/Gütersloher Verlagshaus, 2000), 319–20: "Although I understand and to some extent also share the concern that so-called 'natural' femaleness (and maleness) could lead to a renewed fixation of role patterns, this, in my opinion, should not lead to a cessation and obliteration of all questions concerning sexual differences. . . . These merit their space within a hermeneutics of suspicion in an *ekklesia gynaikon* as well as in the context of a hermeneutics of creative imagination. The discussion on sexual difference in a feminist perspective, when studied in more detail, demonstrates that the issue is not the 'essence' of woman or her biological fixation to already existing female characteristics, the issue is *becoming* woman as something that is in the future."

perspective is part of an open process of Christian storytelling, which has to do with the openness of the theological story of an eschatological future.

Such aspects are crucial for attempts to reformulate women's identity and are closely linked to the reformulation of Christian identity from a feminist perspective.[259]

Identity as the Question of Reformulating Christian Identity

Some aspects of this debate are elaborated in the excellent doctoral dissertation by Manuela Kalsky, recently published as *Christaphanien: Die Re-Vision der Christologie aus der Sicht von Frauen in unterschiedlichen Kulturen.*[260] In the last chapter of her book, she draws attention to three issues she considers crucial in reformulating Christian identity from a feminist perspective: (1) With regard to the problem of anti-Judaism, she highlights the need for a relation-oriented intersubjective definition of Christian identity, recognizing differences. (2) Messianic images and women's stories need to be found to relocate the Christ event in contemporary women's lives. (3) The otherness of the other needs to be recognized and appreciated, as well as pluralism with respect to assumptions about salvation. Kalsky mentions the stress on relationality in feminist reformulations of Christian identity, but she emphasizes that in her view relationality implies the recognition of differences as real differences. Nevertheless, in a new definition of Christian identity, it is necessary to renounce a logic of contrast such as "we and the others."

We should not find identity only in contrast with, but in relation to, the other. Identity then cannot be something stable that one possesses, but something that is in relation to others, and thus in an ongoing process. Identity is happening in a process of recognizing difference and commonality in relation to others and thus is always subject to changes. In this approach the beginning of finding one's own identity is in recognizing distance and differences in relation to others. Moreover, it is crucial to endure the opacity of the other.[261] Relationality does not mean to become one and the same but rather to leave room for distance, the "between," between those who are and remain different.

Kalsky's approach has far-reaching and challenging implications for a reformulation of Christian identity,[262] but here we cannot elaborate on this in detail. In her attempt to break through the hegemonic logic of traditional Christian identity formulations, she comes to the insight that, from a feminist perspective sensitive to anti-Jewish tendencies in any theologies, it is

---

259. E.g., Schüssler Fiorenza, *Jesus,* 73–76.
260. See note 258 (above).
261. Kalsky, *Christaphanien,* 313–14.
262. Ibid., 319–29.

necessary to overcome the logic of sameness and fusion to achieve relationality or *"koinōnia."* She states that "theoretic-synthetic harmony is replaced
by practical dissonance."[263] In this approach Christians need not give up their
particularity, nor do they have to universalize their particularity and impose
it on others. Kalsky explains:

> The totalitarian perception of universalism which presupposes the universaliza-
> tion of one's own particularity is replaced by the search for an *interactive uni-
> versalism*. This presupposes that one has to encounter the "Other" as well as
> to appreciate his/her diversity and his/her opacity. Differences and disso-
> nances are thus the point of departure of common reflection and practice.[264]

Kalsky's approach is just one among others that seek to reformulate
Christian identity from a feminist perspective. Her emphasis on difference,
the recognition of the opacity of the other, and relationality—all appear to
some extent in other approaches as well. Nevertheless, throughout her book
she consequently keeps two aspects in mind—anti-Judaism and misogyny—
in traditional definitions of Christian identity. This makes her work a valuable reference for our study.

Difference and Diversity

As in feminist theory, so also in feminist theology, women from backgrounds
different from the white Western one have drawn attention to the particularity of feminist approaches in the early 1980s. Alice Walker published *In
Search of Our Mothers' Gardens* in 1983. With the creation of the term "womanist," she flagged the difference between white feminist theologians and
African-American women doing theology. The early feminist theological
approaches often stressed the commonality and sameness of women's experiences, and especially the commonality of oppressive experiences. Over against
that, African-American women demonstrated that to be a woman and to
experience life as a woman means quite different things to different women,
depending on the context in which they live and the traditions into which
they were born. Following womanist theologians, the *mujerista* theologians,
Jewish women, and women from the so-called third world soon developed

---

263. Ibid., 326, with my translation of the German: "An die Stelle einer theoretisch-synthetischen
Harmonie tritt die praktische Dissonanz."
264. Ibid., 327, with my translation of the German: "An die Stelle einer totalitären Auffassung von
Universalität, die auf der Verabsolutierung der eigenen Partikularität zugunsten eines einheitlichen
Ganzen beruht, tritt die Suche nach einer auf Begegnung hin angelegten *interaktiven Universalität*, die
die Vielfalt und Opazität der Anderen zulässt und die damit verbundenen Differenzen und Dissonanzen
zum Ausgangspunkt der gemeinsamen Reflexion und Praxis macht."

theological approaches that really took into account the particularities and the contextualities of women's lives. They thereby relativized any universalizing claims of white middle-class Euro-American feminist theologies.

Theologians such as Delores Williams have shown that it actually does make a difference from which perspective women talk about oppression. It is not possible to speak of equal experiences for all women; we need to value differences positively. Since we need to appreciate diversity in creation, we also need to recognize and appreciate diversity among people, including women. In her famous definition of "womanist," Alice Walker stated: "That a womanist is traditionally universalist, as in: 'Mama, why are we brown, pink, and yellow, and our cousins are white, beige, and black?' Ans.: 'Well, you know the colored race is just like a flower garden, with every color represented.'"[265] What divides and separates women are not the differences between them but the negation or devaluation of these differences. Audre Lorde emphasized that it is crucial to use these differences positively to support the struggles for liberation.[266]

Since womanist, mujerista, and third-world theologians protested against being merely "included with" other women, the issues of diversity and difference among women have also found their ways into feminist theologies of white middle-class European and American feminist theologies. Particularity and contextuality as well as the appreciation of different experiences are as much "canonical" in feminist theologies as is the issue of relationality. Manuela Kalsky even entitles the last chapter of her re-vision of Christology "Heilsame Differenzen." But with regard to anti-Judaism, she critically warns that irrespective of the emphasis on the particularity and contextuality of feminist theologies in different cultures, we never should formulate feminist Christian approaches at the expense of any "other."[267]

Kalsky also draws attention to a further aspect in the debate about difference and diversity, an aspect closely related to the identity question in feminist theory and theology. Women of the early feminist movement stressed the equality of women, but this later led to the question "Equal to what?" What did women want to be, and in which respect? I have referred to this debate in the context of the identity question (see above).[268] Some feminist theologians have called attention to the difference of female identity from male identity, whether with reference to nature or to social constructions of

---

265. Alice Walker, *In Search of Our Mothers' Gardens: Womanist Prose* (San Diego: Harcourt Brace Jovanovich, 1983).

266. See Audre Lorde and Adrienne Rich, *Macht und Sinnlichkeit: Ausgewählte Texte* (Berlin: Orlanda Frauenverlag, 1983).

267. Kalsky, *Christaphanien*, 311.

268. See subsec. "Identity and the Question of Women's Nature," in sec. "Contemporary Ways of Thinking," 97ff.

identity. Schüssler Fiorenza, however, regards the thinking in terms of sex and/or gender differences as part of a dualistic perception of the world that is inherently hierarchical and thus part of the universalistic and essentialist Western perception of the world.[269]

Over against this position, Kalsky asks whether it is appropriate to exclude one particular difference among human beings, the difference of sex and gender, from feminist discourse. She contends that as long as we regard sex and gender differences as just one among many differences, we are in minimal danger of having a dualistic theoretical framework for perceiving the world and doing theology. A feminist approach has to take into account sex and gender differences because it is beyond doubt that women live in female bodies.[270]

Relationality and Mutuality

What Schüssler Fiorenza notes with regard to feminist Christology, applies to feminist theology in general: no issue is more fundamental than that of relationality.[271]

Feminist approaches such as Isabel Carter Heyward's or Mary Grey's explicitly base themselves on the concept of relationality; others such as Dorothee Sölle and Elisabeth Schüssler Fiorenza emphasize this aspect more generally in their work.[272]

The title of Carter Heyward's doctoral thesis could serve as the programmatic heading for her entire theological work: *The Redemption of God: A Theology of Mutual Relation.*[273] It is based on the presupposition that in the beginning there is relation. In contrast to traditional Christian theology—which in her view presupposes loneliness, brokenness, and isolation as basic to the human condition—she instead emphasizes that relationality is the fundamental human condition. She perceives relationality as essentially good because through it human beings can empower each other to develop fully their potential as the persons they are.[274] The absence or destruction of relationships is evil because it necessarily implies the destruction of life.

---

269. Schüssler Fiorenza, *But She Said: Feminist Practices of Biblical Interpretation* (Boston: Beacon, 1992), 105–14; idem, *Jesus,* 64; see subsec. "Identity or the *Imago Dei* Question," in sec. "Issues of Identity," 112f.

270. Kalsky, *Christaphanien,* 319.

271. See also ibid., 306.

272. I could mention many more feminist theologians, but these few exemplify the topic.

273. Carter Heyward, *The Redemption of God: A Theology of Mutual Relation* (Washington, D.C.: University Press of America, 1982).

274. Carter Heyward, *Touching Our Strength: The Erotics as Power and the Love of God* (San Francisco: Harper & Row, 1989), 193.

Carter Heyward bases her feminist theological approach on the "I-Thou" concept of the Jewish philosopher Martin Buber and on Elie Wiesel's literary analysis of his own experience of absolute darkness during his imprisonment in Auschwitz. Redemption thus has to do with the reconstruction, or the healing, of relationality in mutuality. The only way to find meaning in life and to overcome evil and darkness is through relationality. She states: "We, you and I, you and we, we were born now and always struggling for power to effect in relation to mother, father, friend and stranger the world itself, into which we come in relation and in which we do not survive except in relation—intimate and immediate bonding."[275] This has implications for Carter Heyward's image of God. Her approach perceives God not as a separate power but as the basis of mutual relation. God is incarnate in the process of mutual relation.

Mary Grey also generally bases her theological approach on relationality.[276] In its innermost structure the world consists in relationality. God is the relational power of the universe, and relationality is also our true human nature. In their emphasis on relationships and appreciation of them, even when socially and culturally transmitted, women play a paradigmatic role for a world in need of redemption, for a world longing for just and satisfying relationships. Relationality is the power to overcome personal and structural brokenness and woundedness, difference and otherness.

The relational power of the Christian community constitutes a redemptive reality over against conflict and struggle. Part of the redemptive process through redeeming connectedness is the need to be aware of and to name factors that hinder or destroy true relationships. It implies the perception of difference and conflict and the avoidance of leveling differences to achieve relationship. To be able to recognize differences and diversity and live with them is part of the vision of healing and redeeming relationships. Grey further stresses that it is not sufficient to state the mere need for relationships. Mutuality in relationships is crucial; otherwise they cannot exercise redemptive and healing power. Yet we should not confuse mutuality with reciprocity. Mutuality would be perverted if it would seek for reciprocity. But inherent in the free flow of mutuality, we find redemptive power.

---

275. Heyward, *Redemption of God,* 152

276. See the following publications: Mary Grey, *Redeeming the Dream: Feminism Redemption and Christian Tradition* (London: SPCK, 1989); idem, "Jesus—Einsamer Held oder Offenbarung beziehungshafter Macht? Eine Untersuchung feministischer Erlösungsmodelle," in *Vom Verlangen nach Heilwerden: Christologie in feministisch-theologischer Sicht* (ed. Doris Strahm and Regula Strobel; Lucerne: Exodus, 1991), 148–71; idem, *The Wisdom of Fools? Seeking Revelation for Today* (London: SPCK, 1993); idem, "Expelled again from Eden: Facing Difference through Connection," *Feminist Theology* 21 (May 1999): 8–20.

Others such as Rita Nakashima Brock,[277] and more recently Manuela Kalsky,[278] have contributed new aspects to the role of relationality in feminist theologies. Elisabeth Schüssler Fiorenza is critical of these approaches: she views them as emphasizing the interpersonal, existentialist aspects of relationality and mutuality, thereby negating the sociopolitical implications of relations, which always include aspects of hierarchical power. She doubts whether feminists can take the focus on interpersonal aspects of relationality and combine it with the demand for sociopolitical justice.

In her critique, Schüssler Fiorenza does not do justice to the approaches mentioned above. Carter Heyward is well aware of the political dimension of relationality in her chapters on the absence of relationality during the horrors of the Shoah.[279] She develops her concept in discussing these very sociopolitical crimes. For her there is no love/justice dichotomy since there can be no loving relation that is not just, and no just relation that is not loving. Also, we cannot reduce Mary Grey's approach to the interpersonal, individual level, although this level is important in her work. She stresses the personal aspects of relationality as part of, and in relation to, sociopolitical and even global contexts.[280] Both scholars see the interpersonal and the sociopolitical dimension of relationality as inseparably related and intertwined with each other, necessarily impacting on each other.

Schüssler Fiorenza and Dorothee Sölle strongly emphasize the sociopolitical dimensions of relationality. But Schüssler Fiorenza draws attention to the fact that relational work, if it is reduced to privatized relations, can have the

---

277. Rita Nakashima Brock, *Journeys by Heart: A Christology of Erotic Power* (New York: Crossroad, 1988).

278. On Kalsky, see subsec. "Identity as the Question," in sec. "Issues of Identity," 114f. Although strongly emphasizing the relational aspect of Christian identity, Kalsky, *Christaphanien,* 182, warns against an idealizing or romanticizing use of this aspect. Over against Carter Heyward, she asks whether the emphasis on the redeeming power of human relationships is possibly not too high an expectation, which tends to forget the relativizing aspect of faith *sola gratia.* Kalsky, ibid., 184, also queries Carter Heyward when she talks of relationships in terms of fusion or becoming one, since this inherently tends to see the other as an alter ego rather than as different from myself. Over against this tendency, Kalsky emphasizes the mystery or the opacity of "the other," which in contrast to modern Western tradition does not try to understand and illuminate all and everything. She says: "This thought implies that moments of the divine, moments of the power-in-relation, are not primarily found in a harmony of paradise but in the confrontation with differences. The possibility to 'tran(s)-cendere,' to transcend, to go beyond the limits to which every person is limited by as a human being, emerges in and through the irritation of my own history caused by the history of 'the other.'" This is my translation of the German: "Dieser Gedanke führt dazu, dass Momente des Göttlichen, Momente der Macht-in-Beziehung, in erster Linie nicht in paradiesischer Harmonie zu finden sind, sondern in der Konfrontation mit dem Verschiedenen. In der Störung der eigenen Geschichte durch die Geschichte des/der Anderen entsteht die Möglichkeit für 'tran(s)-scendere,' für das Überschreiten von Grenzen, an die jede Person mit ihren begrenzten menschlichen Möglichkeiten gebunden ist. Paradoxerweise sind es in diesem Sinne die Unterschiede, die verbinden."

279. Heyward, *Redemption of God,* 120ff.

280. See, e.g., Grey, "Jesus—Einsamer Held?" 166.

function of stabilizing and supporting an otherwise oppressive world. Even religion and church can serve this function when we see them as safe havens where people can recover from a hostile outside world.[281] She even views the concept of relationality as counterproductive while feminists search for a suitable reformulation of Christian identity. Over against this, she highlights the need for feminist scholars in religion to "firmly situate their theological discourses within the emancipatory movements of wo/men around the globe."[282] She says: "The Living One is present wherever the disciples of the *basileia* [kingdom] practise the inclusive discipleship of equals, making it a present reality among the poor, hungry, abused, and alienated wo/men."[283] Though from a different perspective and with a different purpose, this feminist approach again underlines the centrality of relational aspects.

German feminist theologian Dorothee Sölle does not develop relationality explicitly as a theological concept, but in her political theology she teaches that sin has to do with the unrelatedness of individuals as well as systems of oppression, which try to control others and make them submit. In Sölle's approach, God is "the power of life as loving interrelationship, who is present in and through those times and places where such life is happening."[284]

In this chapter we have seen that feminist theory and feminist theology have changed perspectives in their respective disciplines, radically introducing new paradigms and demonstrating that there is more than one and the same universal perspective in scholarship. From within such changing feminist perspectives, these theologies and theories prominently deal with the issues of particularity, identity, diversity, and relationality. They are crucial aspects in the process of searching for new theological discourses beyond hierarchies and domination.

Perspectives have been and are changing also in Pauline studies. One focus in those changes is the search to overcome oppressionist and particularly anti-Jewish patterns in the interpretation of Paul and his letters. The leading question of the following chapters is whether and to what extent the changing perspectives in both disciplines, feminist theologies and Pauline studies, could relate to and illuminate each other.

---

281. Schüssler Fiorenza, *Jesus,* 56.
282. Ibid., 189.
283. Ibid., 188.
284. Ruether, *Women and Redemption,* 189.

Paul in Contemporary Studies and Theologies

4

Paul—Beyond
the New Perspective

Gaps in the New Perspective

E. P. Sanders's *Paul and Palestinian Judaism* has led to a paradigm shift in Pauline studies.[1] Although Albert Schweitzer, W. D. Davies, and Krister Stendahl, from different perspectives, had already argued that the doctrine of justification by faith over against works of law was not the center of Paul's thought, it was Sanders's publication that caused major reaction in Pauline scholarship. He has convincingly demonstrated that the traditional image of Paul as the theologian of justification by faith over against Jewish works-righteousness is based on a historically completely false depiction of first-century Judaism. Sanders himself nevertheless viewed Paul's teachings as different from Judaism: he saw Paul as in opposition to Judaism. In his own approach James D. G. Dunn tried to overcome the opposition between Paul and Judaism still present in Sanders's work. But although Dunn actually sees Paul as integrated in Judaism, he creates a new problem: he depicts two contradictory types of Judaism—a particularistic and ethnocentric one that Paul is opposing, and a universalistic one that Paul advocates.[2] Even if this might not be Dunn's intention, this view implies somehow an evaluation of these

---

1. E. P. Sanders, *Paul and Palestinian Judaism: A Comparison of Patterns of Religion* (Philadelphia: Fortress, 1977). On aspects of the history of research, see sec. "Pauline Studies and Feminist Theology," in chap. 2 (above).

2. James D. G. Dunn, *The Theology of Paul the Apostle* (Grand Rapids: Eerdmans, 1998).

types, the latter being the "better" one. Dunn regards Paul as the champion of universalism over against a form of Judaism that is particularistic. Thus, even here and despite best intentions to do otherwise, we find evidence of the traditional pattern of interpreting Paul as being in opposition to Judaism. Recently several scholars have noted this. In her article "Die Lieder und das Geschrei der Glaubenden: Rechtfertigung bei Paulus,"[3] Luise Schottroff argued that Dunn did overcome the traditional anti-Judaism in his interpretation of Paul as the founder of Torah-observant Gentile churches. But with Dunn's contention that Paul set up his mission to the Gentiles over against a wrong and narrow ethnocentric form of Judaism, Dunn still adheres to the anti-Jewish pattern of particularistic Israel versus universalistic gospel. Schottroff observes:

> Here a law-observant Gentile church is seen as being Paul's achievement; thus traditional anti-Judaism is overcome. But the law-observant Gentile church is set up to bring to an end a wrong Jewish understanding of the Torah. The sociological construction of Dunn continues to adhere to an anti-Jewish Christian perception of the narrow particularistic Israel versus the universal gospel.[4]

Others, such as Neil Elliott, have also found "gaps in the 'New Perspective.'"[5] Elliott acknowledges the progress brought about in Pauline studies through the research of scholars of the New Perspective, but he notes: "This approach has not yet gone beyond the fundamental assumption that Paul must be interpreted over against Judaism."[6] The New Perspective still depicts the particularistic ethnocentrism of Judaism as being in contrast to the "universalism" of Pauline theology. Such a universalism leaves little or no room for Torah-observant Jews. Thus, one has to ask whether the New Perspective actually fulfills its initial promise to reverse centuries of theological anti-Judaism.[7] According to Dunn, although Paul only criticizes Judaism's misuse of the law, his position nevertheless has close similarities to the traditional view: Paul's critique of Judaism actually was fully justified (there must

---

3. Luise Schottroff, "Die Lieder und das Geschrei der Glaubenden: Rechfertigung bei Paulus," *Evangelische Theologie* 60.5 (2000): 332–47.
    4. Ibid., 340, with my translation of the German: "Hier wird zwar eine gesetzestreue Völkerkirche als paulinisches Werk gesehen und insofern der traditionelle Antijudaismus überwunden, aber diese gesetzestreue Völkerkirche beendet ein falsches jüdisches Torahverständnis. Die soziologische Konstruktion von Dunn führt die antijudaistische christliche Vorstellung vom engen partikularistischen Israel versus universalem Evangelium weiter." See also John G. Gager, *Reinventing Paul* (New York: Oxford University Press, 2000), 49–50.
    5. Neil Elliott, "Paul and the Politics of the Empire," in *Paul and Politics: Ekklesia, Israel, Imperium, Interpretation* (ed. Richard A. Horsley; Harrisburg, Pa.: Trinity Press International, 2000), 20.
    6. Ibid., 19.
    7. Ibid., 20.

be something wrong with Judaism beyond the fact that it is not Christianity). Hence, this actually leaves a dichotomy between Jewish particularism and Christian universalism.[8]

For all its declared intentions and efforts to undermine the traditional image of Paul as in opposition to Judaism, Dunn's approach seems to fall back in different degrees into old frameworks of interpretation, dating back to Baur and the Tübingen school. Even though representatives of the New Perspective intend to do otherwise, most of them end up with an image of Paul as being a champion of universalism, who has parted from his Jewish heritage. Quite often, again as in the Tübingen school, they attribute Paul's universalism to the fact that he was a Jew "motivated by a Hellenistic desire for the One, which among other things produced an ideal of a universal human essence, beyond difference and hierarchy."[9] Thus, these scholars view Paul as alienated from his Jewish heritage.[10]

Paul and the Judaism/Hellenism Debate

Was Paul enculturated in the Hellenistic world, and if so, to what extent? And/or did he maintain a particular Jewish identity that was based mainly on the Jewish Scriptures? The two options are generally perceived as opposing each other. Tarsus, Paul's native city, represents Hellenistic culture and an open universalistic mind; Jerusalem symbolizes Jewish-Palestinian culture, a conservative mind, and particularity. W. C. van Unnik describes the contrast: "In these two cities, two worlds stand over against one another, radically different, each with its own questions and its own stamp, with its own attitudes to life and its own aims."[11] Following this pattern of dichotomy, researchers sought to demonstrate that Paul was enculturated either in one world or in the other. Often scholars admit that there still is some influence of the opposite world, though at the same time they stress that Paul is mainly and dominantly enculturated in only one. This leaves us with the impression that behind the actual debate about a Hellenistic or a Jewish Paul is a particular agenda that exceeds purely historical interests.

---

8. According to John Gager, *Reinventing Paul*, 49, in some respects Dunn's work represents a step backward from Sanders.

9. Daniel Boyarin, *A Radical Jew: Paul and the Politics of Identity* (Berkeley: University of California Press, 1994), 7.

10. See Troels Engberg-Pedersen, ed., *Paul beyond the Judaism/Hellenism Divide* (Louisville: Westminster John Knox, 2001); and the discussion about Hellenism in sec. "Hermeneutical Presuppositions," in chap. 2, 9.

11. W. C. van Unnik, *Tarsus or Jerusalem, the City of Paul's Youth?* (London: Epworth, 1962), 3–4; for an alternative view, see André Du Toit, "A Tale of Two Cities: 'Tarsus or Jerusalem?' Revisited," in *New Testament Studies* 46.3 (July 2000): 375–402.

There is no doubt that Paul is a child of his time.[12] Since the Hellenistic culture dominated the period in which he lived, it necessarily had some influence on him. In his rhetoric and in his use of the diatribe style, Paul shows knowledge and skills valued highly in Hellenistic culture.[13] There is quite a variety of different stages and aspects of Hellenistic influence on first-century Judaism, even in methods of scriptural interpretation. The crucial questions of the debate then ought not to be whether or not, but *how* and *to what extent* Paul was influenced by Hellenism, especially how and to what extent Hellenism impacted Paul's theological thinking and form of argumentation.

Scholars developed the tendency to see Paul as mostly enculturated in Hellenism in tandem with an image of Paul putting as much distance between him and his Jewish roots as possible. Only in the nineteenth century did scholars, especially in Germany, become interested in Hellenism as a cultural and political phenomenon in antiquity.[14] They attributed an open-minded, universalistic tendency to Hellenism, which they regarded as the main basis for the development of early Christianity. And if they accepted some Jewish influence as important for nascent Christianity, it was Judaism in its Hellenistic form, which they regarded as being on the point of leaving behind its particularistic attitude. With this assessment they see Paul as entirely enculturated in Hellenism, and as the apostle and hero of a universalistic new religion.

Scholars who read and interpret Paul's letters from this perspective look for parallels to his ways of arguing, his rhetoric, and his use of Greek terms in Graeco-Roman culture generally. Thus, one may look for examples of the use of terms such as "obedience" or "power" in Graeco-Roman society and (supposedly) understand Paul's use from that perspective.[15] The same would

---

12. See sec. "Different Ways of Thinking," in chap. 3, 49ff.
13. On this see Peter Tomson, *Paul and the Jewish Law: Halakha in the Letters of the Apostle to the Gentiles* (Minneapolis: Fortress, 1990), 52.
14. Since this interest arose before the political unification of Germany as a nation in 1871, one might ask whether the political and cultural mood that tended to emphasize the universalism of German culture and therefore promoted the unity of the German nation, influenced historical and theological research to a significant extent. Cf. Ismar Schorsch, *From Text to Context: The Turn to History in Modern Judaism* (Hanover, N.H.: University of New England/Brandeis University Press, 1994), 346, who refers to R. A. Wolf, *Vorlesung über den Apostel Jesu Christi: Sein Leben, sein Wirken, seine Briefe, und seine Lehre: Ein Beitrag zu einer Kritischen Geschichte des Urchristenthums* (Stuttgart: Becher und Mutter, 1845). Cf. Dale B. Martin, "Paul and the Judaism/Hellenism Dichotomy," in *Paul beyond the Divide* (ed. Engberg-Pedersen), 29–62; and Philip S. Alexander, "Hellenisim and Hellenization as Problematic Historiographical Categories," ibid., 63–80.
15. See, e.g., Elizabeth A. Castelli, "Romans," in *A Feminist Commentary* (vol. 2 of *Searching the Scriptures;* ed. Elisabeth Schüssler Fiorenza, A. Brock, and S. Matthews; New York: Crossroad, 1994), 285, 289; Cyntia Briggs Kittridge, *Community and Authority: The Rhetoric of Obedience in the Pauline Tradition* (Harrisburg, Pa.: Trinity Press International, 1998); and Sandra Hack Polaski, *Paul and the Discourse of Power* (Sheffield: Sheffield Academic Press, 1999).

apply to the structure of his arguments, or his emphasis on, for example, believers' "oneness" in Christ.[16]

Troels Engberg-Pedersen has stressed that "Hellenistic culture" is a cultural mixture of originally Greek and originally non-Greek elements.[17] The term should not be used to signify the specifically Greek element of this cultural mixture, which is in itself empty, "designating the mixture of cultural elements."[18] This implies that one should not try to locate Paul in a specific context or to retrace the roots of his thinking and arguing. Paul himself is rather seen "as a place of confluence of ideas, motifs, and practices of almost any provenance."[19]

Engberg-Pedersen's approach is valuable for reminding us that cultural interaction never is a one-way-affair but a complex set of mutual influences. Nevertheless, I consider Engberg-Pedersen's approach as idealistic in its "universalistic" and "open-minded" claim. It does not take into account that despite some mutuality in cultural interaction, in these specific historical circumstances, one part of it is the culture of the dominant political power, with universalistic claims (enforced by the Roman legions), and the other part is the culture of the dominated.[20] This has a major impact on the process of influencing, and it certainly limits mutuality since it is not mutuality in a partnership of equals.

Moreover, the demand "not to let any given theological interest colour its comparison of Paul with phenomena in his cultural context"[21] is an idealistic claim of scholarship as being objective, which detaches scholars and their research from any concrete context. This approach somehow has to depict Paul as an empty vessel, or "a place of confluence of ideas," a figure detached from any given context, a sponge soaking up whatever comes from outside without using, shaping, or integrating these influences according to his own roots or purposes. Despite the outspoken claim not to be influenced by any given interests, this approach expresses idealistic claims of objectivity, which are rooted in Greek philosophical tradition. We receive the image of an idealistic Paul, through whom, as a cultural melting pot, a new idealistic religion with universalistic claims begins to emerge.

---

16. Boyarin, *Radical Jew*, 7.
17. On Hellenistic culture, see sec. "Aspects of Platonic/Aristotelian Ways of Thinking," in chap. 3, 53.
18. Troels Engberg-Pedersen, ed., *Paul in His Hellenistic Context* (Edinburgh: T&T Clark, 1994), xx.
19. Ibid., xviii.
20. Compare the slight French-German antagonism in the French-speaking part of Switzerland, and also the Welsh-English antagonism in Wales.
21. Engberg-Pedersen, *Paul in Hellenistic Context*, xviii.

Daniel Boyarin's important contribution in *A Radical Jew* depicts an image of a Hellenistic Paul from a Jewish perspective. This image is founded on the conviction that Paul is "motivated by a Hellenistic desire for the One, which among other things produced an ideal of a universal human essence, beyond difference and hierarchy."[22] Based on this presupposition, Boyarin contends that, for Paul, being in Christ erases all ethnic and gender distinctions. He sees this universalizing tendency developing especially in two aspects of Paul's theological arguing.

Since Paul, according to Boyarin, is influenced by Platonism in ways similar to Philo, his thinking is operating "in a dualistic system in which spirit precedes and is primary over body."[23] This dualistic pattern of thought is hierarchical and shows that Paul, in accordance with Platonism, is subordinating any kind of bodily phenomena to the spirit. Boyarin states: "This universal humanity, however, was predicated (and still is) on the dualism of flesh and spirit, such that while the body is particular, marked through practice as Jew or Greek, and through anatomy as male or female, the spirit is universal."[24]

From this background, Paul in his interpretation of Jewish Scriptures, according to Boyarin, consequently spiritualizes integral Jewish features such as circumcision (Rom 2:25–29) and descent from Abraham (Gal 4:21–31) or Israel according to the flesh (1 Cor 10:18). Through this method he "transforms the rites and the very existence of a particular tribe" into "an ahistorical, abstract, and universal human truth."[25] Thus he minimizes differences between individuals and people to the extent that they are perceived as irrelevant and of minor value. This is what Paul's message promotes, according to Boyarin. It thus implies the eradication of diversity to achieve sameness—"a humanity undivided by ethnos, class, and sex."[26] William S. Campbell comments on this position: "The result is that since the spiritual essence of the supposed generic human ends up looking like male and Christian, women and Jews become the devalued other."[27] From a Jewish perspective, Boyarin's approach has remarkable affiliations with Baur's interpretation of Paul, which he himself also acknowledges with appreciation.[28]

These strands of research operate with the presupposition that Paul is primarily enculturated in Hellenism and therefore to a certain extent alienated

---

22. Boyarin, *Radical Jew,* 7.
23. Ibid., 14.
24. Ibid., 7.
25. Cf. John M. G. Barclay, "Neither Jew nor Greek: Multiculturalism and the New Perspective," in *Ethnicity and the Bible* (ed. Mark G. Brett; Leiden: Brill, 1996), 207.
26. Boyarin, *Radical Jew,* 181.
27. W. S. Campbell, "The Interpretation of Paul: Beyond the New Perspective" (paper presented at the British New Testament Conference, Manchester, U.K., 2001), 13. Cf. also Pamela Eisenbaum, "Is Paul the Father of Misogyny and Antisemitism?" *Crosscurrents* 50.4 (2000–2001): 506–24.
28. Boyarin, *Radical Jew,* 11, 212.

from his Jewish roots. From this approach, his letters show a universalistic Hellenistic thinker, though at some points (e.g., Rom 9–11) with unfortunate retrogression into Jewish particularism. Paul could not quite rid himself of the concept of the Jews as God's favorite people![29]

Dual Identity

From another period in world history, we can get a most interesting insight into the possibilities of living in different cultures at the same time. In his brief but excellent study *German Jews: A Dual Identity,* Paul Mendes-Flohr[30] gives a well-informed analysis of the way German Jews since the Enlightenment have dealt with the challenge of their intention to become part of German culture and its Enlightenment ideals, especially its *Bildungsideal* (cultural ideal), and have continued to be Jewish as well.

Following the Enlightenment ideal of universal humanity, Jews sought to assimilate to German culture as completely as possible. Inherent in the ideal of universalism is its neutralizing effect on the diversity of cultures, traditions, and religions. To achieve an ideal society of tolerance, people have to give up a specific identity, and the individual has to become merely human. Thus, Jews could gain the main society's acceptance as human beings, but in fact not as human beings with a particular identity, not as Jews. Hence, assimilation could not counteract or prevent the rise of anti-Semitism during the nineteenth century. Since for young Jewish intellectuals assimilation had failed, and the way back to the Jewish ghettos was no option for redefining their German-Jewish identity, they sought for new ways of living and defining this identity.

One of the most prominent thinkers of that period was Franz Rosenzweig, who most clearly realized that living in two cultures, living a "dual identity," did not mean that one had to assimilate a part of one's identity to the point of depriving it of its specific contents. Rosenzweig entitled a book of essays on general and Jewish themes as *Zweistromland,* the land of two rivers.[31] There he outlined his view of German Jewry as residing on the banks of two cultures and being nurtured by the flow of two streams, the German culture and Jewish culture. As Mendes-Flohr shows, Rosenzweig captured the mood of his generation (which included, e.g., Martin Buber): "To be genuinely both a Jew and a German, one must take both of these

---

29. C. H. Dodd, *The Epistle to the Romans* (London: Hodder & Stoughton, 1932), 63.
30. Paul Mendes-Flohr, *German Jews: A Dual Identity* (New Haven: Yale University Press, 1999).
31. Franz Rosenzweig, *Der Mensch und sein Werk, Gesammelte Schriften,* Reinhold Mayer, Annemarie Mayer, ed. (Dordrecht: Martinus Nijhoff, 1984), 566.

cultural identities seriously, attending to each with affection and an informed commitment."[32] Rosenzweig viewed Jews and Judaism as bound to some ambivalence from the very beginning of their existence; they have been part of the cultures of others, without being completely absorbed by any of them. They are accustomed to living simultaneously within and beyond culture, which Rosenzweig regarded as the calling of Judaism as a community of prayer and study.

The "both-and" that Rosenzweig defines as essential for the relation of German culture and Judaism is an "emphatic 'both-and,' denoting a tension."[33] For Jews, this meant a way back to the center of Jewish life, while maintaining respect for the cultural and intellectual achievements of German culture. It meant being enculturated in German culture without giving up their distinctive Jewish identity. Rosenzweig tried to find a balance between Jewish and other cultural identities; in doing so, he took seriously the reality of differences and particularity to the point of showing that identity in itself is a matter of complexity and pluralism.

Admittedly, there is quite a distance in space and time between eighteenth- and twentieth-century Germany, and first-century Palestine and the Diaspora in the Roman Empire. Yet the insights gained from a multiple identity in German Jews, as articulated by Franz Rosenzweig, are significant and can serve as an analogy for understanding aspects of the relation and interaction between Jewish and Hellenistic identity at the time of Paul. There is no need to see this relation solely in terms of either one or the other; even the question as to what extent Paul was Hellenized might not prove to be decisive.

Peter Tomson has thoroughly investigated this question not only in relation to Paul but also by looking at the writings of other Greek-writing authors, especially those of Philo. His findings support what is outlined above,[34] that "it was perfectly possible to speak or write fluent Greek and at the same time be a zealous and self-confident Jew."[35] Tomson claims that even Philo, "the proverbial representative of Hellenistic Diaspora Judaism,"[36] was a philosopher[37] who functioned within a traditional Jewish framework and presupposed Jewish rules; he knew and emphasized the precept to teach children Torah as well as the commandment to keep the "unwritten laws."[38]

---

32. Quoted in Mendes-Flohr, *German Jews,* 43.
33. Ibid., 84.
34. See subsec. "Hellenistic Influences," in sec. "First-Century Jewish Interpretation," in chap. 3, 83ff.
35. Tomson, *Paul and Jewish Law,* 34.
36. Ibid., 47.
37. On Philo, see subsec. "Hellenistic Influences," in sec. "First-Century Jewish Interpretation," in chap. 3, 84ff.
38. Tomson, *Paul and Jewish Law,* 40.

"The image we gain from Philo is that of enlightened piety, freely enriched with numerous elements from Hellenistic intellectual tradition, but organized along the lines of Jewish life."[39] From this, Tomson comes to a convincing conclusion. While pointing to Hellenistic influence in both Philo and Paul, Tomson shows that the basic substructure of the thinking and reasoning of both of them, in distinct ways, is Jewish: "It would seem to follow that unless it appears that Paul effectively departed from the ways of Judaism, halakah must have remained a central factor in his life and thought."[40]

John Barclay, in his comprehensive survey of *Jews in the Mediterranean Diaspora*,[41] compares Paul's letters to other writings of Diaspora Jews. What Paul tells about his upbringing and education and what can be guessed about his education from the cultural level of his letters, match quite well. It is certainly appropriate to suggest that Paul was brought up in a Jewish family who knew Hebrew/Aramaic as well as Greek (cf. Phil 3:5; 2 Cor 11:22; Acts 21:37–22:3). His Greek is good but not "stylistically grand,"[42] he shows hardly any knowledge of Greek literature, and he has some knowledge of rhetorical styles used in debates (diatribe, irony); yet he views himself as an "inexpert speaker" (2 Cor 11:6). R. D. Anderson has also drawn attention to the fact that Paul's Greek style seems strongly influenced by the Semitic Greek of the Septuagint.[43] The vocabulary of Paul was not that of an average philosopher or rhetorician; instead, it seems to have been formed primarily by the Septuagint.[44]

Rather than praising a Greek education he underwent, as Philo and other Hellenistic Jews did, Paul emphasizes that he "advanced in Judaism beyond many among my people of the same age," being "far more zealous for the traditions of my ancestors" (Gal 1:14). After his call Paul committed his life to the "inbringing" of the Gentiles (which possibly implied that he spent more of his time among Gentiles than with Jews); nevertheless, he shows hardly any attempt to express the gospel in terms of Hellenistic culture. His world map is based on the scriptural division between Jews and the nations/

---

39. Ibid., 45.
40. Ibid., 47; see also 51ff.
41. John Barclay, *Jews in the Mediterranean Diaspora: From Alexander to Trajan (323 BCE–117 CE)* (Edinburgh: T&T Clark, 1996).
42. Ibid., 383.
43. R. Dean Anderson Jr., *Ancient Rhetorical Theory and Paul* (rev. ed.; Leuven: Peeters, 1999), 281: "It is at least possible, if not indeed very probable, that Paul's paratactic (as opposed to periodic or even certain forms of hypotactic) style had to do with the kind of Greek spoken by Jews generally. Their native Semitic language was paratactic by nature. Their basic religious textbook, . . . even in Greek translation, preserves this characteristic."
44. Ibid., 282: This is "quite a contrast to Philo, who did not let his use of the Septuagint affect his Greek prose."

Gentiles (Gal 2:8-9; 1 Cor 1:23; Rom 3:29; 9:24; et al.).[45] Rather than try-ing to place Jewish ethics within the context of, for example, Stoic ethics, and Jewish monotheism within the context of Greek philosophy, Paul uses tradi-tional, scripturally based Jewish tradition, intending to root the identity of his Gentile converts firmly within this tradition.[46] He does not try to identify in any way with Hellenistic culture as such. His universal adaptability in 1 Cor 9:19ff. can be read as an occasional strategy to suit his own missionary purpose.

From all this we can conclude that the question whether Paul was influ-enced by Hellenism or not is somehow obsolete.[47] There was the possibility of a dual identity for first-century Jews living in a Hellenistic environment, as much as for Jews living in modern German culture. Being enculturated in another culture did not need to weaken Jewish identity and Jewish ways of thinking to any extent. This applies to the most Hellenized Jew we know, Philo, and even more to Paul, as Barclay has shown. Hence, we can plausi-bly argue that Paul, though influenced by Hellenism, was firmly rooted in his Jewish tradition. The fact that the cultural "mood" of his time was doubtlessly Hellenistic must not necessarily have alienated Paul from his Jewish heritage, nor must it have rendered his way of thinking into a Greek, universalistic, or non-Jewish style.

Here a number of scholars have begun to consider: What if we take seri-ously that "Paul is not a Gentile but a Jew and is not going to change that,"[48] a "Hebrew born of Hebrews" (Phil 3:5), and "far more zealous for the tradi-tions of [his] ancestors" (Gal 1:14)? What if we take Paul's Jewishness really and thoroughly seriously as well as other aspects of the particular context in which he lived, acted, and wrote?

From differing perspectives a number of scholars—critical both of the tra-ditional as well as of the New Perspective on Paul—again are emphasizing the need to take into account the variety of contextual aspects in reading Paul's letters. We can label some of the most recent of these approaches as perspectives "Beyond the New Perspective" on Paul. Here I concentrate on four aspects of these approaches: (1) the contextuality of Paul's statements in his letters, (2) rhetorical perspectives, (3) the Jewish pattern of Paul's way of thinking and acting, and (4) the political dimension of Paul's message.

---

45. On this see James M. Scott, *Paul and the Nations: The Old Testament and Jewish Background of Paul's Mission to the Nations with Special Reference to the Destination of Galatians* (Tübingen: Mohr/Siebeck, 1995), 216–18.

46. Contra Troels Engberg-Pedersen, *Paul and the Stoics* (Louisville: Westminster John Knox, 2000).

47. On this see also Stanley K. Stowers, *A Rereading of Romans: Justice, Jews, and Gentiles* (New Haven: Yale University Press, 1994), 328: "Asking whether Paul was Jewish or Hellenistic is like asking whether a certain rabbi from Boston is Jewish or American; Jewish or Western. The question is silly. Paul was both fully Jewish, absolutely dedicated to his people, and fully a person of Hellenistic culture inhabit-ing the life of the early Roman Empire."

48. Tomson, *Paul and Jewish Law*, 280.

The Contextuality of Paul's Statements

In the late 1960s, interest in the form and function of the Pauline Letters began to develop, pioneered by Paul Schubert in his book *Form and Function of the Pauline Thanksgivings* as early as 1939.[49] It became clear that Paul's letters, although not composed as chapters of a systematic theology, were not casual documents he hastily scribbled on missionary travels; instead, he carefully constructed them, following contemporary rhetorical conventions.[50] Following earlier emphases, J. C. Hurd had warned against harmonizing across the letters and claimed that scholars can best understand the precise significance of each letter when its own distinctive contribution is recognized.[51] Robert Jewett further developed this focus on the particularity of each letter by his contextual analysis of Paul's anthropological terms in each precise context in which they occurred. In taking this approach, Jewett also resisted the tendency to generalize from one letter to the other as if anthropological terms had a standard meaning irrespective of context.[52] In the early 1970s the emergence of a sociological perspective further accentuated the stress on the individual *Sitz im Leben* of each letter.[53]

It is a significant sign of the changing perspectives that in 1986 the Society of Biblical Literature (SBL) Pauline Theology group devoted itself to the exegetical principle of reading and interpreting each of the Pauline Letters and its theology without reference or recourse to the other letters of the Pauline corpus. This reading and interpreting process developed over ten years and emerged in the publication of the four volumes of *Pauline Theology*.[54] Despite the fact that it was difficult for the group of participating scholars to come to agreements as to what "the theology of a particular letter" meant, the whole project is an indication of an increasing awareness that

---

49. Paul Schubert, *Form and Function of the Pauline Thanksgivings* (Beihefte zur Zeitschrift für die neutestamentliche Wissenschaft 20; Berlin: A. Töpelmann,1939).

50. See, for example, John L. White, "Introductory Formulae in the Body of the Pauline Letter," *Journal of Biblical Literature* 90 (1971): 91–97; and idem, ed., *Studies in Ancient Letter Writing* (Chico, Calif.: Scholars Press, 1981).

51. Hurd insisted: "Just as the harmonising of the letters with Acts is illegitimate, so too is the harmonising of the letters with one another. Both types of harmonisation are the result of a faulty historical method." J. C. Hurd, "Pauline Chronology and Pauline Theology," in *Christian History and Interpretation: Studies Presented to John Knox* (ed. W. R. Farmer, C. F. D. Moule, and R. R. Niebuhr; Cambridge: Cambridge University Press, 1967), 225–48 (48); quoted in W. S. Campbell, *Paul's Gospel in an Intercultural Context: Jew and Gentile in the Letter to the Romans* (Berlin: P. Lang, 1992), 6.

52. Robert Jewett, *Paul's Anthropological Terms: A Study of Their Use in Conflict Settings* (Leiden: Brill, 1971).

53. Campbell, *Paul's Gospel*, 7.

54. Jouette M. Bassler, ed.,*Thessalonians, Philippians, Galatians, Philemon* (vol. 1 of *Pauline Theology;* Minneapolis: Fortress, 1991); David M. Hay, ed., *1 and 2 Corinthians* (vol. 2 of *Pauline Theology;* Minneapolis: Fortress, 1993); David M. Hay and E. Elizabeth Johnson, eds., *Romans* (vol. 3 of *Pauline Theology;* Minneapolis: Fortress, 1995); E. Elizabeth Johnson, ed., *Looking Back, Pressing On* (vol. 4 of *Pauline Theology;* Atlanta: Scholars Press, 1997).

"Paul's letters should not be read as disparate chapters of dogma or milestones in an ongoing theological biography."[55] Since Paul had not intended to develop a systematic theology, as Campbell has asserted, "we can no longer therefore legitimately use his statements as if they were abstract and timeless theology."[56] We should rather, as he has further urged, "as far as humanly possible . . . interpret Paul's mission and Paul himself as they are presented in this specific text, before we resort to harmonization or revision from any other sources, however significant."[57]

In and with the SBL Pauline Theology group, J. Christiaan Beker strongly emphasized the issue of the particularity of each letter. Beker's primary concern was to show that the particularity and contingency of Paul's letters need not necessarily stand in contradiction to the fact that there is nevertheless a certain coherence in Paul's thought. Without any such coherence, the letters would be nothing else than occasional literature. Beker attempted to see contingency and coherence as related aspects of Paul's letters, often in dialectical tension; but recognition of both aspects is fundamental to any adequate interpretation of Paul. Beker came to this realization in the process of writing his major work *Paul the Apostle*.[58] He rightly recognized that it is only in and through an understanding of the contingency of the individual letters that we can demonstrate the coherence of Paul's thinking.

Paul's letters reveal a logic that is more homiletic and pastoral than systematic and, according to Beker, appear rather like ad hoc literature, written for specific purposes out of specific needs on the side of the addressees as well as of the author, at a particular time. They show a Paul who is concerned about the communities he founded and who becomes involved in the life of these various communities, in their specific questions which, be they practical or theological, arise out of specific situations at particular times. For Beker, it is evident that Paul intended his letters to be substitutes for his personal presence.[59] Thus Beker states: "Paul was a pragmatic missionary and propagandist. Paul seems more interested in persuasion, emotional appeal, and moral exhortation in his letters than in the academic pursuit of coherence and consistency of thought."[60]

---

55. Tomson, *Paul and Jewish Law,* 56.

56. Campbell, *Paul's Gospel,* 81.

57. W. S. Campbell, "Divergent Images of Paul and His Mission," in *Reading Israel in Romans: Legitimacy and Plausibility of Divergent Interpretations* (ed. Cristina Grenholm and Daniel Patte; Harrisburg, Pa.: Trinity Press International, 2000), 208.

58. J. Christiaan Beker, *Paul the Apostle: The Triumph of God in Life and Thought* (Philadelphia: Fortress, 1980).

59. Ibid., 23. W. S. Campbell, *Paul's Gospel,* 30, also stresses this with reference to Romans: ". . . the letter is the written equivalent of the oral presentation which Paul would have delivered to the congregation had he himself been present. . ."

60. J. Christiaan Beker, "Recasting Pauline Theology: The Coherence-Contingency Scheme as Interpretive Model," in *Pauline Theology,* 1 (ed. Bassler): 20, 15–24.

This does not imply that Paul's writing and thinking are perceived as lacking any kind of coherence; he is not a chaotic opportunist, and his letters are not fragmented and accidental expressions of thought. Paul applies his coherent thinking, focused on the apocalyptic triumph of God, to the particular and contingent situations of the communities. However, the term "coherence" is not identical with a "core" or "center" of Paul's thought, which one might find somewhere "behind the text." Beker emphasizes: "The term 'coherence' . . . suggests a fluid and flexible structure. In contrast to a fixed core and a specific center or particular symbol, it points to a field of meaning, a network of symbolic relations that nourishes Paul's thought and constitutes his 'linguistic world.'"[61] This "coherence" is not a fixed message that then is imposed on, or adapted to, particular exigencies in specific communities.

Jewish apocalyptic constitutes the symbolism or symbolic universe that provides the context and grammar by which Paul appropriates and interprets the Christ event. His apocalyptic interpretation of the cross and resurrection of Christ thus constitutes the coherence of his gospel. Coherence and contingency continually interact in a dialogical dialectic in Paul's thought. Beker could also say that "the coherence of the gospel 'incarnates' itself into the contingencies of the mission field."[62] We therefore should not abstract Paul's letters from their contextual particularity into a set of universal doctrines; we should interpret them "as gospel for particular situations, 'enfleshing' the gospel into human particularity."[63] It might not be merely accidental that the church passed Paul's thoughts along to us in the form of letters. This form seems to conform to Paul's way of thinking and doing theology as a direct and multiform response to various contingent situations. Thus Leander Keck has noted: "It is precisely the particularity of the occasions that make Paul's letters perennially significant."[64]

Wendy Dabourne has recently developed a similar approach in her study *Purpose and Cause in Pauline Exegesis.*[65] She declares that we have to consider carefully what it means to understand Paul's letters as letters and as pastoral. If, as is assumed also in traditional approaches, they are Paul's preaching of the gospel, it is important to clarify what is implied in such a statement. Does this mean that Paul gives an outline of his theological thoughts, an abstract exposition of his theology, as implied in earlier interpretations? Or does this actually mean preaching, addressing listeners rather than readers of

---

61. Ibid., 1:16.
62. Ibid., 1:21.
63. Beker, *Paul the Apostle,* 35.
64. Leander Keck, *Paul and His Letters* (Philadelphia: Fortress, 1979), 17.
65. Wendy Dabourne, *Purpose and Cause in Pauline Exegesis: Romans 1.16–4.25 and a New Approach to the Letters* (Cambridge: Cambridge University Press, 1999), 86.

theology? Such a differentiation does make a difference: a text meant for hearing rather than seeing has a different flow of thought.[66]

Dabourne emphasizes that one has to take into account that Paul's and his addressees' culture was much more one of orality than one of literacy:

> Patterns of thought and the functioning of individual and communal memory are different in oral cultures. For us the most important aspect of this is that in a truly oral culture thought has to be much more concrete and presentation has to be shaped by devices like contrast, repetition, and rhythm, because words once spoken are past.[67]

Since we assume that Paul's letters were substitutes for his presence with the addressees, and that they were not read by the addresses but heard, it is most likely that Paul in composing his letters was "speaking" for an audience rather than "writing" for a readership. To call Paul's letters "preaching" means that he tried to bring the gospel to speech in each new situation. Dabourne writes: "Preaching to believers is characteristically concerned with the way the gospel addresses particular believers in their particular situation, with articulating its claim on their obedience."[68] She draws attention to a further aspect of preaching: this presupposes a committed audience involved in some sort of positive relationship with the preacher.[69]

When we thus find theological thoughts in Paul's letters, we have to see them as contextual theology that emerged in relation to his congregations, in concrete situations out of concrete questions of everyday life. Throughout his letters we find pragmatic theology rather than theoretical and systematic theology. It is therefore no surprise to find traces of rhetorical patterns in his letters rather than of philosophical treatises; after all, he is "speaking" to his addressees. We turn to strands of research that analyze the rhetorical aspects of Paul's letters.

Rhetorical Perspectives

The strand of research generally described as rhetorical criticism, or rhetorical interpretation of Scripture, also emphasizes the insight that Paul did not write chapters of systematic theology or philosophical or theological

---

66. Ibid., 81.
67. Ibid., 82. On oral culture, see also Carolyn Osiek, "The Oral World of Early Christianity in Rome: The Case of Hermas," in *Judaism and Christianity in First-Century Rome* (ed. Karl P. Donfried and Peter Richardson; Grand Rapids: Eerdmans, 1998), 151–72.
68. Dabourne, *Purpose and Cause*, 92.
69. Ibid., 96.

treatises.[70] Scholars using this approach assume that—since Paul addressed specific communities and specific situations, and despite the fact they are perceived as conversations in context—they cannot have been merely ad hoc documents but must have pursued specific aims the author wanted to achieve. Acknowledging the contextual and specific purposes of the Pauline Letters, they argue that Paul employed a specific strategy in writing each letter, and that his letters are primarily argumentative.[71] Neil Elliott sees striking resemblances between Beker's "coherence-contingency scheme" and rhetorical approaches since both stress that Paul's letters are discourses "determined by persuasive purpose within a constraining situation."[72]

In his article "Paul's Rhetoric of Argumentation in Romans" (1976), Wilhelm Wuellner initiated the discussion about rhetoric and argumentation in Paul's letters. He proposed:

> In the rediscovery of the nature and purpose of argumentation as a basically rhetorical process, we will find a more satisfactory way of accounting not only for the dialectical and logical dimensions, and for the literary dimensions in Paul's discourses, but also for the situational and social dimensions presupposed in Paul's letters.[73]

In recent years rhetorical criticism has exploded into view as a method of interpreting biblical texts. A vivid scholarly debate has evolved with regard to rhetorical interpretations of the Pauline Letters because it has not always been clear what the terms "rhetoric" and "rhetorical criticism" actually implied when used in differing approaches. We cannot give a detailed overview of this debate.[74] Here it is sufficient to notice the two basically differing positions of

---

70. Stanley E. Porter and Dennis L. Stamps, eds., *The Rhetorical Interpretation of Scripture: Essays from the 1996 Malibu Conference* (Sheffield: Sheffield Academic Press, 1999).

71. See Campbell's chapter "Paul's Strategy in Writing Romans," in *Paul's Gospel*, 136: "The significance of the rhetoric of the letter must now be allowed to influence contemporary discussion of its purpose and content."

72. Neil Elliott, *The Rhetoric of Romans: Argumentative Constraint and Strategy and Paul's Dialogue with Judaism* (Sheffield: Sheffield Academic Press, 1990), 18.

73. Wilhelm Wuellner, "Paul's Rhetoric of Argumentation in Romans: An Alternative to the Donfried-Karris Debate over Romans," *Catholic Biblical Quarterly* 38 (1976): 330–51; reprinted in *The Romans Debate* (ed. Karl P. Donfried; rev., expanded ed.; Peabody, Mass.: Hendrickson, 1991), 128–46. Wuellner himself was influenced by the Old Testament scholar James Muilenburg, whose address to the Society of Biblical Literature in 1968 had set a starting point for "rhetorical criticism." In his address Muilenburg critized form criticism for various reasons and proposed a new approach: "What I am interested in, above all, is in understanding the nature of Hebrew literary composition, in exhibiting the structural patterns that are employed for the fashioning of a literary unit, whether in poetry or in prose, and in discerning the many and various devices by which the predications are formulated and ordered into a unified whole. Such an enterprise I should describe as rhetoric and the methodology as rhetorical criticism." James Muilenburg, "Form Criticism and Beyond," *Journal of Biblical Literature* 88 (1969): 8, 1–18.

74. For an overview of the history of research of rhetorical criticism, see Anderson, *Ancient Rhetorical Theory,* 17–33. Also, for instance, see Dennis Stamps, "The Theological Rhetoric of the

this debate, labeled by Dennis L. Stamps in an article as "Argumentation versus Rhetoric."[75]

The "rhetorical" strand of research primarily applies the categories of Graeco-Roman rhetorical theory, as described in the respective ancient handbooks, to the Pauline texts. In labeling the different parts of a Pauline letter according to categories of Graeco-Roman rhetoric, scholars assume that it is possible to reconstruct Paul's intentions in historically accurate ways. Margaret Mitchell applies these ancient rhetorical methods thoroughly in her study on *Paul and the Rhetoric of Reconciliation*.[76] Elsewhere she also depicts a Paul who "drew self-consciously upon Greco-Roman political commonplaces against factionalism, in order to persuade the tiny church community."[77] She contends that, in analyzing the Pauline Letters according to the standards prescribed in Graeco-Roman oratorical handbooks, we can reconstruct Paul's intentions historically in the most accurate way.[78] George Kennedy set the agenda for this approach in 1984 in his *New Testament Interpretation through Rhetorical Criticism*.[79] He states: "The ultimate goal of rhetorical analysis, briefly put, is the discovery of the author's intent and of how that is transmitted through a text to an audience."[80] This claim is challenged from different and divergent perspectives from within and without rhetorical criticism.[81]

Situating himself within rhetorical criticism, W. Wuellner has used the term "rhetoric" in a broader sense: he defines "argumentation" as the use of discourse "to influence the intensity of an audience's adherence to certain theses."[82] Argumentation is any means of persuasion applied to persuade or convince somebody.[83] In this definition one may perceive rhetoric and argumentation as being identical.

Pauline Epistles: Prolegomenon," in *Rhetorical Interpretation* (ed. Porter and Stamps), esp. 252–57. With regard to the question as to whether it is appropriate to apply rhetorical categories at all for the analysis of the Pauline letters, Porter in a chapter "Paul as Epistolographer and Rhetorician?" (ibid., 222–48) emphasizes: "That Paul was a letter writer . . . is beyond dispute" (226). From that he argues: "A major question in Pauline rhetorical study is whether, in fact, Paul the letter writer is also a rhetorician" (227). Porter concludes that, since epistolary theory and rhetorical theory were not equated in Paul's time (not till the fourth and fifth century), "the Paul of the letters certainly is Paul the epistolographer" (234).

75. Porter and Stamps, *Rhetorical Interpretation*, 253.

76. Margaret M. Mitchell, *Paul and the Rhetoric of Reconciliation: An Exegetical Investigation of the Language and Composition of 1 Corinthians* (Tübingen: Mohr, 1991).

77. Margaret M. Mitchell, *The Heavenly Trumpet: John Chrysostom and the Art of Pauline Interpretation* (Tübingen: Mohr, 2000), xv.

78. Mitchell, *Paul and Rhetoric*, esp. 1–19.

79. George A. Kennedy, *New Testament Interpretation through Rhetorical Criticism* (Chapel Hill: University of North Carolina Press, 1984).

80. Ibid., 12.

81. Postmodern approaches such as reader-response criticism have asked whether it might ever be possible to discover the intention of an author through analysis since a text attains meaning only through reading. On this see John G. Lodge, *Romans 9–11: A Reader-Response Analysis* (Atlanta: Scholars Press, 1996).

82. Wuellner, "Paul's Rhetoric," 128.

83. See Stamps, "Theological Rhetoric," 253.

The so-called New Rhetoric proposed in Chaïm Perelman and Luci Olbrechts-Tyteca's work *The New Rhetoric* (ET, 1969)[84] had influenced Wuellner and those following his approach. Rather than being a guide to ancient and modern rhetorical criticism, this is a philosophical *Treatise on Argumentation,* as claimed in the subtitle, building on Aristotle's work on rhetoric. Rhetoric and dialectic, according to Aristotle, are of lesser value for the recognition of truth than the formal logic of philosophy since they deal with probabilities rather than certainties.

Perelman and Olbrechts-Tyteca perceive a loss in the restriction of philosophical discourse to formal rational logic, especially since Descartes. They emphasize the value of informal logic and argumentation and set out to "break with a concept of reason and reasoning due to Descartes."[85] In their philosophical approach, reasoning and argumentation are relative, not absolute; they have to do with probabilities. Argumentation also cannot take place in a vacuum, without any relation to the context and people addressed. Argumentation unfolds and develops in relation to a specific audience. Distinct from classical rhetoric, this approach does not limit itself to oral discourse but is applied to any kind of verbal argumentation, including literary works.[86]

Basing a rhetorical approach to Paul's letters on this New Rhetoric allows for a wide range of critical methods being used in interpreting the argumentative flow of Paul's thoughts; it does not restrict itself to the categories of Graeco-Roman rhetoric. In a different perspective we also must handle the question of whether or not Paul could possibly have had any knowledge of these categories and whether he had been educated according to Graeco-Roman standards of education. Even if, as is most likely, he had no direct training in classical rhetorical theory, it does make sense to analyze his letters according to rhetorical criticism.[87]

From a feminist perspective Elisabeth Schüssler Fiorenza has challenged especially the rather "technical" application of ancient rhetoric in biblical studies, but also rhetorical criticism as such, for its "half-turn."[88] Noting positively that rhetorical criticism has drawn attention to the argumentative

---

84. Chaïm Perelman and Luci Olbrechts-Tyteca, *The New Rhetoric: A Treatise on Argumentation* (trans. John Wilkinson and Purcell Weaver; Notre Dame, Ind.: University of Notre Dame Press, 1969); original, *Traité de l'argumentation: La nouvelle rhétorique* (2 vols.; Paris: Presses universitaires de France, 1958).

85. Perelman and Olbrechts-Tyteca, *The New Rhetoric,* 1.

86. For a detailed description of Perelman and Olbrecht-Tyteca's approach, see Anderson, *Ancient Rhetorical Theory,* 23–27.

87. See, e.g., Stanley Porter's arguments in his article "Paul as Epistolographer and Rhetorician?" in *Rhetorical Interpretation* (ed. Porter and Stamps), 228ff.; also, Anderson, *Ancient Rhetorical Theory,* 280–90.

88. Elisabeth Schüssler Fiorenza, *Rhetoric and Ethic: The Politics of Biblical Studies* (Minneapolis: Fortress, 1999), chap. 4, "Challenging the Rhetorical Half-Turn: Feminist and Rhetorical Biblical Criticism," 83–102.

character of the Pauline Letters, she nevertheless sees this approach as lacking in consciousness of its own hermeneutical presuppositions. Rhetorical critical approaches, according to Schüssler Fiorenza, "have sought to validate its disciplinary practices in and through the logos of positivist or empiricist science that occludes its own rhetoricity."[89]

She especially criticizes purely rhetorical approaches, such as Margaret M. Mitchell's, since these seem not to recognize, at least not as a relevant factor, that ancient rhetorical techniques "have been created and adapted to argue for existing power relations of domination."[90] But also, approaches based on the New Rhetoric remain in the captivity of empiricist-positivist scientism because they do not take into account their own political roots and space. Schüssler Fiorenza states: "A rhetorical-political full-turn would enable biblical scholars to investigate the discursive arguments that perform particular kinds of actions in particular historical situations and at particular political sites."[91]

Schüssler Fiorenza deplores that rhetorical-critical approaches are taking hardly any notice of feminist rhetorical criticism. She thus proposes the use of a hermeneutics of suspicion with regard to language, sociopolitical situation, and theoretical presuppositions in rhetorical criticism, a turn that would lead this approach out of its empiricist-positivist captivity.[92] As a liberation theologian, Schüssler Fiorenza argues for an engagement of feminist critical studies with "critical" rhetorical criticism as a "tool." It could help to challenge and change traditional malestream discourses in biblical interpretation and "reconstitute the religious-ethical rhetoric of the Bible and its liberating imagination of a more just world as a religious biblical politics of meaning."[93]

Schüssler Fiorenza is not the only scholar drawing attention to the need for a critical reflection on the presuppositions of interpretation and analytical frameworks. Yet her emphasis, especially with regard to a critical reflection of rhetorical criticism's own hermeneutical presuppositions, is valuable and we should take account of it in further rhetorical-critical research, especially in its feminist focus.

Nevertheless, rhetorical criticism, especially in its broader definition, has led to important insights. It has drawn attention to the fact that, beyond aspects of style and figures of speech, we can read Paul's letters as argumentative discourses rather than as pure theological or systematic statements. Richard Horsley has stated:

---

89. Ibid., 86.
90. Ibid., 86. This applies also to Mark D. Given, *Paul's True Rhetoric: Ambiguity, Cunning, and Deception in Greece and Rome* (Harrisburg, Pa.: Trinity Press International, 2001).
91. Schüssler Fiorenza, *Rhetoric and Ethic*, 89.
92. Ibid., 93.
93. Ibid., 96.

Since the social circumstances of Paul's mission do not correspond to the traditional occasions of Greek rhetoric and since he has mixed and significantly adapted the basic rhetorical forms in composing his letters, therefore, we should attend less to the formal types of rhetoric than to the rhetorical situation. In Paul's letters, form is subsumed to function in the act of communication and persuasion.[94]

One emphasis in this broader definition of rhetoric as argumentation is that a persuasive discourse or rhetoric always presupposes as its starting point some basic agreement between the audience/addressees and the speaker/author. The intention of argumentation then is to proceed from this basic agreement to a modification of an audience's convictions regarding the theses being presented.[95]

It thus is important to pay attention to how Paul selects and applies certain topics in his letters, how he construes a basic agreement with the audience, and how he then proceeds to transfer this agreement to new insights.[96] If one is addressing people and tries to influence them through arguments, one refers to a specific situation and is in a living relationship with those addressees. Thus, the speaker is interacting in a particular way, at a particular time, in a particular space, with particular people, for a specific purpose—not in a vacuum or in an ideal world.[97] This means that we have to take into account the political situation of Paul's activity as well as his ways of arguing. Hence, it is not sufficient to state Paul's use of rhetoric even in its broader definition. We need to ask how he applied these forms, and what is the content he transmits in and with the forms he uses.

Richard Horsley stresses that, although rhetoric had developed as the political instrument of the Greek and Roman elite to maintain the imperial order,[98] Paul's use cannot be equated with this "imperialistic" purpose of Graeco-Roman rhetoric. In fact, Paul used this instrument in circumstances that differed fundamentally from the usual circumstances of public oratory, where rhetoric was used. He was teaching in small groups and wrote letters to tiny marginalized communities, thereby using his gospel implicitly to oppose the Roman imperial order. We elaborate on the political dimension of Paul's gospel in a later section (below). With regard to rhetorical criticism,

---

94. Richard A. Horsley, "Rhetoric and Empire—and 1 Corinthians," in *Paul and Politics* (ed. Horsley), 83.

95. On this see Elliott, *Rhetoric of Romans,* 15ff.

96. Ibid., 60f.

97. Burton L. Mack, *Rhetoric and the New Testament* (Minneapolis: Fortress, 1990), 17, states that rhetorical criticism "can place a writing at the juncture of social history and read it as a record of some moment of exchange that may have contributed to the social formations we seek better to understand."

98. Horsley, "Rhetoric and Empire," 78.

it is important to note here that in its broader definition as argumentation within a specific political and historical situation, this approach supports perspectives that stress the contextuality and particularity of Paul's letters and his ways of arguing.

The Jewish Texture of Paul's Way of Thinking and Acting

One cannot speak of the contextuality of Paul and his letters without taking seriously into account that he speaks of himself as "Hebrew born of Hebrews; as to the law, a Pharisee" (Phil 3:4–6). He says he is extremely "zealous for the traditions of my ancestors" (Gal 1:14)—using the Greek term παραδόσεις (traditions), the technical term for the oral law (cf. Mark 7:3). Thus, Peter Tomson has emphasized, "Paul is not a Gentile but a Jew and is not going to change that (1 Cor 7:18)."[99]

As a first-century Jew, Paul was deeply rooted in the traditions of his fathers and mothers: his life, thoughts, and acts were interwoven with Jewish tradition, which is based on the Scriptures. This was the symbolic universe he lived in, which he interpreted, and through which he found meaning in life. As Campbell has stated: "It was the peculiarity of Paul's cultural inheritance that contributed largely to his thought world."[100]

As early as 1948, in his classic *Paul and Rabbinic Judaism*,[101] W. D. Davies had stressed the embeddedness of Paul in his Jewish context. He demonstrated that Paul applied methods and interpretive techniques showing striking analogies to rabbinic methods of scriptural interpretation. Davies stressed the Jewish background of Paul without drawing a boundary between rabbinic and apocalyptic influences, as Schweitzer and scholars after Schweitzer had done, and he drew attention even to the Judaism in Paul's theology.[102] More recently, Peter Tomson has come to similar conclusions in his *Paul and the Jewish Law*.[103] Both scholars count it as legitimate to presume that by this time earlier forms of what later became rabbinical methods of interpretation were already in use. These Jewish ways of interpretation, especially midrash, are ways of relating the Scriptures and actual life in a vivid process of interaction

---

99. Tomson, *Paul and Jewish Law*, 280.

100. W. S. Campbell, "The Contribution of Traditions to Paul's Theology," in *Pauline Theology*, 2 (ed. Hay): 253.

101. W. D. Davies, *Paul and Rabbinic Judaism* (London: SPCK, 1948; 50th anniversary ed.; Mifflintown, Pa.: Sigler, 1998).

102. See Davies, "Paul and Judaism since Schweitzer," a paper presented at the Society of Biblical Literature meeting in 1964, published as the introduction to Davies, *Paul and Rabbinic Judaism* (1998), xxiii–xxxi.

103. See also Dan Cohn-Sherbok, *Rabbinic Perspectives on the New Testament* (Lampeter, U.K.: Mellen, 1990).

rather than using systematic or doctrinal ways of thinking. Instead of mere theory, interpretation is an activity that relates Scriptures to life and life to Scriptures. Thus, it may not be logical according to standards of Western ways of thinking, but this does not mean that it is incoherent with regard to the Scriptures[104] and its relevance for the life of people. In this sense interpretation is an ongoing process that never comes to final conclusions but requires dynamics and dialogue.

Rooted in Scriptures

In his thorough study Peter Tomson emphasizes the Jewish background of Paul's thinking and arguing. It is therefore no surprise that practical questions of daily life seem as important as theological reflections in Paul's letters. While we can recognize that Paul was a former Pharisee from elements of his exegesis, Tomson says, this "has not been sufficiently considered in connection with his way of thinking as such."[105] Paul's thinking evolves around two focal points, according to Tomson: a continuous reference to Scripture, and a concern for the actual situation of the addressees. The way he addresses the actual situation of the recipients of his letters reflects a way of thinking that is reminiscent of rabbinic midrash. This style of thinking, fundamentally different from systematic thinking according to Western philosophical logic, might be one reason for the "systematic" misunderstanding of Paul in traditional approaches.[106] In a detailed analysis of 1 Corinthians, Tomson shows the apostle's halakic way of arguing and thus demonstrates that though Paul is an unsystematic thinker, this does not mean that he was incoherent:

> We may infer that it is precisely this variegated structuring of life by means of halakah which enables and indeed requires the seemingly unlimited flexibility of theological thought in Paul. In other words the basic coherence of Paul's thought is not in any particular theological theme but in the organic structure of practical life.[107]

Paul's way of thinking and arguing was halakic. This is more than a statement about the technique of interpretation and writing he used; it implies Torah observance in actual life. Since Paul obviously never conceived of

104. On this generally, see also Peter Ochs, ed., *The Return to Scripture in Judaism and Christianity: Essays in Postcritical Scriptural Interpretation* (New York: Paulist, 1993); and Peter Ochs, *Peirce, Pragmatism, and the Logic of Scripture* (Cambridge: Cambridge University Press, 1998).
105. Tomson, *Paul and Jewish Law*, 58.
106. Ibid., 58.
107. Ibid., 265.

himself as anything other than a Jew, some form of Torah observance for himself as for any other Jew cannot have been a question: it was a given. Torah observance was an issue in relation to Gentiles in Christ: the dawning of the age to come *(ha-olam ha-bah)* with the ingathering of Gentiles required a definition of their relation and status with regard to Israel. This was a new situation. In Paul's interpretation of the Christ event, it required flexibility in thinking and life, but it would never result in Paul asking his fellow Jews to abandon Torah observance. Thus Tomson states: "An observant life according to Paul's views would of course not be rigid and monolithic but presuppose pluriformity and mutual accommodation in view of Gentile behavior (Galatians) and Jewish sensitivities (Romans), always pursuing the unity of the church."[108]

Abandoning the Torah was as much beyond Paul's own perspective as relinquishing the Scriptures; both were the world of thought in which Paul lived and acted. Throughout Paul's letters we find numerous scriptural citations as well as allusions to Scripture. The texture of Paul's thinking and arguing is shaped by the Scriptures.[109] After all, the Scriptures were, and still are, the basis and the texture of the symbolic universe of Judaism generally. Paul was part of this tradition, and he lived in its framework; from within it he tried to understand and interpret his experience on the Damascus road and the role and identity of the incoming Gentiles. Thus, Campbell has stated: "In a certain way [Paul] understands himself in front of Scriptures, standing before them and answering to them and a form of life that they project."[110] And further, he emphasizes: "Because the apostle lived in a vital tradition of scriptural interpretation, he used the imagery of Scripture, especially that relating to God's call of Israel, as a central theme of his letters."[111] Paul not only uses Scriptures as proof texts for his gospel; scriptural insights permeate his thinking and arguing.

Although Paul is not interested in straightforward modern systematic exegesis of Scriptures or in the systematic retelling of a biblical text, we nevertheless can find his scriptural basis in citations and to an even greater extent in scriptural allusions and echoes. In a careful exegetical study, Silvia Keesmaat recently has demonstrated how the Exodus narrative, the story of the major formative event in Israelite history, shaped Paul's arguing, particularly in Rom 8:14–30. She pays careful attention to key passages such as

---

108. Ibid., 264.
109. On this see also, e.g., Christopher D. Stanley, "'Pearls before Swine': Did Paul's Audiences Understand His Biblical Quotations?" *Novum Testamentum* 41 (Apr. 1999): 124–44.
110. Campbell, "Contribution of Traditions," 241.
111. Ibid., 253.

"those led by the Spirit of God" (8:14) as well as to key words such as ἄγειν, δουλεία, κράζειν, πρατήρ. Then she convincingly shows that if we interpret these key texts and terms in the context of first-century Jewish understandings and with the allusions they might evoke, they clearly indicate the pattern of the Exodus narrative in this text. From this perspective we can gain a more coherent understanding of this passage in the letter.

Keesmaat's interpretation also shows that throughout Rom 8–11 Paul is unfolding a continuous argument, with chapter 8 serving as a bridge between earlier chapters and chapters 9–11.[112] "It can be seen, then, that from start to finish this passage uses imagery which reflects the Exodus narrative."[113] Becoming aware of the scriptural basis of Paul's way of thinking and arguing leads us to perceive a coherence in his letters we would not find according to the logic of systematic Western-shaped thinking. Paul then does not suddenly and out of nowhere address the issue of Israel in Rom 9; instead, allusions to "Israel" can be found earlier in the letter, as Keesmaat has shown:

> Paul does not first turn to the attributes and privileges of Israel in 9:1ff. but these had been introduced already earlier in the letter in chapters 7:1f. but especially in 8:14ff. This enables us to conclude that chapters 9–11 are no afterthought and that there is no major caesura after 8:39.[114]

The argument throughout these chapters, then, has its own specific coherence and is far from being arbitrary or incoherent.

This convincing and promising strategy involves searching for scriptural allusions and echoes of tradition in Paul's letters to obtain a more appropriate understanding of his ways of thinking and arguing. Rather than looking for parallels in Hellenistic literature and philosophy, it is more adequate to interpret Paul from within his own Jewish tradition, a "cultural inheritance that provided him with a tradition in which creative freedom was valued and visibly present. His creative freedom was already inculcated in his religious upbringing."[115] This was an ongoing process of vivid interaction between Scripture and everyday life, which in its diversity was normal for Jewish perceptions of life. Paul's theological thinking as well as his acting

---

112. See William S. Campbell, "All God's Beloved in Rome: Jewish Roots and Christian Identity?" (paper presented at the Studiorum Novi Testamenti Societas 55th annual meeting, Tel Aviv, Aug. 2000), in *Celebrating Romans,* ed. Sheila McGinn (Grand Rapids, Mich.: Eerdmans, forthcoming), 5.
113. Sylvia C. Keesmaat, *Paul and His Story: (Re)Interpreting the Exodus Tradition* (Sheffield: Sheffield Academic Press, 1999), 96.
114. Campbell, "All God's Beloved in Rome," 3.
115. Campbell, "Contribution of Traditions," 254.

took place in this context. "It is an inner-scriptural, intertextual type of thinking, a world full of images and metaphors that can be used and re-used in differing settings, . . . not a world of propositional truths, of abstract theorizing, or even precise concepts."[116] This implies that Paul was in vivid interaction with fellow Jews, not only Jews "in Christ" but also Jews who did not share his interpretation of the Christ event, who did not share his faith in Christ. The scriptural reasoning of Paul was part of a continuing and vivid interaction of Jews—Christ-believers or not—on differing interpretations of the Scriptures.[117]

Paul's Mystical Apocalyptic Worldview

If we truly take the background of Paul's activities and of his interpretation of Scripture into account, we need to include Jewish apocalypticism as one important aspect of first-century Judaism. As Alan Segal has shown, Paul's experience on the Damascus road is similar to apocalyptic-mystical experiences described in other Jewish apocalyptic literature of his time: "Paul's experiences were, when seen in this light, not unique so much as characteristic of Jewish mystical thought."[118] Segal emphasizes that mysticism in first-century Judaism was apocalyptic; it was not about the revelation of "meditative truths of the universe but the disturbing news that God was about to bring judgment."[119] The way Paul describes his mystical encounters with the risen Christ and his heavenly journeys is in no way strange for a first-century Jew. Parallels of such heavenly journeys to the divine throne can be found in other apocalyptic traditions of Judaism.

It is beyond doubt that Paul had visions and that he described and interpreted them in the language and the imagery of the symbolic universe of Jewish apocalypticism. As Segal notes: "Paul's conversion experience and his mystical ascension form the basis of his theology. His language shows the marks of a man who has learned the contemporary vocabulary for expressing a theophany and then has received one."[120] Segal has demonstrated that the throne vision of Ezek 1 is one of the basic texts of Jewish mysticism,

---

116. Ibid., 253.

117. Mark D. Nanos, *Mystery of Romans: The Jewish Context of Paul's Letter to the Romans* (Minneapolis: Fortress, 1996), 73, emphasizes that this also applies for Gentile Christ-believing groups: "How would they learn the Scriptures and the way God deals with his people apart from involvement in the Jewish community? . . . We must come to grips with the fact that outside the synagogue environment the early Christians would have had little opportunity to learn the 'Scriptures.'"

118. Alan F. Segal, *Paul the Convert: The Apostolate and Apostasy of Saul the Pharisee* (New Haven: Yale University Press, 1990), 51 n. 64.

119. Ibid., 34.

120. Ibid., 69.

which later became known as *merkabah* (throne-chariot) mysticism in rabbinic terms.[121] Paul is one of the earliest witnesses of experiences of such heavenly encounters and a kind of predecessor of merkabah mysticism.

In his study Segal finds trajectories of mystical imagery throughout the Scriptures. He emphasizes that the mentioning of a "human figure" or an "appearance of the likeness of the glory of the LORD" (Ezek 1:28), or an angel, is not unusual and is further developed in apocalyptic and other Jewish literature of the first century.[122] Even the thought of resurrection and ascension as a reward for the righteous martyr had already become part of the Jewish symbolic universe during the Maccabean wars (Dan 12:2; 2 Macc 7:9, 11, 14, 23).[123] In a vision to see one "like a human figure" on the heavenly throne (Dan 7:9–13), even to identify a vindicated hero with the image of the "glory" of God, one needed not to be a religious innovator. Paul, however, interpreted his visionary experience as a call to the Gentile mission and identified the "glory" he had seen as Christ Jesus; this renders his vision specific.[124]

J. C. Beker in *Paul the Apostle* has also emphasized that apocalyptic is "the indispensable means for [Paul's] interpretation of the Christ event."[125] The symbolic structure of Paul's entire thinking is perceived as apocalyptic. Apocalypticism is thus not just the language in which Paul expresses the meaning of the Christ event;[126] it is also not just a "*Kampfeslehre* (combat teaching)" against Hellenistic-Christian enthusiasm.[127] Instead, it is the heart of Paul's gospel. To understand Paul's apocalyptic thought world, Beker says, we should keep in mind that apocalypticism expresses a deep existential concern and awareness of the profound discrepancy between what is and what should be. Contrary to the realities of this world, the apocalyptists maintain hope. They believe that in the end God will keep his promises to his people Israel and will vindicate himself as he vindicates his people and establishes his universal reign.[128]

This has been the specific texture of Paul's thought not only after his call; even before this event, it had been his perception of the world.[129] Such texture

---

121. Ibid., 39.
122. Ibid., 40–52.
123. Ibid., 56.
124. "Whatever the date of Daniel or the earliest son of man traditions, this angelic figure, the figure that the Bible sometimes calls the *Kavod* or the principal angel of God, is pre-Christian and is a factor in Paul's description of Christ." Ibid., 51.
125. Beker, *Paul the Apostle*, 19.
126. This is in opposition to Bultmann's program of demythologizing.
127. As Käsemann had seen it; nevertheless he recognizes the central role of apocalypticism as the "mother of Christian theology." On the different perceptions of apocalypticism see Beker, *Paul The Apostle*, 17.
128. On this see also Luzia Sutter Rehmann, *Geh frage die Gebärerin: Feministisch-befreiungstheologische Untersuchungen zum Gebärmotiv in der Apokalyptik* (Gütersloh: Chr. Kaiser/Gütersloher Verlagshaus, 1995), 17.
129. Beker, *Paul the Apostle,* 144: "Paul's apocalyptic conviction was not initiated by his conversion to Christ but formed the background of his Pharisaic world view."

provided the material or the symbolic language by which Paul interpreted his call as an apostle to the Gentiles. Beker emphasizes that Paul does not use the language of conversion but the language of a prophetic call when he mentions his experience on the Damascus road. Paul's own interpretation of this experience "concentrates on its function and absorption into God's plan for this world rather than on a mere retelling of the experience itself."[130] Thus, Paul relates this experience to the symbolic world in which he lives and thinks—the language of apocalyptic Judaism—and interprets it accordingly.

Apocalypticism generally shapes Paul's hermeneutic and his interpretation of the Christ event as the turning point in history, announcing the end of time and the coming triumph of God. For Paul, therefore, apocalyptic is not peripheral, and we cannot regard it as an incidental linguistic husk from which some core can be abstracted; it is the "fundamental carrier"[131] of Paul's thought: content and medium are inseparable. Beker stresses the theocentric focus of Paul's apocalyptic interpretation of the Christ event. Although Paul perceives the Christ event as the turning point in time, we must not confuse that with an ontological meaning of the Christ event as the center of salvation history. If "the final triumph of God at the end of history becomes so identified with the triumph of God in the Christ event that the theocentric apocalyptic focus of Paul is absorbed into the Christocentric triumph of Christ,"[132] this causes severe misinterpretations of Paul's view of the Christ event. It deprives Paul's gospel of its future dimension by claiming that the future of God is eternally present in the here and now, and it spiritualizes the promises to Israel. Moreover, this misinterpretation runs the risk of producing an ecclesiology that identifies the church with the kingdom of God and lets the church either separate itself from the world or compete with the world for imperial power.[133]

In different ways both Segal and Beker draw attention to the specifically apocalyptic texture of Paul's thinking in his interpretation of his own call and of the Christ event. Nevertheless, they both emphasize the differences between Jewish apocalypticism and Paul's thought pattern. But even if Paul's interpretation of the Christ event is unique, I nevertheless argue that it was a genuinely Jewish apocalyptic interpretation, one that was possible within the boundaries of first-century Judaism. Segal has clarified his stress on the differences between Paul and contemporary Judaism as differences within the boundaries of the same religion:

---

130. Ibid., 10.
131. Ibid., 181.
132. Ibid., 356.
133. Ibid., 355–56.

It seems clear to me that Paul never doubted that he remained Jewish and part of the Jewish community. Nor did he ever doubt that his new community was part of God's plan. The problem was that the wider Jewish community did not agree with him, just as they did not entirely agree with each other.[134]

As recent studies by Judith Lieu and Daniel Boyarin have shown, those boundaries were much less "iron walls" than perceived until recently.[135] Moreover, Beker's stress especially on two aspects of Paul's gospel show the Jewishness of the apostle's interpretation: the theocentricity of Paul's interpretation of the Christ event and the priority of Israel form the condition sine qua non of the truth of the gospel.[136]

"To the Jew First and Also to the Greek"

Beker's statement indicates that giving credit to Paul's use of Jewish interpretation techniques, his dialectical dialogical way of arguing, his use of apocalyptic language, his embeddedness in the Scriptures—all can lead also to the recognition that his "faith in Christ" need not necessarily have alienated him from first-century Judaism. We need not portray an image of a Paul who deliberately set up his gospel in order to breach with Judaism. As shown above, scholars of the New Perspective seem to hesitate to come to such a conclusion, to follow the consequences of the perspective they themselves have helped to open up.[137]

Even with regard to such a "theological" term as "justification," Tomson emphasizes that although justification theology and halakah are on two different levels and exist independently from each other, they are not mutually exclusive. The stress on "justification by faith" does not necessarily exclude the observance of commandments.[138] In the explicitly halakic sections of

---

134. Alan F. Segal, "Response: Some Aspects of Conversion and Identity Formation in the Christian Community of Paul's Time," in *Paul and Politics* (ed. Horsley), 184–90, esp. 189.

135. Judith M Lieu, "'Impregnable Ramparts and Walls of Iron': Boundary and Identity in Early 'Judaism' and 'Christianity,'" *New Testament Studies* 48.3 (July 2002): 297–313; and Daniel Boyarin, *Dying for God: Martyrdom and the Making of Christianity and Judaism* (Stanford: Stanford University Press, 1999); cf. n. 43 in chap. 2, 17.

136. Beker states: "The gospel cannot have any authentic validity or legitimation apart from the people of Israel because the theological issue of God's faithfulness (Rom 3:3) and righteousness determines the truth of the gospel." J. Christaan Beker, "The Faithfulness of God and the Priority of Israel in Paul's Letter to the Romans," in *The Romans Debate* (ed. Karl P. Donfried; rev., expanded ed.; Peabody, Mass.: Hendrickson, 1991), 330, 327–32.

137. See W. S. Campbell's critique of Dunn in "The Interpretation of Paul: Beyond the New Perspective," 15 (paper presented at the British New Testament Society, Manchester, U.K., 2001): "I would like therefore to take Dunn's critique of Sanders and apply it also to Dunn himself: 'The most surprising feature of Sanders' (and Dunn's) writing is that he has failed to take the opportunity his own mould-breaking work offered.'"

138. Tomson, *Paul and Jewish Law*, 66–68, refers to examples in other ancient Jewish literature where the emphasis on faith does not preclude observance of the commandments.

Paul's letters, there is no reference to justification theology; yet in Gal 5:3, for example, he supports justification theology by reference to a halakah. Moreover, Tomson sees justification theology itself as having the character of a midrash and thus as Jewish.[139]

Dunn also demonstrates that even this most Pauline theological term "justification by faith" is deeply rooted in Hebrew-Jewish thinking. He stresses that the background of the Greek term is Hebrew. This implies the Hebrew/Jewish understanding of "righteousness (δικαιοσύνη)," which expresses a relational concept rather than a legal one. The term encompasses the obligations of someone who is part of a relationship. Scholars have not yet fully thought through the consequences of this understanding for the theological explication of "justification by faith." God's righteousness is his faithfulness to his chosen people. God is righteous: he is faithful in a relationship he once entered, and faithful despite the unfaithfulness of his people.[140]

Throughout his writings Campbell has argued that God is faithful toward his people and that his promises to Israel are irrevocable. In this emphasis the Scandinavian school and particularly Johannes Munck have influenced him; against widespread general assumptions, Munck had argued that Paul's letters, and particularly Romans, had to be read in the context of the apostle's mission and work.[141] This reevaluation of Paul's letters as "a missionary's contribution to a discussion"[142] paid special attention to Romans 9–11, which traditional approaches neglected as irrelevant for the theology of the letter as a whole. Bultmann's existentialist approach, with its focus on the individual, left no room for the theme of the people of God or the possibility of relation between different groups within the Christ-believing communities.[143] Munck's ability to read ancient texts with fresh eyes enabled him to see Paul as apostle to the Gentiles, called to a special mission in the context of salvation history. In this context insight also came from Krister Stendahl's essay "Paul and the Introspective Conscience of the West,"[144] as well as his teaching that Paul was concerned primarily with the relationship and the future of the two peoples Jews and Gentiles. This emphasis on the corporate and

---

139. Ibid., 68.

140. Dunn, *Theology of Paul*, 340–44.

141. See Campbell, *Paul's Gospel*, 2–3.

142. Johannes Munck, *Paul and the Salvation of Mankind* (trans. Frank Clarke; London: SCM, 1959), 200.

143. Nils A. Dahl, in his review of *Theology of the New Testament*, by Rudolf Bultmann, *Theologische Rundschau* 22 (1954): 21–40, noted that Bultmann in fact dehistoricized Paul in his individualistic approach. Reginald H. Fuller, *The New Testament in Current Study: Some Trends in the Years 1941–1962* (London: SCM, 1963), 72, also critiqued the limitations of Bultmann's existentialist approach, which became evident in relation to Romans 9–11.

144. Krister Stendahl, "Paul and the Introspective Conscience of the West," in his *Paul among Jews and Gentiles and Other Essays* (Philadelphia: Fortress, 1976), 78–96. Not till 1996 was it published in German: "Der Apostel Paulus und das 'introspektive' Gewissen des Westens," *Kirche und Israel: Neukirchener theologische Zeitschrift* 11 (1996): 19–33.

contextual aspect of Paul's statements in his letters also led to further research on the relationship of "Israel and the nations" as two distinct entities.

Paul wrestles with the fact that only some of his Jewish brothers and sisters follow his own perception of the Christ event as the dawning of the age to come. However critical he might be of his own people, he would never perceive Israel as rejected by God (Rom 11:1).[145] Not only would Paul demolish any assertion that God has cast off his people; he also stresses, especially in Romans, that there is nothing the Gentiles could ever boast of over against the Jews, since the Jews are the root supporting the ingrafted Gentile branches (Rom 11:18). Such a possible boasting of Gentiles could have emerged from a misunderstanding of Paul's mission to the Gentiles, as Campbell has recently argued in his article "Divergent Images of Paul and His Mission."[146] He notes: "Paul may have been understood by the Roman Gentile Christians as being pro-Gentile and, conversely, as being indifferent to Jews. Paul's inclusion in the letter of phrases such as 'to the Jew first' may indicate a correction of their viewpoint in this area."[147] This misunderstanding of Paul's mission apparently led to a denigration of Israel and an intolerance toward a Jewish lifestyle. His strong arguments for "the Jew first" (Rom 1:16) might indicate that Paul was facing an early supersessionism in Gentile Christ-believing groups.[148]

Paul had to oppose and correct such a misunderstanding not only out of concern for the Jews and as an act of respect to those who are and remain different. It was also crucial for understanding the "faith in Christ" as such because this faith has no identity apart from its roots in Judaism and is by no means self-supporting.[149] To recognize the priority of Israel and the faithfulness of God to his promises to Israel is absolutely crucial for the truth of the gospel. If God were not faithful to his earlier promises to Israel, how could the Gentiles have any indication that he would be faithful and remain faithful to them? Thus, Beker concludes: "[The] gospel cannot have any authentic validity or legitimation apart from the people Israel. . . . The priority of Israel is the necessary consequence of God's character as being faithful to himself and as manifesting this faithfulness in his saving actions."[150]

---

145. See Campbell, *Paul's Gospel*, 44; Nanos, *Mystery of Romans*, 21: "Even more important, he does not believe that God has rejected Israel, though some have been 'hardened.' On the contrary, in spite of how circumstances may presently appear, through Paul's apostolic ministry God is demonstrating the irrevocable priority of Israel in the faithful fulfillment of his promises to the fathers (1:1–7, 11–17; 11:11–15, 25–29; 15:7–9)."

146. Campbell, "Divergent Images," 189–211.

147. Ibid., 191.

148. See also Nanos, *Mystery of Romans*, 16.

149. Campbell, *Paul's Gospel*, 151; see also Peter J. Tomson, *"If This Be from Heaven . . .": Jesus and the New Testament Authors in Their Relationship to Judaism* (Sheffield: Sheffield Academic Press, 2001), 208–13.

150. Beker, "Faithfulness of God," 327–32.

This does not imply that the Gentiles have to adopt a Jewish lifestyle in Christ, a proposal Paul is strongly opposing in his Letter to the Galatians. What Paul stresses in his emphasis on the priority of Israel is the positive relation of the Christ-believing Gentiles to their Jewish roots as well as the necessity of these two peoples being distinct in Christ. Paul thus argues against any conception of the Christ-believers, or the church as the "true Israel."[151] This title is exclusively reserved for "the historic people of God to whom the promises were given," as Campbell stresses.[152] But the Jews are also not to become Gentiles, not to abandon their Jewish identity in Christ. Paul says: "Let each of you lead the life that the Lord has assigned" (1 Cor 7:17ff.). There are two possibilities: either one is called as a Jew or one is called as a non-Jew. According to Paul, one should not attempt in any way to change this. As Tomson explains: "Paul's 'gospel for non-Jews' assumed that Jews and non-Jews respect each other's way of life and remain faithful to their own life-style."[153] "Oneness in Christ" does not imply that all become the same but that they are a unity in diversity.

To tolerate and respect each other as different is not just a virtue "in Christ"; it also is imperative for God's sake. If Jews had to become non-Jews or non-Jews had to become Jews "in Christ," God would not be God for all, God of Jews and Gentiles, but only God for the one or the other. This would imply that one had to universalize one identity in Christ, which would be universalizing one particular identity, reducing God to be God only if all were the same. Yet God gave the promise of salvation through Abraham to Israel *and* the nations. If the age to come is indeed dawning with the coming of Christ, as Paul and his fellow believers are convinced, then the Gentiles have to come in as Gentiles. According to the prophets, this influx of Gentiles is a sign of the dawning age to come. Hence, the Jews must remain faithful to their heritage, particularly when the age to come is dawning.[154]

The emphasis on the priority of Israel and of the need to maintain differences between people who are different is rooted in the theocentricity of Paul's gospel, according to Beker.[155] Paul's emphasis on the Christ event as the

---

151. I think Israel in Gal 6:16 is referring to historic Israel and by no means to the church. See Krister Stendahl, *Final Account: Paul's Letter to the Romans* (Minneapolis: Fortress, 1995), 5.

152. Campbell, *Paul's Gospel,* 48.

153. Tomson, *"If This Be from Heaven,"* 182.

154. Nanos, *Mystery of Romans,* 18.

155. Beker, *Paul the Apostle,* 356. Dahl similarly noted: "For more than a generation the majority of New Testament scholars have not only eliminated direct references to God from their works, but also neglected detailed and comprehensive investigation of statements about God. Whereas a number of major works and monographs deal with Christology, . . . it is hard to find any comprehensive or penetrating study of the theme 'God in the New Testament' . . . O. Cullmann has stated that 'early Christian theology is in reality almost exclusively Christology.' It is not clear whether or not it has ever occurred to him that this statement might also be turned the other way round." Nils A. Dahl, "The Neglected Factor in New Testament Theology," *Reflection* 73.1 (1975): 5–8. See also Halvor Moxnes, *Theology in Conflict: Studies in Paul's Understanding of God in Romans* (Leiden: Brill, 1980).

beginning, inauguration, or dawning of the world to come has as its ultimate focal point not Christ, but God and his coming reign. Paul understands the Christ event as the fulfillment of God's promises, not in the sense of the end point of a process, but as the confirmation of the faithfulness of God to his people, the nations, and the whole of creation. In fact, it is probably more appropriate to speak of *confirmation* of the divine promises in Paul's gospel rather than of their fulfillment.

We must see Paul's insistence on the incoming of the Gentiles as Gentiles in this light. It has nothing to do with a devaluation of Judaism or the Torah, but with the demonstration of God's faithfulness.[156] What others perceive as typical for Paul's Hellenism and rupture with Judaism—his concern for the Gentiles or his so-called universalism—Nanos sees as genuinely Jewish: "The purpose of Israel's special call was in the service of universal salvation, not triumphant exclusivism."[157]

The insistence on the remaining distinctiveness and diversity of people who are different also in Christ—Jews remain Jews and Gentiles remain Gentiles—is crucial not only for anthropological reasons but also for theological reasons. If God is the one God of Israel and of all nations and of the whole of creation, his oneness necessarily implies diversity. Since in the beginning God created diversity and "saw that it was good" (Gen 1), he will redeem Israel and the nations and all of creation in their distinctiveness. To do otherwise would annul what he himself in the beginning had perceived as good: it would imply annulling creation. In the perspective of the Scriptures (which at the time of Paul were nothing else than Jewish Scriptures), redemption is always the restoration of creation. If God is to be faithful toward himself, he cannot obliterate the diversity he once created and make a uniformity of sameness. Thus, from a Jewish perspective, the oneness of God implies the diversity of people and creation.[158]

This is the background from which we have to read and try to understand Paul. He is focusing on the oneness of God under the apocalyptic preview of the dawning of the age to come. This oneness has to be reflected in the diversity of people and all of creation. Otherwise, the one God of Israel is not the

---

156. Mark Nanos has argued: "Gentiles were forbidden to become Jews not because becoming Jewish and keeping Torah are no longer valid acts of faith; they are forbidden because to do so would be to deny the universalistic Oneness of God." Nanos sees Paul's ministry to the Gentiles as closely related to the assertion of the oneness of God as expressed in the Shema. It is thus a thoroughly Jewish concern, consistent with Paul's commitment to his own people and to the Torah. Nanos views Paul as a "good Jew" who believes in Jesus as Israel's Christ, "who did not break with the essential truths of the Judaism(s) of his day, [and] who was committed to the restoration of his people as his first and foremost responsibility in the tradition of Israel's Deuteronomic prophets." Ibid., 9.

157. Ibid., 9.

158. Jonathan Sacks, "The Other—Jews and Christians," *The Other as Mystery and Challenge* (Martin Buber House) 25 (spring 1998): 31–41.

one God of the whole world. Paul's insistence on being "one in Christ " (Gal 3:28) is never to be confused with all becoming "the same in Christ."

Such confusion can occur only when people read Paul through lenses shaped by Greek philosophical traditions, with their perception of oneness as sameness, and of God as an ultimate high figure who is monistic rather than monotheistic. If we presuppose that this is the pattern of thought in and with which Paul argues, then we end up with a Paul who "is motivated by a Hellenistic desire for the One."[159] This Hellenistic ideal obliterates difference and diversity in its zeal to attain one and same universal human essence. But if we presuppose Paul being entirely embedded in Judaism and in Jewish ways of thinking and arguing, then oneness is something different from, but not in contrast to, diversity.

The oneness of God's people, the oneness in faith, then implies the difference of people because their oneness is a reflection of the oneness of God, who is the one God for all only as they are different. For Paul, then, faith in Christ Jesus in no way compromises Jewish monotheism and thus also does not oppose Torah. Monotheism and Torah are as inseparable for Paul as for any Jew.[160]

The Political Dimension of Paul's Message

Recognizing the Jewishness of Paul's gospel and his ways of thinking also has political implications, which we need to consider. Paul was not embedded in an abstract and ahistorical form of Judaism but in first-century Judaism under the political dominance of the Roman Empire. In stressing the contextuality of Paul's thinking, we cannot ignore this aspect. Scholars such as Richard Horsley, Neil Elliott, and Dieter Georgi contend that the political situation was a far more significant aspect of Paul's gospel than scholars have until recently acknowledged.[161]

Over against traditional interpretations of Paul and their tendency to depict nascent Christianity as a universal, purely spiritual religion, these scholars claim that it started as an anti-imperial movement.[162] They draw attention to Paul's use of specific terms such as gospel, cross, and salvation as well as to his use of rhetoric. On these matters, it seems obvious that Paul used or alluded to "imperial" language, but he used it "upside down," to present his gospel in opposition and competition to the Roman imperial

---

159. Boyarin, *Radical Jew,* 7.
160. Nanos, *Mystery of Romans,* 176.
161. Elliott, "Paul and the Politics of the Empire," 39.
162. On this see Richard A. Horsley, ed., *Paul and Empire: Religion and Power in Roman Imperial Society* (Harrisburg, Pa.: Trinity Press International, 1997), 1.

order, which he regarded as "the present form of this world," which "is pass-
ing away" (1 Cor 7:31). Assuming political overtones in Paul's gospel, we
need to ask whether such were also present in Paul's persecuting activity
before his call. The Jewish communities in the Diaspora often depended on
the support of local authorities for protection. The proclamation of a savior
other than Caesar, even more the proclamation of a savior crucified by the
Roman authorities meant a real threat for the whole Jewish community.
Paula Fredriksen suggests: "News of an impending Messianic kingdom, originating from Palestine, might trickle out via the *ekklēsia's* Gentiles to the
larger urban population. . . . The open dissemination of a Messianic message,
in other words, put the entire Jewish community at risk."[163]

In *Liberating Paul*, Neil Elliott has argued that a political perception of
Paul's pre-call activities implies a political perception of his call/conversion as
well. If we take seriously the imperial context of first-century Judaism, apocalyptic visionary experiences would most likely have served "to provide self-
authorizing scripts for differing policies of accommodation or resistance to
Rome."[164] From this, Elliott concludes that Paul as an apocalyptic-minded
Pharisee would easily have recognized the political implications of a revelation/
apokalypsis of a crucified Jew who "now stood vindicated at the right hand of
God in heaven" (cf. Acts 7:55).[165]

Paul's gospel thus opposes not Judaism or the Law, in whichever form,[166]
but rather the "rulers of this age," the Roman Empire.[167] Dieter Georgi has
analyzed key terms used by Paul in relation to their significance in Roman
imperial language and has gained some insights that are worth noting.
Especially terms such as εὐαγγέλιον, πίστις, δικαιοσύνη and εἰρήνη must
have evoked allusions to Roman imperial ideology, as Georgi contends. They
were omnipresent throughout the empire, even on the coins people carried
around with them.[168] Thus, εὐαγγέλιον alluded to the "gospel," the "good
news of victory" of the imperial savior; πίστις meant the "loyalty" of the
emperor, to which his subjects had to reciprocate by delivering "loyalty";
δικαιοσύνη was the "justice" imposed by the emperor; and εἰρήνη was the

---

163. Paula Fredriksen, "Judaism, the Circumcision of Gentiles, and Apocalyptic Hope: Another Look
at Galatians 1 and 2," *Journal of Theological Studies* 42.2 (1991): 556, 532–64.

164. Elliott, "Paul and the Politics of the Empire," 23.

165. Neil Elliott, *Liberating Paul: The Justice of God and the Politics of the Apostle* (Sheffield: Sheffield
Academic Press, 1995), 23.

166. Since the New Perspective still perceives Paul's gospel as opposing some form of Judaism (ethno-
centric, particularistic), it remains within the traditional paradigm of Pauline interpretation, which used
Judaism as the counterimage to the ideal universalistic religion Paul had actually founded. See Horsley,
Paul and Empire, 5; and Elliott, "Paul and the Politics of the Empire," 19, 22.

167. Horsley, *Paul and Empire*, 6–7.

168. See Dieter Georgi, "God Turned Upside Down," in *Paul and Empire* (ed. Horsley), 148–57;
idem, *Theocracy in Paul's Praxis and Theology* (trans. David E. Green; Minneapolis: Fortress, 1991).

"peace" secured by the Roman order, imposed by Roman military conquest. The παρουσία was the arrival of the king or military leader at the city gates. And the proclamation of a κύριος as lord of an οἰκουμένη of different nations was without doubt alluding to Roman political ideology.[169] In using language that could so easily be associated with imperial political ideology with its religious overtones, Paul actually presented his gospel as in competition with the gospel of Caesar.[170] Horsley thus has stated: "In his use of key terms and symbols from political public oratory and imperial ideology, Paul was thus proclaiming an alternative gospel of an alternative emperor."[171]

Language is one indication of the anti-imperial tendency of Paul's gospel. As Neil Elliott declares, the message of the cross as such is anti-imperial. In Paul's interpretation, Jesus' death at the hands of the Romans marked

> the beginning of God's final "war of liberation" against all the Powers that hold creation in thrall through the instruments of earthly oppression. The death of Jesus unmasks the rulers of this age as intractably opposed to the wisdom of God.[172]

Nevertheless, the death and resurrection of Jesus are not yet themselves the complete overcoming of these evil rulers, but only the beginning of the process through which they would be dethroned. To interpret the Christ event, Paul uses apocalyptic language and symbolism with political implications. He sees current historical struggles as related to, and caught up in, God's struggle against the evil powers. This interpretation of historical political struggles differs from merely denying or avoiding the political powers.[173] Paul sees the existential powers of sin and death as revealing themselves and being present in the "rulers of this age" (1 Cor 2:8) and the system of power, violence, and death they uphold.[174]

This system was omnipresent throughout the Roman Empire, and hardly anyone could escape its influence. Paul is opposing this contemptible establishment strongly and without compromise. In this perspective, the beginning of the Letter to the Romans is a contrast between the justice of God and the injustice of human society. (The contrast between faith and works is not made until Rom 3:20.) Paul is not so much concerned with the conscience of individuals as with the political and communal aspects of the structures of

---

169. Elliott, "Paul and the Politics of the Empire," 25.
170. Georgi, "God Turned Upside Down," 140.
171. Horsley, "Rhetoric and Empire," 92.
172. Neil Elliott, "The Anti-Imperial Message of the Cross," in *Paul and Empire* (ed. Horsley), 180.
173. See Horsley, *Paul and Empire,* 143.
174. See 1 Cor 15:24–26.

sin and their devastating implications.[175] These structures or powers of sin and death still exist but the *"the resurrection of Christ the crucified . . . reveals the imminent defeat of the Powers, pointing forward to the final triumph of God."*[176]

The political system of the Roman Empire was not political in a modern sense, but interwoven with religious overtones, as for instance in the cult of the emperor. Hence, the use of words that had a specific meaning in the imperial system and the proclamation that "the rulers of this age are doomed to perish" (1 Cor 2:6), could not be heard as purely religious statements. Since there was nothing purely political, there was nothing purely religious. The spheres could not be separated.

In Romans, Paul contrasts two forms of worship: the shameful idolatry of the Roman world (1:18–32), which asks for the surrender of the human body to the power of sin and injustice; and the "reasonable worship" (12:1, my trans.), which calls for those in Christ to serve God's justice with their bodies (6:19). All this has aspects not merely spiritual.[177] Proclaiming a savior other than the emperor and a peace other than the Pax Romana was a political statement, if not explicitly then certainly implicitly. Under the circumstances of the first century, as formulated from the "Jewish corner," proclaiming Jesus Christ as the Savior must have been heard as a political provocation even if Paul had not intended it so. Proclaiming not just another savior but one crucified by the Romans, was not just provocative, over against the dominant values of the elite; it also was suicidal, as Horsley has said:

> To speak of a gospel of the crucified was also "foolish" in the sense of politically suicidal, because it would bring the Romans down on one's head—to maintain the peace with military violence when persuasion and intimidation did not suffice.[178]

---

175. Luise Schottroff has elaborated on this in her excellent analysis of what she calls "strukturelle Sünde (structural sin)," in *Schuld und Macht: Studien zu einer feministischen Befreiungstheologie* (ed. Christine Schaumberger and Luise Schottroff; Munich: Chr. Kaiser, 1988), 32: "In order to understand the Pauline theology of sin, it is useful to consider the perceptions that describe the relation between sin and Adam, that is, between sin and human beings. These perceptions originate in the realm of domination: in the political domination of the Romans in the Roman Empire, in the domination of masters over slaves, and in the domination of the demons over human beings who are possessed by them." My translation of the German: "Um die paulinische Sündentheologie nachzuvollziehen, ist es sinnvoll, die Vorstellungen zusammenzustellen, die die Beziehungen zwischen Sünde und Adam bzw. den Menschen beschreiben. Durchweg stammen diese Vorstellungen aus dem Bereich von Herrschaftsausübung: der politischen Herrschaft der Römer im römischen Weltreich, der Herrschaft der Herren über Sklaven, und der Herrschaft der Dämonen über die von ihnen besessenen Menschen." See also Luise Schottroff, "Die Schreckensherrschaft der Sünde und die Befreiung durch Christus nach dem Römerbrief des Paulus," *Evangelische Theologie* 39 (1979): 497–510.

176. Elliott, "Anti-Imperial Message," 181.

177. See Elliott, "Paul and the Politics of the Empire," 39.

178. Horsley, "Rhetoric and Empire," 92.

To read Paul's letters in the context of Roman imperial propaganda depicts a Paul at the margins of mainstream imperial society and its hierarchical power structures. He is trying to set up alternative satellite communities as forerunners of another peace and another justice. The peace and justice of the one God of Israel's reign was beginning to dawn.

Schüssler Fiorenza challenges this political approach, even though she is much in favor of it, for not being critical enough over against the imperialistic tendencies within Pauline rhetoric. She sees Elliott's and Horsley's approach still remaining within traditional malestream paradigms. They identify with Paul as the main authority of the early church. This makes them unaware of the imperial rhetoric that Paul still uses, thus reinscribing, according to her, hierarchical power relations within his communities. In her interpretation, Paul tries to suppress any voices differing from his own in order to establish his personal authority in his communities. She states:

> If one focuses on the marginal and powerless, such as slaves and wo/men, one is no longer able to argue that Paul's rhetoric calls into question rather than re-inscribes the social values and dominant relations of Greco-Roman imperialism.[179]

Over against this image she stresses the need to hear Paul as one of many voices within the emerging church. His letters are part of an ongoing debate and show evidence of legitimate discussions within the communities of those "who sought to live God's alternative society."[180]

Schüssler Fiorenza's critique of Elliott and Horsley may not be adequate. I do not see the contradiction she depicts between her request to develop "a reconstructive historical politics of interpretation that valorizes difference, plurivocality, argument, persuasion, and the democratic participation of all those excluded from, or subordinated by, theological discourses"—and Elliott's and Horsley's approach. In their emphasis on the political allusions of Paul's language, they show that he uses this same language in diametrical opposition to the hegemonic and suppressing power of the imperial state. In his upside-down use of elements of imperial language, Paul is seen as implicitly yet radically criticizing the imperial state by questioning its claim of dominion over the world. However, we cannot take this as indicating that Paul did not understand himself as part of an ongoing discourse of an egalitarian movement. Carolyn Osiek states what she often rightly sees in his letters:

---

179. Elisabeth Schüssler Fiorenza, "Paul and the Politics of Interpretation," in *Paul and Politics* (ed. Horsley), 50.
180. Ibid., 51.

Paul draws upon the language of the city-state . . . to imply that all Christians, male and female, have the responsibility of full participation in the commonwealth in which they belong most appropriately. This is the basis for any vision of a discipleship of equals in the Pauline churches. In a world of social inequalities, Christians are to live in the consciousness of their heavenly equal citizenship here and now.[181]

Thus, we must not perceive the use of elements of imperial language as a reintroduction of hierarchical power relations into an absolutely egalitarian movement. We need to take two aspects into account here:

1. It is not surprising that Paul used the language of his time, nor that he used patriarchal language and imagery. As recognized above, it is impossible to escape thought and language patterns known to us.[182] Paul is not exempt from this. He develops his understanding of the gospel within the thought and language patterns known to him, applying those same patterns to serve the emancipatory purpose of the gospel.[183] Also, we need to remember the sociological situation of Paul and his communities. It does make a fundamental difference whether elements of imperial language are used upside down by a tiny marginal minority in the Roman Empire, or by the propaganda machinery of this imperialistic power.

2. The radically different contexts of Paul and of the contemporary interpreter are of particular significance in this issue: the contrast is like the difference between a pre- and post-1789 situation as the French Revolution began. We should not judge Paul's use of language according to post-revolutionary categories of equality and democracy. Moreover, we must not argue as if words have fixed connotations in and of themselves, irrespective of the construction within which they are situated. Otherwise, we are guilty of decontextualizing language.[184]

Conclusion

The different strands of research depicted in this section elaborate, in different ways, on an image of Paul that presupposes insights gained by the New

---

181. Carolyn Osiek, "Philippians," in *A Feminist Commentary* (vol. 2 of *Searching the Scriptures,* ed. E. Schüssler Fiorenza, A. Brock, and S. Matthews), 246.

182. See the discussion (above) on the definition of women's identity from a feminist perspective, in sec. "Contemporary Ways of Thinking," in chap. 3, 92ff.

183. On this aspect, see also Elsa Tamez, "Der Brief an die Gemeinde in Rom: Eine feministische Lektüre," in *Kompendium feministische Bibelauslegung* (ed. Luise Schottroff and Marie-Theres Wacker; Gütersloh: Chr. Kaiser/Gütersloher Verlagshaus, 1998), 557.

184. On the need to analyze words in their semantic networks, see, e.g., James Barr, *The Semantics of Biblical Language* (London: Oxford University Press, 1961); and Jacques Derrida, *Points . . . : Interviews, 1974–1994* (ed. Elisabeth Weber; trans. Peggy Kamuf et al.; Stanford: Stanford University Press, 1995), 373.

Perspective but in certain distinct ways move beyond it. They portray a different image of Paul by taking seriously into account the contexts of Paul's letters, the characteristics of his arguing in them, the Jewish texture of his life and thought, and the political dimension of living in the first-century Roman Empire. The emerging image differs radically in shape, contours, and "background" from traditional ones. It is the portrait of a man who is part of a movement of men and women inspired by the vision of the dawning age to come in the Christ event. They are in vivid interaction and dialogue not against, but with, each other within this movement, which is part of first-century Judaism under the conditions of Roman domination.

This image of Paul is based on different hermeneutical presuppositions and should have an impact also on feminist approaches to the Pauline Letters. Chapter 6 focuses on this question, but first chapter 5 will analyze hermeneutical presuppositions in some feminist interpretations of Romans.

⎇ **5** ⎇

Paul in Feminist Perspectives

In the following section I investigate how different hermeneutical presuppositions, or different images of Paul, make a difference for feminist interpretations of the Pauline Letters. I focus this analysis on Paul's Letter to the Romans.

Here I do not concentrate on texts dealing specifically with women. Others have done so at length; the result is that we receive an image of Paul ranging from misogynist to not being as bad a patriarch as one might at first suppose.[1]

My own presupposition is that Paul, like any other New Testament writer, was a person of his time, living in a culture and using a language patriarchal through and through. We cannot expect him to dissociate himself completely from this context.[2] Nevertheless, in antiquity we can find tendencies toward more equality or more mutual appreciation.[3] In Paul's letters we can find statements that cannot be of relevance for us anymore if we take seriously the feminist liberation impetus for equality and mutuality. On the

---

1. E.g., Elisabeth Schüssler Fiorenza, *In Memory of Her: A Feminist Theological Reconstruction of Christian Origins* (New York: Crossroad, 1983), 160–204, esp. 168ff. Luise Schottroff, "Wie berechtigt ist die feministische Kritik an Paulus? Paulus und die Frauen in den ersten christlichen Gemeinden im Römischen Reich," in *Befreiungserfahrungen: Studien zur Sozialgeschichte des Neuen Testaments* (Munich: Chr. Kaiser, 1990), 229–46; cf. also Else Kähler, *Die Frau in den paulinischen Briefen* (Zurich: Gotthelf, 1960).

2. See also Elsa Tamez, "Der Brief an die Gemeinde in Rom: Eine feministische Lektüre," in *Kompendium feministische Bibelauslegung* (ed. Luise Schottroff and Marie-Theres Wacker; Gütersloh: Chr. Kaiser/Gütersloher Verlagshaus, 1998), 559–60.

3. Kathleen E. Corley, *Private Women, Public Meals: Social Conflict in the Synoptic Tradition* (Peabody, Mass.: Hendrickson, 1993), 78–79.

other hand, we also recognize other issues in his letters that are remarkable, considering the context in which he lived; for example, in Rom 16 Paul mentions many women co-workers, with whom he obviously cooperated, apparently on a basis of equality and mutuality.[4]

I do not particularly want to add to this specific discussion about Paul and women. It is an important issue in feminist interpretations of the Pauline Letters, but in concentrating only on it, feminist theology separates and isolates itself from other central aspects of these writings.[5] This is relevant particularly in dealing with letters such as Romans, where women are hardly mentioned explicitly until chapter 16 (though some recent versions use inclusive language). To engage with texts like this, we need, as Sheila McGinn has put it, "to break out to a new approach, one which requires a deeper engagement with the text, its author, and its history."[6]

Introduction to Feminist Interpretations of Romans

Some feminist interpretations of Romans tend to presuppose that Paul "was motivated by a Hellenistic desire for the One, which among other things produced an ideal of a universal human essence, beyond difference and hierarchy."[7] In their view, "the text of Romans invites a continual interrogation of the problematic of *inclusion* insofar as inclusion is one of the letter's themes, and creating an image of the universal human is a central ideological interest of the letter's author."[8] This Pauline universalism as found in Romans, according to Elizabeth Castelli, is mainly based on a general, overarching dualistic discourse: "The logic of Romans depends on an overarching hermeneutical and philosophical use of dualism."[9] With reference to Gal 3:28, Elisabeth Schüssler Fiorenza has also argued that Paul reintegrates this egalitarian early Christian vision into a dualistic framework.[10]

---

4. On this see Margaret Y. MacDonald, "Reading Real Women through the Undisputed Letters of Paul," in *Women and Christian Origins* (ed. Ross S. Kraemer and Mary Rose D'Angelo; Oxford: Oxford University Press, 1999), 199–220.

5. On the issue of isolation tendencies in feminist theologies, see Deborah F. Sawyer and Diane M. Collier, eds., *Is There a Future for Feminist Theology?* (Sheffield: Sheffield Academic Press, 1999), esp. 198–206, "Feminist Theology—Out of the Ghetto?" by Linda Woodhead.

6. Sheila McGinn, "Feminist Approaches to Romans: Rom 8:18–23 as a Case Study" (paper presented at the SBL conference, Nashville, 2000), 3.

7. Daniel Boyarin, *A Radical Jew: Paul and the Politics of Identity* (Berkeley: University of California Press, 1994), 181.

8. Elizabeth A. Castelli, "Romans," in *A Feminist Commentary* (vol. 2 of *Searching the Scriptures;* ed. Elisabeth Schüssler Fiorenza, A. Brock, and S. Matthews; New York: Crossroad, 1994), 184.

9. Ibid., 285.

10. Elisabeth Schüssler Fiorenza, *Rhetoric and Ethic: The Politics of Biblical Studies* (Minneapolis: Fortress, 1999), 149–73, esp. 169.

In some selected examples I investigate the textual and ideological bases for such and similar contentions by feminist scholars, since they as any interpreters operate within a hermeneutical circle of presuppositions that determine the outcome of their research. By this critical approach toward some feminist interpretations of Paul and his letters, I do not mean to question feminist exegesis as such. It is beyond dispute that it is essential to do theology and exegetical work from a feminist perspective. Nevertheless, after three decades of substantial feminist research, there is also a need for critical self-reflection. We should do this, as Ursula King has declared, "in a spirit of openness and critical reflexivity."[11] She further emphasizes:

> We need to acknowledge the deeply haunting presence of *ambivalence* and *ambiguity,* which runs through all attempts of interpretation and existential transformations. These afflict all human endeavours everywhere with deep resonances of contingency, incompleteness, and ultimate unsatisfactoriness, and feminist theological efforts are no exception to this.[12]

Feminist research also has its presuppositions and is influenced by traditional ways of doing research. Unconscious implications influence feminist approaches as any other. As a theology that seeks for the aspects of hope, justice, and liberation in the Christian tradition, as well as for the open and hidden history of distortion and domination in this tradition, it needs to be aware of its own presuppositions and limitations.

Platonic Dualism in Romans: Elizabeth A. Castelli

In her commentary on Romans in *A Feminist Commentary,* the second volume of *Searching the Scriptures,*[13] Elizabeth A. Castelli shows some awareness of hermeneutical presuppositions in any kind of commentary:

> [A] commentary's claim to represent knowledge (truth) rather than a reading (interpretation) cannot exist unproblematically in an intellectual frame that sets high relief in the primacy of interpretation as a mode of understanding. . . . Feminist interpretation, in short, reads against the grain of the tradition and its revered texts.[14]

---

11. Ursula King, "Feminist Theologies in Contemporary Contexts: A Provisional Assessment," in *Is There a Future for Feminist Theology?* (ed. Deborah F. Sawyer and Diane M. Collier; Sheffield: Sheffield Academic Press, 1999), 101.

12. Ibid., 109.

13. Castelli, "Romans," 272–300.

14. Ibid., 274.

In her view, a feminist commentary "will critically gloss the text by examining the ways in which language, ideology, and imagery underwrite certain relationships while rendering others impossible."[15]

With these statements in mind and the author's goal to give just one possible reading of Romans in her commentary, it is somewhat of a surprise to find her contentions about dualism (as cited above). She does not give any textually based explanation, nor is she referring to the work of any other exegete, for the Platonic dualism which, according to her, shapes the texture of Romans as a whole. We are confronted with the statement that there is an ideology prior to the actual text and its imagery and metaphor, which is underlying Paul's arguing throughout the letter. Castelli claims to have found this ideological basis in the concept of a dualism

> that explains the nature of things through recourse to binary opposition, arranging all ideas, things, and phenomena into pairings of mutually exclusive elements. . . . Finding its classic articulation in the philosophy of Plato, dualism characterized much of the thinking in the ancient Mediterranean and greatly influenced Paul's thought. For feminism, the problem of dualism is not simply the binary opposition itself but also that the opposition created is never a balanced one but rather a hierarchical relation.[16]

One page earlier she stated that the central ideological interest of the letter's author is "in creating an image of the universal human."[17] This later quote thus implies that in the dualistic pairings the superior part serves this "central ideological interest" of universalism.

Castelli turns to the actual text of Romans only after expressing these ideological presuppositions. She especially studies chapters 8 and 9–11, where she finds this dualistic perception of the world confirmed.

The ideology Castelli presupposes for her reading of Romans, especially of chapters 8 and 9–11, has significant similarities to the image of Paul in the aftermath of the Protestant Reformation and its emphasis on the dualistic opposition of "law and gospel." The Tübingen school varied and further developed this dualistic image of Paul, based on the dialectical Hegelian philosophy of history. In this perception of history and philosophy, dualistic oppositional pairings are essential for the unfolding of the spirit (Geist) in

---

15. Ibid., 276.
16. Ibid., 285.
17. Ibid., 284.

history to its full and universal validation. These scholars viewed Christianity as the religion of universalism, which has paved the way for this unfolding of the spirit. They perceive Paul as the one who has overcome Jewish particularism and brought Christianity to its own self-understanding: universalism. According to this view, Paul achieved the universalism due to his enculturation in Hellenism.

Hence, the ideology of dualism and universalism Castelli finds as the logic and central interest of Romans is not necessarily the ideology of Paul and his Letter to the Romans itself. Instead, it arises from the Hegelian perception of history and philosophy as applied to Paul and his letters by F. C. Baur. Thus, this feminist approach that claims to read "against the grain of tradition" presupposes unquestioned a traditional and, as shown above, disputable image of Paul before producing any textually based statements. Admittedly, any textually based statement is influenced by ideological presuppositions. As I have mentioned several times (above), there is no way out of this hermeneutical circle. The point of critique is recognizing that these ideological presuppositions are applied without any reference to, or awareness of, their origins. Without such awareness, we already set the results of analyzing the texts, and they are anything but surprising or new. The only difference from the traditional (male) interpretations based on the same ideological presuppositions is that these results, supposedly from the text, are counted as problematic or negative instead of positive.

When the author comes to the textual basis of her arguments, these passages serve only as proof texts for what has been previously stated. Romans 8 offers a number of contrasting expressions. Castelli interprets them as proof of Paul's Platonic dualism. This implies that the imagery evoked by those words is associated with a Platonic perception of the world or our image thereof, which again, the Enlightenment perception of ancient philosophy has shaped. This perspective associates flesh, sin, death, and the material, created world with each other as belonging to the inferior, unreal world of the visible. It associates spirit, life, and the spiritual world with each other as belonging to the superior, real world of the invisible. Castelli merely states this without further comment and then seeks the implications of the Platonic association of women and the feminine with the realm of flesh, sin, and death. This indeed is a crucial question for feminist research, given the ongoing negative history in depicting women, bodily existence, and the material world in Christianity. Admittedly, Castelli does not blame Paul directly for these associations and their awful implications. But the fact that Paul perceives the world in this kind of dualism nevertheless renders him, in her perspective, the initiator of a disastrous development, since in all those dualistic pairings mentioned in Rom 8, the dualism male-female is implicit even though not explicitly mentioned.[18]

Reinforcing this perceived dualism is the author's view that Romans is a general theological treatise rather than a letter addressed to a particular situation in a particular community. She does not contradict the view that this letter is the "culmination of Paul's theological writing, his 'last will and testament,'" as Günther Bornkamm stated.[19] Thus, she regards the statements Paul made therein as general theological statements—as the theology of Paul—again similar to traditional, malestream perceptions of this letter.

Castelli bases her interpretation of Romans mainly on the work of Daniel Boyarin, who attributes to Paul a fundamental interest in producing an ideal humanity beyond any difference and hierarchy.[20] Boyarin is aware of his close connection to the image of Paul held by the Tübingen school and especially by Ferdinand Baur himself,[21] thus reflecting on his own presuppositions to some extent. I cannot find any indication of such an awareness in Castelli's commentary; this is contrary to the intention she formulated in her introduction.

Castelli explicitly mentions Paul's Jewish context only after depicting his way of thinking as entirely in accordance with the philosophical and mythic framework of the Hellenistic world. This indicates that she perceives the Hellenistic context as the one from within which Paul is best understood.

Although Castelli noticed Paul's interpretation of the Scriptures[22] earlier in her commentary, she did not mention that the Scriptures he is dealing with are the Scriptures of the Jewish people. The emphasis on Paul's Jewishness occurs only in the context of referring to the law. This suggests allusions that identify Judaism with legalism: the title of this section of her commentary is "Legal Discourses."[23] Castelli distances her exposition from the deplorable type of interpretation that identifies the "Jewish or rabbinic background" of Paul with whatever is regarded as objectionable in Paul's thought. But she herself only mentions Paul's Jewish background when she comes to speak about the law. Nevertheless, it cannot only be "his attention

---

18. Ibid., 286: "It is perhaps notable that the opposition female-male is not explicitly mentioned in Romans; however, there are two reasons for thinking that this is not unreasonable to see it implied. First, the *structure* of dualism is present throughout the letter (including its analogical dimension), and the opposition of male and female was, in the Greco-Roman context, a fundamental element in the overarching hierarchical dualism that dominated its philosophical discourse."

19. Günther Bornkamm, "The Letter to the Romans as Paul's Last Will and Testament," *Australian Biblical Review* 11 (1963): 2–14; cf. Castelli, "Romans," 272.

20. Boyarin, *Radical Jew,* 181.

21. Ibid., 11.

22. Castelli, "Romans," 287.

23. Ibid., 289.

to the question of the law" that "must certainly be understood in the context of his position as a Jewish thinker and reformer."[24] Instead, his thinking, arguing, and actions as a whole, and especially his being—all are rooted in the Scriptures.

As noted above, Castelli never explains that these Scriptures are the Scriptures of the Jewish people, the Scriptures of Israel. She first leaves us with the impression that the Jewish heritage does not make any difference for understanding Paul's way of thinking, then admits that it does make a difference for understanding him when he is dealing with the law. Admittedly, in referring to Paul's Jewish background in this context, Castelli emphasizes that Paul's critique of the law is not the critique of an outsider but the critique of an insider. She thus tries to avoid an anti-Jewish understanding of Paul's critique. Nevertheless, the structure of her interpretation still follows traditional anti-Jewish patterns of interpretation.

In her explanation of Paul's use of the law, Castelli mainly concentrates on the problem of male language and metaphors. She refers to the male identity marker circumcision and the debate about whether women felt included in the community of the "circumcised." With regard to the relationship to God, she problematizes the use of the metaphor of $\upsilon\iota o\theta\varepsilon\sigma\iota\alpha$ and "adoption as sons of God" (Rom 8:15–16).[25] I do not want to discuss these aspects here, but rather look at Castelli's general remarks about Paul's use of the law. She states:

> One might be further confused by Paul's apparent inconsistencies with respect to the Jewish law itself, rejecting its capacity to bestow identity and religious status but retaining its ability, for example, to circumscribe sexuality. These are strategic choices on the part of a writer who takes very seriously the tradition he critiques and challenges. They are not simply pragmatic solutions to immediate problems faced by Paul but rather are constitutive of his hermeneutic and his theology.[26]

Many scholars find inconsistencies in Paul. Whether we should understand Paul's statements about the law in the way she describes them is a matter of ongoing debate. Her perception is similar to the interpretation of the New Perspective, which distinguishes different perceptions of the law in the Pauline Letters.[27] There is a negative aspect of the law, which is rejected or

---

24. Ibid., 289.
25. On this see McGinn's analysis in "Feminist Approaches," 7–9.
26. Castelli, "Romans," 292.
27. As done, for example, by James D. G. Dunn; see sec. "Pauline Studies," in chap. 2, 27ff; and all of chap. 4, 123ff.

overcome by Paul, and a positive aspect, to which Paul adheres. Hence, many conclude that if there is a negative aspect of the law, there must be something wrong at least with this aspect as well as with those who consider it of importance, as Jews do until today. Again, we can find structural anti-Judaism in this type of interpretation.

Nevertheless, Castelli does offer helpful remarks about the effect of such interpretation of Paul's perception of the law, especially the effect for women. If Paul actually did depart from the law, we still do not have enough knowledge about the women's relationship to the law so as to determine whether this had a liberating effect for women or not.[28]

The Platonic dualism Castelli has found in Rom 8 is also the basis for her comments on chapters 9–11. Here again, she finds the dualistic opposition between spirit and flesh. Castelli sees Paul creating a "disjuncture between the real descendants of Abraham and those who are descendants κατὰ σάρκα, according to the flesh."[29] By this Paul perceives ethnic connections, of primary importance in Judaism, as irrelevant. Although Castelli does not explicitly say so, her conclusion that the real descendants of Abraham are the Christians, whereas the descendants according to the flesh are the Jews, is not far from the view that the church in fact has replaced the Jews as the real Israel. Castelli notes Paul's extensive references to the Scriptures in these chapters. She takes this fact as an indication of some kind of dualism, since Paul shows himself as an interpreter of the Torah, which for Castelli is in contradiction to his claim to be an apostle to the Gentiles.

Here Castelli is unclear as to whether Paul and the actual text are inherently anti-Jewish. This is a question she considers irrelevant. Instead, she refers to the problematic history of interpretation, in which these chapters have been used to justify Christian anti-Judaism.

In her commentary Elizabeth Castelli clearly shows the need and the relevance for feminist exegesis to find new ways of approaching texts like Romans. But for her own writing, she does not perform what at the beginning of her essay she declares as most relevant for a feminist exegesis of Romans: the obligation to examine critically the ideology that underwrites the text. The presuppositions behind her exegetical comments have close similarities to traditional malestream interpretations of Paul and their inherent anti-Judaism. Castelli's feminist interpretation of Romans is in fact an

---

28. Castelli, "Romans," 292, states: "Indeed, we know far too little about Jewish women's relationship to the law in this period to know how Paul's attacks upon it would have been experienced by them. Insofar as Judaism attracted women converts in significant numbers in the Roman period, we must assume that the law was not perceived as a burden but rather possessed appeal for these women."

29. Ibid., 293.

interpretation of a specific perception of the letter rather than an interpretation of the Pauline text itself. This has its own merits, but it is not what the author claims to do.

Justification by Faith or by the Law: Elsa Tamez

In the *Kompendium feministische Bibelauslegung,* edited by Luise Schottroff and Marie-Theres Wacker, Elsa Tamez gives an introduction to Romans: "Der Brief an die Gemeinde in Rom: Eine feministische Lektüre."[30] Here too, as in Castelli's interpretation, we can find an inherent dualistic pattern of interpretation, although it is not declared or criticized as such and is thus less obvious.

This introduction does not claim to be a commentary; instead, she calls it a "feminist reading that reads Romans as the result of a specific, varying, and challenging context rather than as a dogmatic theory."[31] Elsa Tamez thus briefly outlines this context in terms of Paul's situation, place of writing of the letter, and future travel plans. Her main emphasis lies in describing the sociopolitical circumstances of the imperialistic Roman Empire: "[Paul] had been traveling a lot and had been an eyewitness to the presence of the Roman domination in economic, political, and military issues that proclaimed 'peace and security' in the occupied territories in exchange for unconditional subordination."[32] She gives a differentiated description of Paul's attitude toward women (including a broad discussion of the essential role of Phoebe as deliverer and interpreter of the letter). Then she presents a historical investigation into the situation of the early Christ-believing groups in Rome before coming to her feminist reading of the text itself. She thereby takes Paul's androcentric language and the patriarchal context as a given fact, which she consciously does not further analyze. Her aim is rather to look at certain theological statements in the letter from a feminist perspective.

In contrast to traditional interpretations of the letter that developed abstract doctrines out of certain specific key words such as *sin, grace, election,* and so on, she points to the need to interpret Romans out of its specific socioeconomic, cultural, and religious context. In Tamez's perception the key

---

30. See n. 2, 161.
31. Tamez, "Der Brief," 557, with my translation of the German: "Eine feministische Lektüre wird den Römerbrief als Ergebnis eines besonderen Kontextes lesen, der verändert und herausfordert, und nicht als eine abstrakte, dogmatische Abhandlung."
32. Ibid., 557, with my translation of the German: "Er war schon viel gereist und war Augenzeuge der Präsenz der römischen Herrschaft in wirtschaftlichen, politischen und militärischen Angelegenheiten, die in den besetzten Gebieten 'Frieden und Sicherheit' verkündete im Gegenzug zu einer bedingungslosen Unterwerfung."

to a feminist reading of Romans is the issue of (former) exclusion. Paul's main purpose, according to her, is the inclusion of Jews and Gentiles in God's promises.

In her commentary she divides the letter into three sections: chapters 1–8, the righteousness of God; 9–11, election; and 12–15, ethical issues.[33]

In analyzing chapters 1–8, Tamez depicts the imperial power of Roman society as the context that chiefly influenced Paul's arguing. She perceives sin as the power inherent in the structures of the Roman system of oppression, injustice, and violence. Since the power of the Roman Empire was at its peak in the Second Temple period, it was impossible for anyone to escape its influence.[34] Sin and injustice were dominant, and according to Paul, there was no possibility for any human being to do justice, Tamez claims. Only the righteousness of God can empower men and women to do justice and live according to his will. Justification is God's gift, and nobody can earn it, certainly not by human works. Tamez contends that this is a radical critique over against Roman society, which was based on works and merits, and also a general critique of any kind of law, and of the Mosaic law in particular.

Tamez is aware of the inherent danger of such a statement, since it might lead again to an anti-Jewish interpretation. Yet she depicts what she views as Paul's critique of the Mosaic law: a first-century Jew's radical self-criticism. She sees Paul as criticizing a perception of the law as a means of salvation and as a possibility to achieve some changes toward a better world. Over against this perception, Paul has found the power of the gospel, the gospel of grace, which is a free gift of God to all human beings without any distinction. Thus the former discrimination between Jews and Gentiles has come to an end in Christ. In the realm of faith the inclusion of the formerly excluded (Gentiles) has become possible.[35]

According to Tamez, Paul goes even further in his critique of the law:

> In setting the law in opposition to faith and grace, [Paul] discovers in various types of law—be they legal law or "hidden," such as the law or the logic of tradition, of institutions, of culture or of doctrine—a dark, obscure domination . . . Paul criticizes this law and puts it in contrast with the law of the Spirit, with another logic, which is named as grace or faith.[36]

---

33. Ibid., 560.
34. Ibid., 561.
35. Ibid., 566.
36. Ibid., 567, with my translation of the German: "Indem er das Gesetz dem Glauben und der Gnade gegenüberstellt, entdeckt er in verschiedenen Gesetzestypen, sei es legales Recht oder 'unsichtbares'—wie das Gesetz oder die Logik der Tradition, der Institutionen, der Kultur oder des Dogmas—eine finstere Herrschaft. . . . Paulus kritisiert dieses Gesetz und stellt es dem Gesetz des Geistes gegenüber, einer anderen Logik, die auch Gnade und Glaube genannt wird."

Tamez emphasizes that this is not peculiar to Mosaic law; this tendency is inherent in any kind of law. It enslaves men and women in that it values them according to their works and merits, which implies that men and women who cannot do what the law requires are of lesser value. Tamez maintains that this attitude had disastrous consequences, especially for women in patriarchal societies, with their specific image of women and the tasks they should fulfill.[37]

Tamez is aware of anti-Jewish tendencies in traditional Pauline interpretation, especially when the question of the law is concerned; she is aware that an image of Paul as critical of the law and circumcision has led to anti-Judaism in the past. But in her interpretation, she actually follows traditional patterns of interpretation to some extent. She perceives Paul as a self-critical Jew who is just relativizing the law, since he has found the power of grace. Nevertheless, when she elaborates further on the role of the law, she sees Paul setting faith and grace in contrast to the law. According to Tamez, Paul sees a tendency toward domination in any kind of law, and thus also in the Jewish law.[38]

She is aware of the need to contextualize Romans in the specific contemporary context of the first century. Therefore, Tamez draws attention to the fact that sin and oppression are not merely individual deficiencies but are inherent in political and socioeconomic structures. Her contextualization, however, is limited to this particular aspect of the situation of the first-century Roman Empire. What is missing here is a specific contextualization of the letter in the concrete situation of the Christ-believers at Rome. In addition, Tamez does not take into account the closest context of Paul's life and thought: first-century Judaism.

Especially in her analysis of the role of the law over against the gift of grace, we can easily discover the well-known traditional pattern of interpreting Romans mentioned above. It is this same pattern of depicting the law as in contrast to, and in contradiction with, the gospel, or justification by faith over against works of the law—what has shaped Pauline interpretation particularly since the Reformation period. Tamez's prevailing emphasis on the gift of grace and justification by faith clearly echoes Luther. As W. S. Campbell states: "The path to righteousness is not . . . by doing righteous acts, but may only be found through faith, because 'the righteousness of God' is that righteousness by which he makes us righteous, just as the wisdom of God is that by which he makes us wise."[39] And further, Luther declares: "To

---

37. Ibid., 562.
38. Ibid., 566.
39. W. S. Campbell, "Martin Luther and Paul's Epistle to the Romans," in *The Bible as Book: The Reformation* (ed. Orlaith O'Sullivan; London: British Library, 2000), 108.

want to be justified by works of the Law is to deny the righteousness of faith."[40] This interpretation treats the Jews as a category of people who are boasting of being God's elect and of having received the law. The Lutheran emphasis on grace and faith, together with the theological categorization of the Jews as those representing the wrong attitude of faith, has become the general pattern of subsequent Pauline interpretation.

Ferdinand Christian Baur and the Tübingen school had produced this type of Pauline interpretation, with its inherent anti-Judaism, and it undoubtedly contributed to the rise of political anti-Semitism in the nineteenth century. Ernst Käsemann, in contrast to his great teacher Rudolf Bultmann, stressed the communal as well as the cosmic character of the doctrine of salvation by faith, but he nevertheless still used "the Jew" as the category of people who represented "the apostle's real adversary."[41]

This pattern of interpretation has shaped Elsa Tamez's exposition even though she interprets this doctrine from a feminist perspective: she investigates the implications it has for women and all those who are marginalized and excluded. Thereby she discovers a liberating potential in the traditional doctrine of justification by faith:

> Therefore, the issue of grace is a liberating message for women. First of all, grace stands against any norms that ask for merits, in order to be regarded as human beings with their own dignity. . . . Grace, moreover, opens up free space to live together and to celebrate everyday life. The urge/yearning for efficiency or to do the right thing in order to be a "superwoman," is not dominant in the realm of grace.[42]

She continues in traditional vein, stating that "Romans as well as Galatians is emphasizing that God justifies human beings through faith rather than through works."[43]

Tamez tries to weaken what she interprets as "Paul's radical critique of the Mosaic law and circumcision,"[44] by describing Paul's critique as a self-critique

---

40. Ibid., 112, quoting Luther from his 1535 lectures on Galatians.

41. Ernst Käsemann, "Paul and Israel," in *New Testament Questions of Today* (London: SCM, 1969), 184, 183–87.

42. Tamez, "Der Brief," 566, with my translation of the German: "Darum ist die Rede von der Gnade eine befreiende Botschaft für die Frauen. In erster Linie steht die Gnade gegen die Normierungen, die Verdienste fordern, um Menschen mit eigener Würde zu sein. . . . Schliesslich erschliesst die Gnade Freiräume, um zusammenzuleben und den konkreten Alltag mit seinen Festen zu feiern. Der Drang zur Effizienz oder dazu, das Richtige zu tun, um eine 'Superfrau' zu sein, beherrscht nicht den Bereich der Gnade."

43. Ibid., 566, with my translation of the German: "Der Römerbrief führt ebenso wie der Galaterbrief aus, dass Gott die Menschen durch den Glauben und nicht die Werke gerecht macht."

44. Ibid., 566.

from within Judaism, criticizing what is perceived to be a misunderstanding of the law. But she universalizes what she at first had described as an intra-Jewish problem, making it a general critique of any kind of "bad" law, which she then develops into a general critique of any kind of law. With this universalization of a specific critique, she implies that there must be something wrong also with the Jewish law, the Torah, and to adhere to this Jewish law must at least be somehow anachronistic. With the "discovery" of the free gift of grace by Paul, the Torah is an expression of a wrong perception of life, a conservativism that should be overcome. At certain points her use of language evokes undue associations, as when she claims that Paul "discovers in different kinds of law . . . some dark power."[45]

I cannot see much structural difference between this kind of interpretation and the traditional malestream interpretation of Paul. The interpretative pattern of law over against the gospel, law over against grace, is just another type of dualism imposed on Paul. Again we have a traditional interpretation of Paul—now interpreted from a feminist perspective, but not a truly feminist interpretation of the Pauline texts.

Gnostic Dualism: Rosemary Radford Ruether

In *Gaia and God: An Ecofeminist Theology of Earth Healing*, Rosemary Radford Ruether finds a different kind of dualism in Paul.[46] This work is not a commentary on a Pauline letter, yet Ruether refers to Paul and especially to the Letter to the Romans at some length in chapter 5 of her book, where she outlines "Classical Narratives of Sin and Evil."[47] In her view Paul has laid the foundations of a concept of sin and evil that was a fusion of "the Jewish ethical and the Greek metaphysical views of evil. Evil is located both in the freedom of the human will and its choice of disobedience against God, and in the flawed ontology of mortal being."[48]

In contrast to Castelli and Tamez, Ruether locates Paul's theology within the apocalyptic and gnostic thought world. With regard to apocalypticism, she is in accordance with some of the recent Pauline scholarship (e.g., Segal, Beker); on the other hand, her perception of Paul as a gnostic does not find much basis in malestream Pauline exegesis.[49] She does not give any reference to the exegetical work on which her contention is based and states:

45. Ibid., 567, with my translation of the German: "Er entdeckt in verschiedenen Gesetzestypen . . . eine finstere Herrschaft."
46. Rosemary Radford Ruether, *Gaia and God: An Ecofeminist Theology of Earth Healing* (London: SCM, 1993).
47. Ibid., 115–42.
48. Ibid., 126.
49. Elaine Pagels, *The Gnostic Paul* (Philadelphia: Trinity Press International, 1992).

> Basic to [Paul's] theology is a profound dualism between two modes of exis-
> tence: existence according to the "flesh," which he characterizes as a state of
> slavery to sin and death, and existence in the Spirit, which he sees as freeing
> the Christian, through their rebirth in Christ, both to virtuous and loving life
> and also to the promise of immortality.[50]

Paul's description of these two modes of existence, his identification of sin
with death and goodness with immortal life, seems to imply that the created,
material human body or even creation has to be overcome or transformed
into a celestial type of existence. Ruether considers this as a clear expression
of a quasi-gnostic, dualistic cosmo-anthropology, based on "the two-storied
cosmology of contemporary philosophy."[51] This philosophy divides the
world into two realms: the spiritual, immortal one; and the earthly, material
one, "governed by demonic powers that trap us in sin and death."[52]

She depicts the Jewish law as standing between the two realms, and its
commandments as belonging to the spiritual realm. But those who try to
obey them without "the Spirit" only reveal themselves as being still enslaved
by the powers of this world. Only baptism in Christ frees human beings
from enslavement by demonic spirits. Paul, according to Ruether, stresses
that people cannot achieve salvation by observance of the law; instead, salvation is a free gift of God, received through faith.

Ruether states that Paul, with his critique of the law as a means of salvation, is not an antinomian. Rather, she sees him as strongly emphasizing the
importance of an ethics of relationship. This is based in Paul's "understanding of the Church as the Body of Christ. The prime indicator of being in
Christ is to be in the Church as a community of loving relationship."[53]

Although Ruether mentions the apocalyptic thought world of Paul, she
does not really contextualize him within first-century Judaism. She perceives
Romans and bits and pieces of other letters (Galatians, 1 Corinthians) as
universal theological treatises detached from any concrete situation. She does
not even put Paul's ethical exhortations in relation to the ethics of the Torah.
Thus again, inherent in her interpretation we find patterns of Pauline exegesis that are quite traditional.

First, there is the dualism of "flesh and spirit," which originates, as
Ruether contends, in "contemporary philosophy," described as being dualistic
in a Platonic way. As I have shown in my analysis of Castelli's commentary,

---

50. Ruether, *Gaia and God*, 127.
51. Ibid., 129.
52. Ibid.
53. Ibid., 131.

this perception of Paul has close analogies to Enlightenment interpretations of Paul, especially in Baur's Tübingen school. The same applies to Christian faith overcoming the Jewish law as a means of salvation, which Ruether briefly mentions. The difference from traditional interpretations consists mainly in her evaluation of what she finds. Ruether sees these concepts, although not yet fully developed in the Pauline Letters, as responsible for the later fully developed, problematic Christian view that set the spiritual over against the carnal, the immortal over against the mortal life, and all in a hierarchical order. This view identified women with the carnal and mortal aspects of life, which true Christians have to overcome.[54] I agree with Ruether's critique of this interpretation of the Christian perception of life. Nevertheless, I do question her interpretation of Paul as the one "who laid the foundations of this concept of sin and evil."[55]

Conclusion

In different ways and with different purposes, these three feminist interpretations of Paul show similar inherent hermeneutical patterns. They interpret the Letter to the Romans as well as Paul's letters generally through the lenses of a dualistic generalizing pattern, whether through Platonism as viewed in the Enlightenment tradition or through the Lutheran law/gospel dualism. In her interpretation from the margins, Elsa Tamez finds liberationist aspects in the doctrine of justification by faith for feminist theology. Elizabeth A. Castelli and Rosemary Radford Ruether make a negative valuation of what they interpret as Paul's Platonic dualism. They regard it as the foundation for devaluing the created, material world generally in Christianity, and particularly for devaluing women and associating them (more than men) with the material world.

Elsa Tamez emphasizes the need for a contextualized interpretation, but her contexualization is limited to the impact of the socioeconomic and political circumstances on Paul's writings. She gains important insights from this. Yet she does not mention either the concrete situation of the addressees in Rome or the Jewish context of Paul's theologizing. We thus receive the idea that Romans still is a general theological treatise, mainly about the law and justification by faith, which Paul formulated under the general circumstances of the empire under Roman rule. Castelli and Ruether completely neglect any concrete context of the letter and interpret as if it were a treatise of timeless theological doctrine.

---

54. See ibid., 139–41.
55. Ibid., 127.

Through this type of interpretation, an image of Paul emerges depicting him as a lonely fighter, who tries to replace Jewish particularism with an overarching universalism. These scholars have derived the idea of this universalism from Graeco-Roman philosophical ideas of an all-encompassing oneness in which differences are eradicated. They see Paul's message and behavior as hierarchical, as he tries to establish his own authority over against his communities and leaves no room for different meanings and interpretations of the Christ event.[56] According to such an interpretation, anti-Judaism and the teaching of subordination of, and contempt for, anybody who is different (particularly women), are inherent in Paul's letters. We end with an image of Paul as an anti-Jewish misogynist. As mentioned above, this image has close similarities to the image of Paul in traditional Pauline scholarship. We may rightly criticize it from feminist as well as other perspectives.

Nevertheless, this is not the only possible image of Paul. As we have demonstrated above, this image is based on presuppositions challenged particularly by approaches Beyond the New Perspective. This movement is depicting new images of Paul, locating him within Judaism rather than in opposition to it.[57] It thus is not enough to criticize the traditional images of Paul as anti-Jewish, hierarchical, and misogynist. Instead, we need to ask what the result of a feminist interpretation of the letters of Paul would be if it were not based on traditional images of Paul, and if it would take into account aspects of new images of Paul such as those Beyond the New Perspective.

---

56. See, for instance, Elizabeth A. Castelli, *Imitating Paul: A Discourse of Power* (Louisville: Westminster/John Knox, 1991); and Cynthia Briggs Kittredge, *Community and Authority: The Rhetoric of Obedience in the Pauline Tradition* (Harrisburg, Pa.: Trinity Press International, 1998).

57. See "Paul—Beyond the New Perspective," chap. 4, 123ff.

༺ **6** ༻

"That We May Be Mutually Encouraged"
(Rom 1:12)

A Feminist Perspective—Beyond the New Perspective

By analyzing the approaches of Castelli, Tamez, and Ruether to Romans, I have demonstrated that we must maintain a critical distinction between the *Wirkungsgeschichte* (history of the impact) of Paul's letters and the texts themselves. The critical study of the history of interpretation and critiquing it as a history of injustice are important steps toward a new reading of the Pauline Letters from feminist and other perspectives. Becoming aware of the specific hermeneutical presuppositions of an interpretation allows for fresh and at times surprisingly new ways of approaching Pauline texts. This is particularly evident when we take into account hermeneutical insights such as those expressed in *Christianity in Jewish Terms*. This book draws attention to the fact that Western post-Enlightenment rationality is just one among other ways of perceiving reality and interpreting it. If we start with this outlook, we may discover that Paul and early Jewish-Christian relations follow a different kind of logic than traditionally assumed.[1]

Thus, in strands of research Beyond the New Perspective, an image of Paul begins to emerge that is depicted in the colors of first-century Judaism. It is the portrait of a Jew who followed his call as a missionary to the

---

1. Tikva Frymer-Kensky et al., eds., *Christianity in Jewish Terms* (Radical Traditions; Boulder, Col.: Westview, 2000).

Gentiles, not as a lonely fighter isolated from the world, but in a specific historical and social context, always surrounded by, and working together with, other members of the movement of Christ-believers. We can see Paul as "one link in a chain of those who taught him hope (1 Cor 15:3) and those who sought to give form to the new life with him and [were] also in confrontation with him."[2] Common to such approaches is an increasing awareness of the limitations of Western philosophical discourse and its universal claims, which have shaped biblical interpretation, and through it the perception of early Jewish-Christian relations, and specifically, the image of Paul. These scholars are rediscovering modes of scriptural reasoning that, in the wake of "modern reasoning," have long been ignored, depreciated, or suppressed. Such postcritical approaches (e.g., as advocated in the series Radical Traditions) might reveal fresh insights into Paul's way of thinking and arguing, insights based on Scripture and thus more responsive than originative, more dialogical than logical (in a traditional philosophical way).[3]

The relevance of what I recommend here is clearer when we look at specific examples of the interpretation of Paul's letters. At first sight it seems quite reasonable that we find only a few feminist writings on Romans since in this letter Paul addresses hardly any issues that are relevant from a specifically feminist perspective (except 1:26–27, chap. 16 and perhaps chap. 7). But this is only a first impression or the result of an ongoing presupposition that Romans is, as perceived in traditional interpretation, the core of Paul's theology, his last will and testament, the summary of Paul's thought as such. Since feminist theologians emphasize the need to account for the contextuality of any kind of theologizing and exegesis, we rightly need to regard claims of universal truths and timeless theological statements as the claims of the dominant discourse in power. As such, we must critically analyze traditional interpretations of Paul and particularly of Romans. As shown above, this traditional perception of Paul and thus of Romans is not the only possible one: there might be more positive relevance in this letter than previously assumed, even from a feminist perspective.

---

2. Luzia Sutter Rehmann, "German-Language Feminist Exegesis of the Pauline Letters: A Survey," *Journal for the Study of the New Testament* 79 (2000): 11.

3. Thus Peter Ochs, in *Christianity in Jewish Terms* (ed. Frymer-Kensky), 68, has stated: "The Christian theologian Robert Jenson and the Jewish philosopher Emmanuel Lévinas offer overlapping criticisms of one of these forces: the tendency toward 'totalistic thinking' that affects secularists as well as religious Christians and Jews. This is thinking that claims to identify the one set of clear principles upon which all human life should be based. . . . Jenson argues that a major source of this totalistic tendency is an admixture of biblical religion with the Greek philosophic concept of 'timeless being'—the concept that for something to exist truly, it must be immune to change and to relationship with whatever changes. . . . When this God is assimilated to the Greek philosophic concept of deity, what often results is the portrayal of an absolute deity whose intentions are unchangeable but knowable by at least a select portion of humanity. This portion may be elected to comprehend the entire world and also to rule over it. For Lévinas, worship of 'timeless being' in this way is a source of modern totalitarianism, secular as well as religious."

Here I analyze specific texts, especially of Romans, from hermeneutical presuppositions known as Beyond the New Perspective, paying special attention to the relevance of such a perspective for a feminist perspective on Paul that seeks to free itself from being based on traditional malestream interpretations of Paul's letters. In this analysis I concentrate on three key issues that are jointly emphasized in recent feminist theory and theology[4] as well as in recent Pauline studies: universalism and/or particularism, hierarchy and/or mutuality, sameness and/or diversity.

Universalism and/or Particularism

As we have seen, traditional malestream interpretation and some feminist commentaries on Paul locate the apostle entirely within Greek patterns of thought. They thus depict him as a man driven by the desire to overcome any kind of particularities, especially ethnic particularities, in anticipation of his vision of the world to come, where God's reign will eradicate all differences and distinctions between peoples and nations.. This scenario portrays the universal claim of the gospel as implying that all must become the same in order to become "one in Christ." Such a perspective depicts Paul as closely related to a universalistic perception of the world that, especially when paired with political and military power, has devastating impacts on those who are different in a society—different from those in power on the political as well as ideological level. It does not allow ethnic as well as other identities to be different from the one declared to be the universal identity and therefore the only right one. Since white "Christian" men have dominated Western civilization for centuries, it is no surprise that the ideal human being tends strongly to resemble a white Christian man. It has therefore not been to one's advantage if one happened to be Jewish or/and a woman and/or black.

Feminists and others have rightly criticized this Christian hierarchical universalism from various perspectives. It is inherently anti-Jewish as well as misogynist since it leaves no room for difference and particularity, certainly not on the basis of equality and equal rights. If Paul actually had been advocating this kind of universalism, it would be better, from a feminist perspective, to move beyond him.

But we need not necessarily view Paul as the champion of a law-free universal and hierarchical Gentile church, adhering to a Christianity freed from the limits of that ethnocentric particularism to which Judaism was still adhering.

---

4. See sections "Contemporary Ways of Thinking," 92ff, and "Issues of Identity, Diversity, and Mutuality," 110ff, in chap. 3.

A number of scholars have emphasized that we come to a better under-standing of Paul's letters if we read them as written from a particular perspec-tive at a specific moment in time, addressing specific people in a particular situation. These approaches draw special attention to religious, social, politi-cal, and other contexts of Paul's life, activity, and thought.[5]

This context is primarily and essentially that of first-century Judaism, of which Paul was a part during his entire life, before as well as after his call. Several statements in his letters show that he did not view Judaism in a nega-tive way, and certainly not as something that had to be overcome because of its ethnocentricity or particularism (e.g., Rom 3:1–2; 9:1–5). Paul rather emphasized the right to, and necessity of, Jewish particular identity and the irrevocability of the promises and election. As J. C. Beker has stressed: "The gospel cannot have any authentic validity or legitimation apart from the people Israel because the theological issue of God's faithfulness (Rom 3:3) and righteousness determines the truth of the gospel."[6]

The gospel Paul proclaims in Romans is actually a genuinely Jewish mes-sage addressed to "the Jews first and also to the Greek," the Gentiles (Rom 1:16). And even when Paul addresses Gentiles, as he mostly does in his let-ters, he does so as a Jew deeply rooted in the traditions of his ancestors, in the Scriptures. These Scriptures specifically shaped his thinking and the con-tents of his arguments. As Peter Tomson has explained, Paul's theological arguing to a great extent consists in doing exegesis in the light of an apoca-lyptic interpretation of the Christ event.[7] This in itself reveals the particular-ity of Paul's statements. Doing exegesis from within a Jewish context implies that one is dealing with concrete issues of everyday life. For Paul to have faith in the one God of Israel has very practical implications. The nature of his Jewish exegetical traditions, the Scriptural traditions of his ancestors, tied Paul to the particularities of halakic issues, and this despite the fact of his recognition that the God of Israel is also the God of all nations.

---

5. On this see e.g. W. S. Campbell, *The Purpose of Paul in the Letter to the Romans*. PhD Thesis, University of Edinburgh, 1972. Already in 1971 in a remarkable small publication, *Die Juden im Römerbrief* (Theologische Studien 107; Zurich: Theologischer Verlag, 1971), Friedrich-Wilhelm Marquardt explained: "Romans is a real letter, rather than an epistle, situated in a unique and certainly limited historical situation. . . . Paul belongs to the church not with his timeless ideas but in the unity of his person and work and in the diversity and pluralism of his solidarities and identifications." My trans-lation of the German: "Der Römerbrief ist ein wirklicher Brief, nicht Epistel, und hat eine einmalige bes-timmt begrenzte historische Situation. . . . Paulus gehört der Kirche nicht in seinen zeitlosen Ideen, sondern in der Einheit seiner Person und seines Werkes und gerade in der Vielfalt der von ihm eingegan-genen Solidaritäten und Identifizierungen" (44). "Uns scheint . . . dass sich der Apostel jeder Verallgemeinerung und Ausweitung eines von ihm konkret gebrauchten Begriffs mit Leidenschaft entge-gengestellt hat" (46). See chap. 4, 133ff.

6. J. Christiaan Beker, "The Faithfulness of God and the Priority of Israel in Paul's Letter to the Romans," in *The Romans Debate* (ed. Karl P. Donfried; rev., expanded ed.; Peabody, Mass.: Hendrickson, 1991), 330.

7. With reference to the justification motif, see Peter J. Tomson, *"If This Be from Heaven . . .": Jesus and the New Testament Authors in Their Relationship to Judaism* (Sheffield: Sheffield Academic Press, 2001), 188.

Mutuality and Diversity: The Particularity of Paul's Theology

In Rom 14–15 Paul explicitly addresses practical issues deriving from everyday life in particular communities in Rome.[8] Scholars are still debating the significance of these chapters: Are they just some ethical additions to his crucial theological statements in the previous chapters?[9] Or are there inherent and in fact decisive connections between this section and chapters 1–11?[10] There is also an ongoing debate about the identity of the groups Paul actually addresses here, about the identity of the "weak" and the "strong."

I consider these chapters to be linked both in structure and in content to the issue that is central throughout the letter, the issue of the relationship of Jews and Gentiles.[11] Thus, rather than being a mere appendix, Rom 14–15 is central to the letter as such and serves as a prime example of the particularity of Paul's theology.

We cannot easily answer the question of the precise identity of the groups involved in the problems Paul addresses. There is less debate about the identity of the "strong" since most scholars identify them as Christ-believing Gentiles. But who these "weak in faith" are is more of a problem. Scholarly identifications range from gnosticizing pagans to nonbelieving Jews.[12] It is

---

8. According to a vast scholarly consensus.

9. As, for instance, their position at the end of Dunn's huge volume on Paul's theology implies; see James D. G. Dunn, *The Theology of Paul the Apostle* (Grand Rapids: Eerdmans, 1998), 680–89.

10. On this see the respective section in these commentaries: C. E. B. Cranfield, *The Epistle to the Romans* (2 vols.; 6th ed.; International Critical Commentary; Edinburgh: T&T Clark, 1975–79); James D. G. Dunn, *Romans 1–8* and *Romans 9–16* (Word Bible Commentary 38A–38B; Dallas: Word, 1988); Joseph A. Fitzmyer, *Romans* (Anchor Bible 33; New York: Doubleday, 1993); Douglas J. Moo, *The Epistle to the Romans* (Grand Rapids: Eerdmans, 1996). Also see W. S. Campbell, "The Rule of Faith in Romans 12:1–15:13: The Obligation of Humble Obedience as the Only Adequate Response to the Mercies of God," in *Romans* (vol. 3 of *Pauline Theology*; ed. David M. Hay and E. Elizabeth Johnson; Minneapolis: Fortress, 1995), 259; Mark D. Nanos, *The Mystery of Romans: The Jewish Context of Paul's Letter to the Romans* (Minneapolis: Fortress, 1996), 85, 102, 114.

11. W. S. Campbell emphasizes this: "In 11:13ff. Paul, after a long discussion begun in 9:1, addresses himself pointedly to the Gentile Christians and specifically warns them not to boast over the fate of the unbelieving Jews. . . . This is no hypothetical situation and the dialogue style gives no warrant for the belief that Paul does not address himself to a real situation in Rome, where current anti-Judaism was threatening the unity of the church. Paul's carefully constructed conclusion in 11:30–32 [and] his exhortations in 12:1ff. and in [chapters] 14–15 support this interpretation of chapter 11. An even clearer indication in support of the above is the concluding scripturally substantiated imperative in 15:7f. . . . In view of the direct connection of 15:7f. with 14:1ff., it is clear that the division between the weak and the strong is one along Jew-Gentile lines, and it is then easy to read back via 12:3 and to relate [chapters] 9–11 with 4:16ff. and 6:11ff. to a particular set of circumstances in the Christian community in Rome." W. S. Campbell, "Romans III as a Key to the Structure and Thought of the Letter," *Novum Testamentum* 23 (1981): 22–40; now in his *Paul's Gospel in an Intercultural Context: Jew and Gentile in the Letter to the Romans* (Berlin: P. Lang, 1992), 33, 25–42. Also see Nanos, *Mystery*, 84f. Moo, *Romans*, 828, emphasizes that the relationship between Jews and Gentiles is the leitmotif of the whole letter.

12. See Nanos, *Mystery*, 85–165. Nanos argues strongly in favor of a non-Christian Jewish identity of the weak. I am not convinced by his arguments; instead, I perceive the weak as Christ-believers. But since Boyarin's and Lieu's research demonstrates the fluidity of these boundaries and categories, I consider the precise definition of the identity of the weak somewhat obsolete—perhaps there was no precisely defined identity at all; perhaps the outside, pagan world perceived all of them, "weak" or "strong," as "Jewish."

sufficient for this study to recognize that the issue addressed here makes it most likely that the division is one along Jew/Gentile lines.[13] I therefore draw attention to insights Daniel Boyarin and Judith Lieu have presented: the boundaries between the different Jewish, Gentile, and Christian groups remained fluid and open over a much longer period than we have perceived until recently.[14] What implications this may have for the identification of the "weak" and the "strong" must be a matter of further research.[15]

We could take the fluidity of boundaries as an indication that a clear identification of groups is impossible: there might have been more than just two groups that could simply be divided according to ethnic origin.[16] Nevertheless, W. S. Campbell has concluded: "What is required to make sense of the content is not Jewish Christians as such but a context in which Judaism plays a role."[17] The groups obviously differ on matters related to food and drink and also to certain days. In 14:2–3 the text mentions meat and vegetables; 14:21 adds wine to the list, and 14:5 mentions regard for days. All this strongly indicates that Jewish matters are at stake, most likely questions about kosher meals.[18] This points to the presence of Jewish Christ-believers, but it could also imply that at least some Gentile Christ-believers or proselytes are living a Jewish lifestyle.

Whatever their precise identity, however, the groups involved must have been socially related to each other in such a way that the quality of their relationship did actually matter since it impacted upon both. The context of this relationship was such that "Jewish affairs" mattered. Hence, Paul most likely was addressing Christ-believing groups within, or at least with links to, the

---

13. See Campbell, *Paul's Gospel*, 33; James C. Walters, *Ethnic Issues in Paul's Letter to the Romans: Changing Self-Definitions in Earliest Roman Christianity* (Valley Forge, Pa.: Trinity Press International, 1993), 88; Moo, *Romans*, 828; Campbell, "Rule of Faith," 277; Robert Jewett, "Following the Argument of Romans," in *Romans Debate* (ed. Donfried), 265–77; James D. G. Dunn, "The Formal and Theological Coherence," in *Romans Debate* (ed. Donfried), 245–50.

14. See Daniel Boyarin's chapter "When Christians Were Still Jews," in his *Dying for God: Martyrdom and the Making of Christianity and Judaism* (Stanford: Stanford University Press, 1999), 1–21; and Judith M. Lieu, "'Impregnable Ramparts and Walls of Iron': Boundary and Identity in Early 'Judaism' and 'Christianity,'" *New Testament Studies* 48.3 (July 2002): 297–313. Already in 1991 W. S. Campbell, *Paul's Gospel*, 115, emphasized: "In practice, there was probably great fluidity and diversity concerning the relationship between those Christians of Jewish and those of Gentile origin in the earliest period of the church."

15. In Rom 14–15 Paul uses the terms "weak" and "strong" (defined below) in a provisional rather than absolute sense, perhaps even with tongue in cheek, gaining rapport with the strong by using a flattering designation for them even while taking them to task. With that understanding, I thenceforward do not put quotation marks around these terms unless they are embedded in a longer quotation.

16. See Moo, *Romans*, 12.

17. Campbell, "Rule of Faith," 267, where he continues: "But even if the great majority of the Roman Christians were Gentile, . . . we are not obligated to accept the hypothesis that the weak were all Jewish by birth (and the resultant correlation of Jewishness and weakness). It is feasible that many of them were Gentiles influenced in different degrees by Jewish practices."

18. See Peter J. Tomson, *Paul and the Jewish Law: Halakha in the Letters of the Apostle to the Gentiles* (Minneapolis: Fortress, 1990), 239.

synagogue.[19] The quality of the relationship or interaction between the groups involved was, in Paul's view, of central importance for ethical as well as for theological reasons.[20] The quality of this actual relationship directs us toward the proper understanding and living of faith.[21]

Paul uses two different labels when he addresses these different groups in Rome. He mentions welcoming "τὸν ἀσθενοῦντα τῇ πίστει (the one who is weak in faith)" (14:1) and the obligation that "we οἱ δυνατοί (who are strong)" have (15:1). These labels clearly show that inequalities in terms of power are involved.[22] The ἀσθενῶν (the one being weak, 14:2) is considerably more vulnerable than the δυνατοί (strong ones, 15:1). Whether this is also an indication of the quality of their faith seems at least worth a question. In 14:1 the scholarly opinion almost exclusively relates τῇ πίστει (in faith) to τὸν ἀσθενοῦντα (the weak person), assuming that the weak are weak with regard to their faith. But throughout the rest of chapters 14 and 15, Paul speaks only of the weak and the strong, without any further qualification. "In faith (τῇ πίστει) could also be related to the imperative to "welcome (προσλαμβάνεσθε) one another" (14:1; 15:7)—meaning that "the strong (οἱ δυνατοί)" should "in faith (τῇ πίστει) welcome the weak person (τὸν ἀσθενοῦντα" (14:1). Although "to be weak in faith (ἀσθενεῖν τῇ πίστει)" and "to be strengthened in faith (ἐνδυναμωθῆναι τῇ πίστει)" are terms Paul applies in 4:19–20, the near textual context of 15:7 rather supports the reading suggested here: Paul admonishes the Christ-believers: "Welcome one another, therefore, just as Christ has welcomed you, for the glory of God."

Moreover, Paul counsels that the "strong (δυνατοί)" should "bear (βαστάζειν) the weaknesses (τὰ ἀσθενήματα) of the weak (ἀδυνάτωνοι)," using the same word βαστάζειν he used in 11:18, where he reminded the boasting Gentiles "in Christ" that "it is not you that bear the root, but the root that bears you ([my trans. of] οὐ σὺ τὴν ῥίζαν βαστάζεις ἀλλὰ ἡ ῥίζα σέ." This indicates a theology of mutuality and accommodation rather than of hierarchical dualism. There is no room here to elaborate on this in more detail. The interrelationship of δυνατοί, ἀδύνατοι and βαστάζειν in this passage is a topic for further research. It is sufficient to note that the terminology

---

19. See Campbell, "Rule of Faith," 275; also 277: "We have envisaged competing communities and leaders along a continuum that stretched from 'synagogue' Christians to 'Gentile' house-churches with an aversion to Judaism and the law."

20. Campbell, *Paul's Gospel,* 55, emphasizes with regard to the purpose of the letter as a whole that "Paul had to be involved in the discussion at Rome because his gospel and mission were at stake. . . . Gentile Christians need to understand God's grace to Israel in order to understand his grace to them."

21. As Campbell, "Rule of Faith," 278, has stated: "Both righteousness and faith were practical issues for the Romans. Orthopraxy rather than orthodoxy was a central concern."

22. See John M. G. Barclay, "'Do We Undermine the Law?' A Study of Romans 14.1–15.6," in *Paul and the Mosaic Law* (ed. James D. G. Dunn; Tübingen: Mohr, 1996), 302, 287–308; also Dunn, *Romans 9–16,* 837.

of weak and strong points to inequalities in terms of power rather than in terms of faith.[23]

Throughout these chapters, moreover, Paul addresses the strong far more than the weak; he actually asks them to change their concrete behavior in relation to the weak. To a lesser extent he addresses the weak; he does not ask them to change their behavior or mature to a stronger form of faith: Paul in no way asks them to give up their specific "opinions."

We could interpret this as indicating several things: (a) Paul regards the strong as much more in need to be addressed. (b) Paul regards them as more responsible for what is causing the conflict. (c) He regards them as being in a more powerful position than the weak, or they regard themselves as being in a more powerful position. (d) The practices of the strong rather than the "opinions" of the weak are a threat to "oneness in Christ." I refer here to practices, behaviors, and not simply to attitudes, because this is what Paul is concerned about: the weak may have little power to effect change, whereas the strong do. The issue is orthopraxy rather than orthodoxy.

Here Paul addresses conflict along Jew/Gentile lines, and chapters 14–15 are inherently connected to chapters 1–11. Hence, the position and behavior of the strong likely has something to do with the "boasting" of the Gentiles, whom Paul, according to interpretations in the school Beyond the New Perspective, is addressing most strongly throughout the letter.[24] Labeling them as strong thus might not only have a positive connotation: there could also be an implied allusion to former warnings not to "be wise in your own conceit" (11:25, my trans.), warnings against any kind of boasting or arrogance. The strong are the ones who are about to forget that the gospel is "to the Jew first and also to the Greek." They are about to forget their roots, that they are "grafted in" as wild shoots into a cultivated olive tree, borne by its roots (11:17–24). They are about to forget that the advantage of the Jews is much in many ways, above all that they "were entrusted with the oracles of God" (3:2; cf. 9:4ff.). They are about to forget that "the gifts and the calling of God are irrevocable" (11:29).

They are strong, "filled with all knowledge, and able to instruct one another" (15:14). Paul hopes that when he is able to visit them, they "may be mutually encouraged by each other's faith" (1:12). Nevertheless, Paul feels the urge to write to them "boldly by way of reminder" (15:15) about what they are in danger of forgetting: their Jewish roots and the role of Israel in salvation history. This is not simply a matter of nice human relationships.

---

23. Cf. Mark Reasoner, *The Strong and the Weak: Romans 14:1–15:13 in Context* (Society for New Testament Studies Monograph Series 103; Cambridge: Cambridge University Press, 1999), esp. 61–62, 202.
24. See, e.g., Nanos, *Mystery,* 98ff.

What is at stake in and through concrete relationships between different peoples are the faithfulness of God and the oneness of God as the God of Israel and the nations and all of creation.[25]

Seen in this context, Rom 14–15 is not a mere ethical appendix to the previous "highly" theological chapters but the concrete testing ground of what otherwise would be a purely theoretical faith. If believers do not live out the consequences of faith in Christ in concrete everyday life with people who are different, then faith has no relevance at all. It is either practical or it is nothing at all.

Thus, taking the context of chapters 14–15 within the letter into account, we see that the strong in Rome most likely are the ones more in need to be addressed than the weak. They were about to forget central aspects and implications of their new faith in Christ. This led them to the conclusion that the insistence on Jewish identity was a hindrance for true κοινωνία (oneness, fellowship). Paul admonishes them "to bear (βαστάζειν) the weaknesses (ἀσθενήματα) of the weak (ἀδυνάτων)" (15:1) As indicated by his counsel, the strong presume that the only way to achieve κοινωνία (oneness) in Christ would be for all Christ-believers to become the same, with Gentile Christian identity as the norm for the true and proper identity in Christ. Throughout the letter Paul reminds them that Jewish identity is not in contradiction to faith in God through Christ; it is not a preliminary stage that has to disappear when a more mature stage is achieved. Since Gentile identity is not an obstacle to being "one in Christ," and since Gentiles do not have to become Jews, Jewish identity also is not an obstacle to being "one in Christ." Particular identities of different people are the presuppositions for, and not obstacles to, experiencing real κοινωνία, "oneness in Christ." Jewish identity is the root, the condition sine qua non, of Gentile identity in Christ and thus the strong ones not only have to tolerate it, but also to accept it and appreciate it—not only for the sake of their Jewish co-believers in Christ, but also for their own sake. Only thus could there be genuine acceptance for those who are all "one in Christ" but yet remain different.

The presupposition that Christ-believing communities need to overcome all internal differences to be really "one in Christ," is in itself a threat to exactly this same being "one in Christ." If the Christ event and being in Christ mean that the age to come is dawning, this implies the beginning of

---

25. On this see ibid., 179–201; also, with a slightly different emphasis, Tomson, *Paul and Jewish Law*, 256, saying it is not incidental that the issue of glorifying the Creator occurs in context with discussions about food and wine. God is blessed at meals, and to do so with an insecure or idolatrous consciousness would be a blasphemy to the Creator. This aspect certainly applies to 1 Cor 8–10. It is unclear whether food offered to idols is the issue in Rom 14–15, where I see Paul giving attention more to the issue of different identities in Christ rather than on food offered to idols.

realizing the Jewish messianic hope, that the God of Israel will reveal himself as the God of Israel *and* of the nations. A sign for this is that, together with the people Israel, the nations are beginning to praise the Lord. The dawning age maintains and does not eradicate the difference between Israel and the nations; hence, the messianic vision Paul relays in 15:9–12 implies a κοινωνία of worshipers who are and remain different.[26] To ask for the assimilation of one identity to the other, to ask for sameness as a presupposition for "oneness in Christ," actually means to pervert the meaning of the gospel.

Paul regards the position of the strong as powerful enough to pervert the gospel. Their attitudes and behavior could actually "injure" or even "destroy" the brother or sister for whom Christ also died (14:15, 20–21; cf. 1 Cor 8:11). This could refer to an actual and real threat to the very identity of those who are maintaining a Christian lifestyle different from the strong. Here Paul addresses a dangerous development within Gentile Christ-believing groups in Rome who have formulated their own self-understanding at the expense of, and in opposition to, Jewish identity. As the history of later Jewish-Christian relations demonstrates, Paul's warnings were obviously not well heard and appreciated.

Paul addresses the weak as well. Though they do not have to give up their διαλογισμοί (opinions, 14:1), they nevertheless are not to κρίνειν judge, 14:3–4) those who eat meat. Paul reminds them that they are not in a spiritually more advanced position than the strong, and thus must give up even that excuse for judging them. Since the strong are accepted by God, it is only his judgment that is essential (14:10). But apart from this, Paul supports the weak in their "opinions," in their adherence to their specific identity. He does not require them to change either now or in the future.

Paul reminds both the weak and the strong that the different lifestyles and food customs to which they are adhering are intimately related to their faith. In different ways they both give thanks to God and glorify him—in eating meat and in not eating meat. They should not try to convert each other to their own opinions about this but be convinced in their own minds, respectively (14:5). In this whole debate the crucial aspect about eating and drinking is that whatever they do, they should do because they are convinced that what they do is appropriate with regard to their faith. Both lifestyles are accepted by God since both can be expressions of faith in him. Both the weak and the strong should equally appreciate and accept this.[27]

---

26. On this see the work of Emmanuel Lévinas: The beginning of relationship, the beginning of ethics, is the recognition of difference, the recognition of the other as other, as different from myself. See also C. Keller, chapter 3, note 240, 109.

27. Cf. Tomson, *Paul and Jewish Law*, 250.

Nevertheless, when it comes to irritations and problems between the two groups because of the behavior of those who eat meat and drink wine, then the latter should abstain from doing so in order not to endanger peace and justice within the group. If food is a matter of debate and doubts, then the meat-eaters are the ones to give in and accommodate to those who have their doubts.

Paul asks both groups to mutually respect and accept each other in their differences. When it comes to conflicting situations, however, those in the "stronger" power position have to accommodate. Paul does not ask the "weaker" to mature or give up their peculiarities; that would actually mean asking them to give up what is related specifically to their Jewish identity, which they have to respect by all means. So, to sustain and thus to maintain peaceful relationships within these groups, they need to show mutual acceptance—not just tolerance, but real acceptance of difference between Jewish and Gentile identity—since what these groups do as people who are different is done to glorify God.

In this passage Paul clearly demands mutuality in relationships of equals, but he is well aware that even if there are only slight inequalities, it is still primarily the identity and integrity of the weaker ones that the Christ-believers need to respect. They can ensure mutuality only when they respect and protect minorities. Thus, rather than strengthening the position of the strong, to which Paul allocates himself ("we," 15:1), he strengthens the position of those who are different from him!

I do not regard this as patronizing the weak from a position that stands above such matters of indifference.[28] This would only be the case if Paul himself regarded these issues as matters of indifference, and if he himself had abandoned the law and thus given up his own Jewish identity. But Paul never calls these issues matters of indifference. They are not unimportant things that either could, or in fact should, be abandoned for higher values. God has accepted them all in their differences, as people who are and who decide to remain different. It is also not evident that Paul, although counting himself as among the strong, is in fact eating meat (cf. 1 Cor 8:13). I am not convinced that the strong and the meat-eaters are completely identical here. If they were, this might mean that Paul had actually given up his Jewish identity!

Paul rather says that meat-eating by Gentiles in Christ can be an acceptable way of life if they do it with thanksgiving and praise for the Lord (14:6; cf. 15:9–12). Accepting this, whether as a Jew or as a Gentile in Christ, indicates being strong in faith.

---

28. Contra John M. G. Barclay, "Neither Jew nor Greek: Multiculturalism and the New Perspective," in *Ethnicity and the Bible* (ed. Mark G. Brett; Leiden: Brill, 1996), 171–96.

I prefer to see here an analogy or close link to the ethics of mutuality and protection of the rights and integrity of the weaker partner in power relations, according to the ethics of the Scriptures. This is more precisely expressed in the ethics of the covenant: I am your God, and you are my people, with obligations to obey the commandments to protect and respect the strangers, widows, and orphans (e.g., Exod 19–20; Deut 26).

This interpretation is based on the presupposition that Paul was firmly rooted in Judaism and that we can most appropriately understand him from this perspective. The flow of his argument in this crucial practical issue addressed in Rom 14:1–15:13 is thoroughly halakic.[29] But again, Paul's way of thinking is not only rooted in Judaism in a "technical" way; the background of his practical arguing also is Jewish, as parallels in rabbinic and Hellenistic Jewish literature indicate.[30] His strong emphasis on difference and diversity reflects the highly esteemed pluralism of the Pharisaic-rabbinic tradition.[31] Paul's thinking is rooted in, and part of, this tradition, which itself in turn is rooted in the Scriptures. Paul's exhortation that "each of us will be accountable to God" (14:12) resonates with Prov 16:2: "All one's ways may be pure in one's own eyes, but the LORD weighs the spirit."

Here we have an example of Scriptural reasoning in Paul, as is his exhortation to "pursue what makes for peace and for mutual upbuilding" (Rom 14:19). This verse is based on Ps 34:15 and is also paralleled by a saying of Hillel: "Be of the disciples of Aaron, loving peace and pursuing peace, loving mankind and bringing them nigh to the Torah" (*m. 'Abot* 1:12). Paul is theologizing and developing thinking, not in a set of systematic theological statements, but in a process of negotiation that is always related in various ways to the people, the context, and the actual situation. These may change, and thus theologizing in a Pauline way means to be involved in an ongoing dialogical process of negotiation.

This perspective on Paul could present the apostle as a source of inspiration and a model for a feminist perspective in several respects:

---

29. See Tomson's analysis of Rom 14:1–15:13 in his *Paul and Jewish Law,* 236–58, esp. 236–37.

30. See ibid., 248–49, reporting discussions about purity laws and showing that Paul's statement, "Nothing is unclean in itself" (Rom 14:14; cf. 14:20), is not, as traditionally taken, a sign for Paul's abandonment of the law. Instead, it conforms well with an example Tomson cites, Rabban Yohanan ben Zakkai's reason for the purity ritual with the red heifer (Num 19): "By our lives! A corpse would not render impure, nor water purify, were it not for the decree of the Holy One, blessed be He" (from the medieval *Midrash Tanhuma,* quoted at www.mtholyoke.edu/~cemulshi/whatis.html).

31. See ibid., 251: "Although not widely recognized as such, pluralism was highly esteemed within the dominant Rabbinic tradition and was in a way essential to it. In the last few generations before the destruction of the Temple, the Pharisaic-Rabbinic movement was divided into the schools of Shammai and Hillel. They differed on such a large number of haggadic and halakic issues, sometimes quite powerfully, that it may be justified to speak of two movements. According to Rabbinic tradition, this was accepted as a fact of life and both schools cultivated mutual relations."

1. We see Paul as thinking theologically in a particular context and communicating with specific Christ-believing communities in an ongoing theological and practical dialogue about specific issues arising from the everyday life of these communities.

2. We see Paul as focusing on the relationality of faith, both theologically and practically. He is paying special attention to the need for mutual respect and acceptance in a relationship of equals.

3. Paul is aware of power issues involved in relationships and emphasizes the need for special respect and protection for the ones in the weaker position in a situation of conflict, to maintain mutuality in the relationship.

4. As a presupposition for a proper relationship and real mutuality in Christ, Paul stresses the need for diversity rather than sameness.

We thus gain a picture of Paul not in opposition to, but as part of, first-century Judaism. He is strongly arguing for mutual recognition and support for people who were and remain different. What he teaches with regard to human relations, in his anthropocentric focus, he roots firmly in his theocentrism.[32] Thus, Paul gives the admonition, "Let all be fully convinced in their own minds" (14:5), because "we will all stand before the judgment seat of God" (14:10). The Christ-believers ought to "welcome one another, therefore, as Christ has welcomed you, for the glory of God" (15:7). In mutually appreciating their differences, their aim is that together, as Israel and the nations, they may glorify and bless God as the God of all nations and of the whole creation.

These issues, which the school Beyond the New Perspective is intensely examining in Romans, resemble some of the key matters that feminist theologians address, as they search to reformulate women's identity and gender relations from a feminist perspective. Although feminist issues are not identical with those Paul is addressing in Romans, the way he approaches the problems of the early Christ-believing groups in Rome can be of interest for contemporary feminist theologians.

Feminist Issues and Paul's Theologizing

Particularity

One of the key issues stressed in feminist theologies is the strong emphasis on particularity and contextuality. To do theology means always to do it from a particular perspective and from within a specific context. Thus, any

---

32. See ibid., 250.

interpretation is particular and contextual, either implicitly or explicitly.[33] There is no detached neutral position of objective scholarship. We can see the relevance of this, for example, in the issue of the definition of female identity.[34]

Traditional interpretation has used women as the negative foil in depicting the ideal human being. This is similar to the tendencies of formulating Christian identity in antithesis to Judaism, or using Judaism as a negative foil—which Paul seems to address in Rome and which has been dominant throughout Christian history. The traditional ideal human had close similarities to the white "Christian" man and identified the highest ability attributed to him as his capacity for reasoning. This idealism saw women as being all that men were not. It universalized the identity of the white Christian rational man, thus oppressing and devaluing anything that did and does not conform to the ideal. This false ideal has had a major impact especially on women but also on people of other faiths and cultures. It did not allow for differences and diversity on a basis of equality. In such an ideal, there has been room for difference only in a negative way and to fit a male perspective. The other—the woman—was of lesser value. Relationships of equals were possible only among those who were the "same." There was no possibility for women to formulate their own identity from their own perspective.

After critically deconstructing this universalization of one—male—identity, feminist scholars could demonstrate that this was an expression of one particular perspective, a male perspective only. Feminists in theology also began to formulate their own identity from within their own perspective. This enterprise has similarities with discovering new territory: it means to do something for which no given patterns actually exist. Thus, feminist theorists and theologians have been and are traveling on a variety of routes in the search to formulate women's identity.[35] Apart from claiming their own perspective, feminists emphasize that any formulation or definition of identity is specific, contextual, and particular. This context includes the concrete experience of everyday life of women (and men), that encompasses the material aspects of life as well as the psychological and social ones. We need to root these theological insights in, and relate them to, these concrete aspects

---

33. Thus declares Elizabeth Linell Cady, *Religion, Theology, and American Public Life* (Albany: State University of New York Press, 1993), 143: "The interpretation and evaluation of religious narratives and symbols cannot be prosecuted in abstraction from their instantiation in specific contexts. Far from having static, essential meanings that can be retrieved from a text, they are cultural strategies that cannot be *deciphered except through their embodiment in local settings.*"

34. In chap. 3, see subsec. "Identity and Question," 97ff, in sec. "Contemporary Ways of Thinking"; sec. "Issues of Identity, Diversity, and Mutuality," 110.

35. See subsec. "Identity and Question," in sec. "Contemporary Ways of Thinking," in chap. 3, 97ff.

of life if we are going to make sense and find any meaning for women in the contemporary world.[36]

As shown above, this project coheres with strands in recent research that stress the need to understand interpreters in their specific contexts, including Paul and his own theologizing.[37] Feminist scholars maintain that the theological statements in Paul's letters are expressions not of a universal but of a particular theology, addressing particular problems of specific Christ-believing groups. They see Paul as theologizing in a way similar to what feminist theologians are advocating. Consistent with this kind of theologizing is Paul's emphasis on the legitimacy of particular identities, contrasting with any attempts to universalize different identities into one and the same Christian identity. In Romans we see Paul resisting tendencies of Gentiles "in Christ" to formulate their own identity at the expense of others, Jewish Christians. He strongly warns these Gentiles "in Christ" against universalizing their particular identity and making it the norm for all those "in Christ." Here again, we find Paul stressing aspects similar to those flagged in feminist theologies.

Difference and Diversity

The emphasis on particularity implies a further study on difference and diversity. As feminists came to recognize the particularity and contextuality of any interpretations and theological statements, they also accepted the need to recognize positive value in diversity and difference. Because theological statements can only be made from particular perspectives, one has to allow for different perspectives, for pluralism within theology. This applies to feminist as well as other theologies. Consequently, in a volume of essays about the future of feminist theology recently published, the authors mostly speak of "feminist theologies" rather than of feminist theology.[38]

When looking again at the identity issue, we find feminist research in general—and in theology in particular—stressing the need to recognize differences between women. The first wave of feminism had stressed the sameness of women in their struggles for emancipation. In further development,

---

36. In this context some feminist theologians speak of "body theology" or "embodiment." See, e.g., Melissa Raphael, *Thealogy and Embodiment: The Post-Patriarchal Reconstruction of Female Sacrality* (Sheffield: Sheffield Academic Press, 1996); Sally MacFague, *The Body of God: An Ecological Theology* (Minneapolis: Fortress, 1994); Elisabeth Moltmann-Wendel, *I Am My Body: New Ways of Embodiment* (London: SCM, 1994).

37. In chap. 4, 133ff, see sec. "Contextuality of Paul's Statements" and following sections.

38. See Deborah Sawyer and Diane M. Collier, eds., *Is There a Future for Feminist Theology?* (Sheffield: Sheffield Academic Press, 1999).

women recognized the need to positively appreciate difference and diversity among themselves.[39]

There is no one and the same female identity everywhere and at all times. What it means to be and live as a woman means different things to different women in different places, in different situations, and at different times in history. As feminist theologians maintain, there is a need to recognize the particularity and contextuality of any kind of theologizing. This applies also to formulating male and female identity from a Christian perspective. Since we can live human life only in a particular way in a specific context at a particular time in history, we have to recognize that we can live it only in difference and diversity. Sameness, in fact, is an illusion or an artificial construct, and it cannot be presupposed as a condition for a relationship of equals. This applies to relationships within as well as across gender boundaries. There is no one and the same female identity, just as there is no one and the same male identity. Moreover, what "female" and "male" actually means is not something that we can define once and forever and for all; instead, it is a matter of continuous and new negotiations across fluid boundaries. Feminist research emphasizes that real diversity and the proper recognition of difference definitely provide a presupposition for real relationships of equals.

In Rom 14–15 Paul actually strongly teaches that in order to be "one in Christ" (cf. Gal 3:28), those who are different need not, and in fact should not, become the same. To have "faith in Christ" requires Jews and Gentiles to remain different and to recognize each other as people who are and remain different. Thus Paul urges: "Let each of you lead the life that the Lord has assigned, to which God called you" (1 Cor 7:17). If God is the "one God of Israel and the nations," this requires that Gentiles as Gentiles rejoice with his people who remain his people (cf. Rom 15:8–12). Therefore, we have not found a Paul who, out of a hierarchical position of power, urges people to subordinate themselves to each other. He certainly does not promote and support the position of those who obviously have more power, the strong. In his urgent teaching on the positive recognition of difference and diversity as well as his special attention to the needs of those with less power, the weak, we find counsels that strongly support contemporary feminist issues.

Mutuality and Relationality

Feminist theologies have also promoted the issues of relatedness and mutuality. People could use the emphasis on diversity and difference as an argument

---

39. See subsec. "Difference and Diversity," in sec. "Contemporary Ways of Thinking," 103ff; and sec. "Issues of Identity, Diversity, and Mutuality," 110ff.

in favor of the separation of those who are different into discrete entities that have nothing to do with each other. They could use it as justification for ethnocentrism or apartheid, and also with regard to gender differences and relations. Feminist theologians certainly do not so intend; instead, they stress the need to recognize and appreciate difference, and most of them are aware of possible dangers inherent in this focus. They stress the acknowledgment of difference and diversity (as noted above) as a presupposition behind real relationships, rather than in support of separation.

Sheila Greeve Davaney sees positive values in this view:

> Relatedness and dependency do not vitiate distinctiveness; on the contrary, they provide the bases out of which uniqueness emerges and upon which it depends. Distinctiveness and difference are not the corollary of autonomy and separation but of connectedness and the capacity for relation.[40]

Over against the ideal of the autonomous rational man, feminist theologians teach that relatedness and mutuality are basic factors not only of human life but also of life generally.[41] Even such an individual human activity as "knowing" is always an act of "knowing together," a reciprocal or mutual interaction of subjects. To recognize that we are mutually dependent upon, and related to, each other is the beginning of ethics, as Catherine Keller has stated.[42]

As we have seen, this also actually is Paul's primary concern in the Letter to the Romans. He addresses most prominently the relationships of people who are different. Paul strongly demands mutual appreciation for those now related to each other "in Christ," stressing that they are all "one in Christ," though they may live as somewhat separate subgroups. Contrary to traditional and some feminist interpretations, this does not mean that they all have to become the same, but that they ought to recognize, bear, and "welcome one another" in their difference as equals (Rom 15:7). Paul is concerned with those "in Christ" as *groups* rather than just as individuals. The apostle thus emphasizes the relational implication of faith, the ethics of relationships. Those "in Christ" ought to "pursue what makes for peace and for mutual upbuilding" (14:19). We "must please our neighbor for the good

---

40. Sheila Greeve Davaney, *Pragmatist Historicism: A Theology for the Twenty-First Century* (Albany: State University of New York Press, 2000), 66.

41. One example is Catherine Keller's "Seeking and Sucking: On Relation and Essence in Feminist Theology," in *Horizons in Feminist Theology: Identity, Tradition, and Norms* (ed. Rebecca Chopp and Sheila G. Davaney; Minneapolis: Fortress, 1997), 76; also MacFague, *Body of God*; Mary Grey, "Expelled Again from Eden: Facing Difference through Connection," *Feminist Theology* 21 (May 1999): 8–20; Elisabeth Moltmann-Wendel, *I Am My Body: New Ways of Embodiment* (London: SCM, 1994);

42. Keller, "Seeking and Sucking," 74.

purpose of building up the neighbor" (15:2). Paul prays that God "may . . . grant you to live in harmony with one another, in accordance with Christ Jesus" (15:5). This ethics of relationality is not a mere appendix to aspects commonly regarded as more central to faith; instead, such ethics is absolutely central to faith in Christ.

Again, we have found similarities between Paul's theologizing and feminist theologians, who maintain that relatedness is basic and central for life on earth and among human beings.

Paul emphasizes such an ethics and presents a theology of mutuality in the context of relationships of people who are different. Hence, the dialogue with Paul in this aspect could be illuminating and inspiring in the contemporary search for an ethics and a theology of mutual relationality in difference, whether in the realm of gender, intercultural, or interfaith relations.

ᗑ **7** ᗑ

Conclusion

The changing perspectives in Pauline studies and feminist theologies outlined in this study indicate that we seem to be at the edge of a process of revolutionary change in theological research. Postmodern/postcritical approaches—which began to emerge in the aftermath of the twentieth-century ruptures of civilization, particularly after the two World Wars—are challenging traditional hermeneutical presuppositions. Scholars have initiated paradigm shifts in a variety of disciplines.

Philosophical strands such as the critical theory of the Frankfurter School or deconstructionism in France have challenged Western Enlightenment rationality and patterns of thinking and their hegemonial claims. These approaches teach that there are different ways and patterns of thinking, different kinds of "logic." Western rationality, based on Graeco-Roman categories of thinking, can think of differences only in terms of dualistic contradictions that are exclusive of each other. To achieve coherence and oneness, rationalists try to eliminate differences and contradictions. The devastating impact of Western Enlightenment ways of thinking, when universalized and combined with hegemonic claims of power, has become obvious. Derrida's "deconstructing" approach of "fragmented thinking," however, opposes any kind of closed or so-called coherent system of thought and any presumption of sameness. He emphasizes, similar to Emmanuel Lévinas, that the recognition of difference, and of the "other" as different from me, is the beginning of thinking as well as of ethics. Deconstructionists regard diversity and contradictions as constituents of human discourse.

Aspects of such postcritical thinking are also present in postcritical theological approaches as expressed in the series Radical Traditions.[1] These writers are advocating a return to the text and rediscovering modes of scriptural reasoning. In these approaches they are formulating a new awareness and viewing understanding and interpretation as part of a process of an interrelationship of texts and communities of interpretation. They oppose universalism and stress the dialogical, contextual, and thus limited character of any interpretation.

Feminist theories and theologies have played a significant role in starting these changing processes. Feminism of the early 1970s began as a liberation movement. Feminist theology shares with other liberation theologies the resolve to bring to speech the perspective and the needs of those oppressed and excluded from mainstream discourse. Various feminist approaches emphasize the particularity, the contextuality, and the limitation of any perspective. Other perspectives and approaches have only just begun to notice the implications and consequences of feminist perspectives. Feminist perspectives have actually also initiated a paradigm shift in the realm of logic and patterns of thinking, a shift that has had and will further have essential implications for other perspectives as well.

In biblical studies the feminist paradigm shift has led women to reread and reclaim the biblical texts and the biblical tradition. Feminist interpretation had to deal with the consequences of centuries of one-sided particular male-dominated patterns of interpretation, along with the fact that the biblical traditions themselves are rooted in a patriarchal worldview. Thus, feminist interpretations face the challenge of trying to look at biblical texts from "nowhere," from somewhere no woman has yet been, because for so long traditional malestream patterns have been the only ones we have known, and we have needed to initiate and develop new ones. From its beginnings, feminist interpretations have successfully established new patterns and developed new tools, such as the "hermeneutics of suspicion," in order to break through layers of traditional patterns of interpretations. Scholars exposed some biblical traditions as being hopelessly repressive and thus needing to be rejected from a feminist liberation perspective; other biblical traditions surprisingly revealed liberating potential when read from a feminist perspective. Feminist scholars have done excellent research in many fields of biblical studies and have gained refreshing and illuminating insights.

---

1. See, e.g., Tikva Frymer-Kensky et al., eds., *Christianity in Jewish Terms* (Radical Traditions: Theology in a Postcritical Key; Boulder, Colo.: Westview, 2000).

With some surprise, therefore, I have noticed that, except for some rare exceptions,[2] the situation is different with regard to Pauline studies. The analysis of some feminist interpretations of Romans has shown that they have not fulfilled their claim to move beyond traditional malestream patterns of interpretation. Instead, these patterns have somewhat unconsciously been the basis of feminist interpretations. The prominent role Paul plays in traditional malestream theology likely does not render him an attractive object of study from a feminist perspective. Although Pauline studies from a feminist perspective are increasing, there still exists no book-length feminist interpretation of a Pauline letter, but only brief overview commentaries and articles on specific texts or topics in Paul. In their interpretations these articles often apply thematic or systematic frameworks that have not previously been critically analyzed. This is a trap that is most likely to lead to the application of traditional malestream patterns of interpretation. It is not surprising that, from a feminist perspective, the images of Paul and his writings emerging from these interpretations are negative. We must conclude that the feminist critique of traditional patterns of interpretation, in most cases, is not radical enough when it comes to the study of Paul.

In general Pauline studies, too, a major paradigm shift is under way. The work of Albert Schweitzer, W. D. Davies, Krister Stendahl, and the Scandinavian school has initiated this change.[3] Nevertheless, the New Perspective on Paul began explicitly to emerge only after E. P. Sanders published *Paul and Palestinian Judaism*.[4] It has its roots in different earlier approaches that did not receive proper recognition in their time, such as the work of Welsh scholar W. D. Davies. Over a period of more than thirty years, substantial research in the Pauline Letters has led to innovative insights, and an image of Paul has begun to emerge that does not stand entirely in opposition to first-century Judaism. But the New Perspective did not fulfill the promises it had evoked. It had started as an approach that was conscious of the anti-Jewish patterns of interpretation in Pauline studies, especially of the devastating impact of the Reformation doctrine of justification by faith. The New Perspective actually did succeed in demonstrating that this pattern of interpretation was in fact reflecting the sixteenth-century conflict between the Reformation movement and the Roman-Catholic church, rather than Paul's theological thinking. Nevertheless, many New

---

2. Such as, for instance, Luise Schottroff; see Claudia Janssen, Luise Schottroff, and Beate Wehn, eds., *Paulus: Umstrittene Traditionen-Lebendige Theologie: Eine feministische Lektüre* (Gütersloh: Chr. Kaiser/Gütersloher Verlagshaus, 2001); ET, *Journal for the Study of the New Testament* 79 (2000).
3. The bibliography lists some of their relevant works.
4. E. P. Sanders, *Paul and Palestinian Judaism: A Comparison of Patterns of Religion* (Philadelphia: Fortress, 1977).

Perspective scholars continue to depict Jewish identity as at least somehow anachronistic in relation to Christian identity.

Some New Perspective scholars see Jewish identity markers, moreover, as an expression of narrow ethnocentrism, and thus again devalue parts of the Jewish law. They see Paul at least as partly in opposition to Judaism and the Torah, and divide Judaism into a "good" part, to which Paul was still adhering, and a "bad" part, which he was strongly opposing. Through this division, anti-Jewish patterns of interpretation are still present in this strand of Pauline studies, despite its declared attempts to do otherwise. In my opinion the New Perspective, in its critique of traditional interpretation of Paul, has not been radical enough.

Since the New Perspective did not fulfill its initial promises, a number of scholars have moved on to a position labeled Beyond the New Perspective. They have continued their research where the New Perspective had hesitated to follow through the possibilities it had opened up. J. Christaan Beker, for example, has convincingly demonstrated that Paul's theological thinking and arguing is always related to the concrete life and problems of his communities.[5]

Nevertheless, Beker did not see that his emphasis on the contextuality of Paul's letters actually implied not only the contextuality in and of his communities, but also the location of Paul entirely within first-century Judaism. Peter Tomson has elaborated on this and demonstrated that Paul, his life, and his ways of thinking are entirely embedded within first-century Judaism. He presupposes no break or critique anticipating that Paul would start to move out of the tradition of his people. The parting of the ways was not yet in sight—but developed only after Paul in a vivid and diverse process until the fourth century. Tomson has shown that Paul's theologizing is an interplay between contemporary issues and the Scriptures, which were the Scriptures of Israel. This in itself contradicts any attempt to universalize Paul's theological thinking. It also is impossible to detach his thinking from the concrete everyday life of actual people. All these aspects indicate that Paul was firmly rooted in first-century Judaism. Mark Nanos and William S. Campbell presuppose close links with, and ongoing interaction between, the synagogues and early Christ-believing communities. Nanos depicts them mostly as still part of the synagogue communities and thus part of Judaism.

The most recent research of Daniel Boyarin and Judith Lieu supports this approach. They both are depicting a scenario of the history of the early relationship of Jews and Christ-believers that is far more complex and indicates

---

5. See, for example, J. Christiaan Beker, "Recasting Pauline Theology: The Coherence-Contingency Scheme as Interpretive Model," in *Thessalonians, Philippians, Galatians, Philemon* (vol. 1 of *Pauline Theology;* ed. Jouette M. Bassler; Minneapolis: Fortress, 1991), 15–24.

far more fluidity in terms of boundaries for a much longer period than so far presumed.[6] These new depictions of early Jewish-Christian relations will have far-reaching consequences for the entire field of theology and biblical studies, and for Pauline studies in particular. My study shows that the results of such research particularly affect the perception of Paul's way of thinking. Paul was rooted in the scriptural traditions of his people and thus familiar with a type of reasoning that does not primarily and exclusively follow Graeco-Roman philosophical categories. Paul was theologizing rather differently from Western Enlightenment rationality. The postcritical challenge of Western traditions of thought—with its emphasis on openness and diversity of life and thought processes—provides us with a contemporary rationale that supports these approaches. Following them, we try to gain a really fresh look at Paul and his letters, beyond the layers of traditional interpretation. When we discover that Paul's life and theological thinking are based on scriptural reasoning, we recognize him as a most interesting dialogue partner for strands of research such as postcritical theology.

This radicalization of the New Perspective promises to be a really new approach in Pauline studies, actually moving beyond the layers of domination, particularly attitudes of anti-Judaism, in the interpretation of Paul. In the formulation of Christian identity, it can lead us beyond the devastating tradition that used the "other" only as a negative contrast.

The analysis of Rom 14–15 in this study has demonstrated that, when we read from a perspective locating Paul consistently within Judaism, we find a Paul who actually is strongly opposing tendencies of the strong dominating the weak in the Christ-believing communities of Rome. Here Paul is clearly advocating the right of people who are different to remain different: he is advocating diversity rather than uniformity in Christ. He is emphasizing a crucial aspect of faith, that people who are different must respect and support each other mutually in their abiding differences. In Christ, they do not have to overcome differences. Instead, they are a presupposition for real unity (Rom 15:5–12).

The misunderstanding of the gospel in the Christ-believing communities of Rome threatened the weak in their particular identity. The balance of power in these groups was not to the advantage of the weak; thus the stronger majorities could dominate the weak. Where one group in power dominates another by universalizing its own position, equality and mutuality in the

---

6. See Daniel Boyarin, *Dying for God: Martyrdom and the Making of Christianity and Judaism* (Stanford: Stanford University Press, 1999), esp. 1–21; and Judith M. Lieu, "'Impregnable Ramparts and Walls of Iron': Boundary and Identity in Early 'Judaism' and 'Christianity,'" *New Testament Studies* 48.3 (July 2002): 297–313.

relationship are at stake. Paul seems well aware of these group dynamics and deals with them in a differentiated way. He addresses these groups not as an appendix to his otherwise theological letter, as perceived in many traditional interpretations, but as the necessary consequences of faith in action. Since he is relating the Scriptures to contemporary issues, he does not formulate consistent, conceptualized theological arguments; instead, he is responding to contextual issues in daily life that determine the parameters of the discussion.

We thus find a Paul who, rather than writing timeless theology in Romans, is relating his theological thinking to a particular social context in a process of negotiation. He is supporting the differing identities of the others and sharply opposing the attempt to homogenize and universalize one particular identity at the expense of another. And he explains that to relate to each other in Christ implies welcoming each other in faith, as Christ has welcomed them. Paul reminds the Christ-believing communities in Rome, and especially the strong ones, that mutual encouragement and support in diversity in the particular contexts of their lives is essential to living in Christ, for the glory of God.

Most Christian traditions have attributed to women the role of the other, and this usually did not imply a positive valuation of their lives and abilities. Hence, feminist approaches pay particular attention to any oppressive and dominating tendencies in Christian tradition and interpretation. They rightly reveal universalism—the formulation of identity at the expense of those who are different, and the urge to uniformity in order to achieve unity—as an oppressive and even totalitarian tool for dominating women and others who do not conform to the dominant ideal. Over against such dominating patterns, not only of interpretation but also of thought categories and structures of society more generally, feminist theories and theologies recognize the need for particularity and contextuality. They stress the formulation of women's identity and Christian identity from a feminist perspective, and count diversity as a presupposition for real unity. There are obvious similarities between such feminist emphases and postcritical approaches, as well as with tendencies in Pauline studies Beyond the New Perspective.

Feminist research on Paul has set out to probe behind layers of traditional interpretation of his letters and to pull out the roots of patterns of domination and oppression inherent in Christian tradition. In my view, most of these approaches are not radical enough. They are right in their critique of the tradition of domination in Pauline interpretation, but they do not actually present an adequate critique of the Pauline Letters themselves. The analysis of Rom 14–15 has demonstrated that an image of Paul differing radically from the traditional one does emerge when we change perspectives radically enough.

The issues of particularity, identity, and diversity are not so remote in the Pauline Letters as traditional interpretation might make us think they are.

Approaches to Paul in the stream Beyond the New Perspective, although from a different perspective, try to view Paul's letters really afresh, and thus they face similar problems and share emphases similar to feminist approaches. They address issues of power, oppression, and domination in Christian tradition and in the formulation of Christian identity. Also, they have emerged from a history of violence against, and devaluation of, others who are and remain different. Insights from Beyond the New Perspective thus might actually reveal interesting aspects of Paul's theological thinking and activity, aspects relevant also to a feminist perspective of Paul.

It could prove interesting and illuminating for feminist research on Paul to enter into dialogue with strands of research Beyond the New Perspective, whose agenda, though different, shows some remarkable analogies to feminist studies. For perspectives Beyond the New Perspective, it would be equally fruitful to enter into dialogue with feminist research on Paul. Over the last three decades feminist theologians have developed important tools and excellent expertise in order to find aspects of domination and tendencies of oppression in biblical texts and their interpretation. As Elisabeth Schüssler Fiorenza has demonstrated with regard to rhetorical critical approaches, we need carefully to address and analyze implicit ideologies of domination. Since it can easily happen that, unwittingly, new research applies traditional patterns of interpretation, such attention is crucial. For instance, some rhetorical analyses are disappointing because they are not aware of the power issues involved in rhetoric.[7] Feminist scholars are not immune to such traps, as the analysis of some feminist commentaries of Romans has shown, but they might be more aware of such hidden presuppositions than are their male colleagues.

Since Paul's theological thinking has been used ideologically as a means to legitimate domination and oppression, we need to make a careful analysis of his letters and focus on these power issues if we want to move beyond the failure to address these aspects of Christian tradition. An exchange of research results, cooperation, and serious dialogue—among feminist approaches, approaches Beyond the New Perspective, and postcritical theological approaches—could be stimulating and lead to illuminating new insights in Pauline studies. Such joint efforts would lead to whole new fields of research, especially surrounding the issues of domination and power. It is

---

7. See sec. "Rhetorical Perspectives," in chap. 4, 136ff.

not the purpose of this study to elaborate further on this matter. This is an issue that requires more than one further book-length study. Just beginning to rise above the horizon are the potentials for serious interrelation and interaction between feminist research and some recent strands of Pauline studies, as well as critical consideration of insights from postcritical theologies and deconstructionism. Such an interaction would be mutually beneficial for all those involved in this dialogue. It could be a significant contribution to a revolutionary shift and development in Pauline studies. And it definitely could be a contribution to a theology of mutuality for the twenty-first century.

✄ BIBLIOGRAPHY ∾

Adorno, Theodor W. "The Actuality of Philosophy." *Telos* 31 (spring 1977): 120–33.

Adorno, Theodore W., and Max Horkheimer. *Dialectic of Enlightenment.* Translated by John Cumming. New York: Herder & Herder, 1972. Translation of *Dialektik der Aufklärung* (1947). Original, *Philosophische Fragmente.* Amsterdam: Querido, 1944.

Alcoff, Linda. "Cultural Feminism versus Post-Structuralism: The Identity Crisis in Feminist Theory." Pages 330–55 in *The Second Wave: A Reader in Feminist Theory.* Edited by Linda Nicholson. New York: Routledge, 1997.

Alexander, Philip S. "Hellenism and Hellenization as Problematic Historiographical Categories." Pages 63–80 in *Paul beyond the Judaism/ Hellenism Divide.* Edited by Troels Engberg-Pedersen. Louisville: Westminster John Knox, 2001.

———. "Jewish Aramaic Translations of Hebrew Scriptures." Pages 217–53 in *Mikra, Text, Translation, Reading, and Interpretation of the Hebrew Bible in Ancient Judaism and Early Christianity.* Edited by Martin J. Mulder. Assen: Van Gorcum, 1988.

———. "Quid Athenis et Hierosolymis? Rabbinic Midrash and Hermeneutics in the Graeco-Roman World." Pages 101–24 in *A Tribute to Geza Vermes.* Edited by R. R. Davies and R. T. White. Sheffield: JSOT Press, 1990.

Anderson, R. Dean, Jr. *Ancient Rhetorical Theory and Paul.* Rev. ed. Leuven: Peeters, 1999.

Arendt, Hannah. *The Origins of Totalitarianism.* New York: Harcourt Brace
    Jovanovich, 1979. Reprint of *The Burden of Our Time.* London: Secker &
    Warburg, 1951.

Armour, Ellen T. *Deconstruction, Feminist Theology, and the Problem of
    Difference: Subverting the Race/Gender Divide.* Chicago: University of
    Chicago Press, 1999.

Baeck, Leo. *Paulus, die Pharisäer und das Neue Testament.* Frankfurt: Ner
    Tamid, 1961.

Barclay, John M. G. "'Do We Undermine the Law?' A Study of Romans
    14.1–15.6." Pages 287–308 in *Paul and the Mosaic Law.* Edited by James
    D. G. Dunn. Tübingen: Mohr, 1996.

————. *Jews in the Mediterranean Diaspora: From Alexander to Trajan
    (323 BCE–117 CE).* Edinburgh: T&T Clark, 1996.

————. "Neither Jew nor Greek: Multiculturalism and the New
    Perspective." Pages 171–96 in *Ethnicity and the Bible.* Edited by Mark G.
    Brett. Leiden: Brill, 1996.

Barr, James. "'Abba, Father' and the Familiarity of Jesus' Speech." *Theology
    Today* 91 (1988): 173–79.

————. "Abba Isn't Daddy." *Journal of Theological Studies* 39 (1988):
    28–47.

————. *The Semantics of Biblical Language.* London: Oxford University
    Press, 1961. Philadelphia: Trinity Press International, 1991.

Barth, Markus. *The People of God.* JSOT Suppl. Series 5. Sheffield: JSOT
    Press, 1983.

————. "St. Paul—a Good Jew." *Horizons in Biblical Theology: An
    International Dialogue* 1 (1979): 7–45.

Bartsch, Hans-Werner. "Die antisemitischen Gegner des Paulus in
    Römerbrief." Pages 27–43 in *Antijudaismus im Neuen Testament?* Edited
    by W. Eckert et al. Munich: Chr. Kaiser, 1969.

Bassler, Jouette M. "Divine Impartiality in Paul's Letter to the Romans."
    Novum Testamentum 26 (1984): 43–58.

————, ed. *Thessalonians, Philippians, Galatians, Philemon.* Vol. 1 of
    Pauline Theology. Minneapolis: Fortress, 1991.

Bauer, W., F. W. Danker, W. F. Arndt, and F. W. Gingrich. *A Greek-English
    Lexicon of the New Testament and other Early Christian Literature.* 3d ed.
    Chicago: University of Chicago Press, 1999.

Baur, Ferdinand Christian. *Das Christenthum und die christliche Kirche der
    drei ersten Jahrhunderte.* 2d ed. Tübingen: Fues, 1860. Reprinted as vol.
    3 of *Ausgewählte Werke in Einzelausgaben.* Edited by Klaus Scholder.
    Stuttgart-Bad, Cannstatt: Frommenn, 1966.

———. "Die Christuspartei in der korinthischen Gemeinde, der Gegensatz des paulinischen und petrinischen Christentums in der ältesten Kirche." *Tübinger Zeitschrift für Theologie* 4 (1831): 61–206. Reprinted as pages 1–144 in vol. 1 of *Ausgewählte Werke in Einzelausgaben*. Edited by Klaus Scholder. Stuttgart-Bad, Cannstatt: Frommenn, 1963.

Beauvoir, Simone de. *The Second Sex*. Translated and edited by H. M. Parshley. New York: Knopf, 1953; Reprinted, London: Pan, 1988. Original, *Le deuxième sexe*. Paris: Gallimard, 1949.

Beck, Evelyn T., ed. *Nice Jewish Girls*. Trumansburg, N.Y.: Crossing, 1982.

Beker, J. Christiaan. "The Faithfulness of God and the Priority of Israel in Paul's Letter to the Romans." Pages 10–16 in *Christians among Jews and Gentiles: Essays in Honor of Krister Stendahl on His Sixty-Fifth Birthday*. Edited by George W. E. Nickelsburg and George W. MacRae. Philadelphia: Fortress, 1986. See also pages 327–32 in *The Romans Debate*. Edited by Karl Donfried. Rev., expanded ed. Peabody, Mass.: Hendrickson, 1991.

———. *Paul the Apostle: The Triumph of God in Life and Thought*. Edinburgh: T&T Clark, 1980.

———. "Recasting Pauline Theology: The Coherence-Contingency Scheme as Interpretive Model." Pages 15–24 in *Thessalonians, Philippians, Galatians, Philemon*. Vol. 1 of *Pauline Theology*. Edited by Jouette M. Bassler. Minneapolis: Fortress, 1991.

Benhabib, Seyla. "The Generalized and the Concrete Other: Visions of the Autonomous Self." *Praxis International* 5.4 (1986): 402–24.

———. *The Reluctant Modernism of Hannah Arendt*. Thousand Oaks, Calif.: Sage Publications, 1996.

———. *Situating the Self: Gender, Community, and Postmodernism in Contemporary Ethics*. New York: Routledge, 1992.

Best, Steven, and Douglas Kellner. *Postmodern Theory: Critical Interrogations*. London: Macmillan, 1991.

Betz, Hans Dieter. *Paulus und die sokratische Tradition*. Tübingen: Mohr, 1972.

Bloch, Renée. "Moise dans la tradition rabbinique." *Cahiers Sioniens* 8 (1954): 211–85.

Bonhoeffer, Dietrich. *Letters and Papers from Prison*. Edited by Bethge Eberhard. Enlarged ed. London: SCM Press 1971.

Bordo, Susan. "Feminism, Postmodernism, and Gender-Skepticism." Pages 133–56 in *Feminism/Postmodernism*. Edited by Linda J. Nicholson. New York: Routledge, 1990.

Bornkamm, Günther. "The Letter to the Romans as Paul's Last Will and Testament." *Australian Biblical Review* 11 (1963): 2–14. GT, "Der

Römerbrief als Testament des Paulus." Pages 120–39 in vol. 2 of his *Geschichte und Glaube.* Vol. 4 of *Gesammelte Aufsätze.* Munich: Chr. Kaiser, 1971.

Borresen, Kari E., ed. *Image of God and Gender Models in Judeo-Christian Tradition.* Oslo: Solum, 1991.

Boyarin, Daniel. *Dying for God: Martyrdom and the Making of Christianity and Judaism.* The Lancaster/Yarnton Lectures in Judaism and Other Religions for 1998. Stanford: Stanford University Press, 1999.

———. *A Radical Jew: Paul and the Politics of Identity.* Berkeley: University of California Press, 1994.

Braidotti, Rosi. "Patterns of Dissonance: Women and/in Philosophy." Pages 108–23 (119–20) in *Feministische Philosophie.* Edited by Herta Nagl-Docekal. Vienna: Oldenbourg, 1990.

Brändle, Rudolf, and Ekkehard W. Stegemann. "The Formation of the First 'Christian Congregations' in Rome in the Context of the Jewish Congregations." Pages 117–27 in *Judaism and Christianity in First-Century Rome.* Edited by Karl P. Donfried and Peter Richardson. Grand Rapids: Eerdmans, 1998.

Brock, Rita Nakashima. *Journeys by Heart: A Christology of Erotic Power.* New York: Crossroad, 1988.

Brooten, Bernadette J. "Jewish Women's History in the Roman Period: A Task for Christian Theology." *Harvard Theological Review* 79 (1986): 22–30. Reprinted in *Christians among Jews and Gentiles: Essays in Honor of Krister Stendahl on His Sixty-Fifth Birthday.* Edited by G. W. E. Nickelsburg and George W. MacRae. Philadelphia: Fortress, 1986.

———. *Love between Women: Early Christian Responses to Female Homoeroticism.* Chicago: University of Chicago Press, 1996.

———. "Paul and the Law. How Complete Was the Departure?" In *The Church and Israel: Romans 9–11.* Edited by Daniel Migliore. *Princeton Seminary Bulletin,* Suppl. Issue no.1 (1990): 71–89.

———. *Women Leaders in the Ancient Synagogue: Inscriptional Evidence and Background Issues.* Chico, Calif.: Scholars Press, 1982.

Brown, Elsa Barkley. "'What Has Happened Here': The Politics of Difference in Women's History and Feminist Politics." *Feminist Studies* 18 (summer 1992): 295–312. Reprinted, pages 272–87 in *The Second Wave: A Reader in Feminist Theory.* Edited by Linda Nicholson. New York: Routledge, 1997.

Brueggemann, Walter. *Theology of the Old Testament: Testimony, Dispute, Advocacy.* Minneapolis: Fortress, 1997.

Bryant, M. Darrol. "Beyond the Enlightenment: An Unfinished Exploration of Modernity." In *The Future of Religion: Postmodern Perspectives: Essays in Honor of Ninian Smart*. Edited by Christopher Lamb and Dan Cohn-Sherbok. London: Middlesex University Press, 1999.

Buber, Martin. *Schriften zur Bibel*. Vol. 2 of *Werke*. Munich: Kösel, 1964.

Bultmann, Rudolf. *Theology of the New Testament*. Translated by Kendrick Grobel. 2 vols. New York: Scribner, 1951–55. Original, *Theologie des Neuen Testaments*. 3 vols. Neue theologische Grundrisse. Tübingen: Mohr/Siebeck, 1948–53.

Burns, Gerald L. "The Hermeneutics of Midrash." Pages 189–213 in *The Book and the Text: The Bible and Literary Theory*. Edited by Regina M. Schwartz. Cambridge, Mass.; Oxford: Blackwell, 1990.

Burrus, Virginia. "Word and Flesh: The Bodies and Sexuality of Ascetic Women in Christian Antiquity." *Journal of Feminist Studies in Religion* 10.1 (1994): 26–51.

Cady, Elizabeth Linell. "Identity, Feminist Theory, and Theology." Pages 17–32 in *Horizons in Feminist Theology: Identity, Tradition, and Norms*. Edited by Rebecca S. Chopp and Sheila G. Davaney. Minneapolis: Fortress, 1997.

———. *Religion, Theology, and American Public Life*. Albany: State University of New York Press, 1993.

Campbell, William S. "All God's Beloved in Rome: Jewish Roots and Christian Identity" (paper presented at the Studiorum Novi Testamenti Societas 55th annual meeting, Tel Aviv, Aug. 2000) in *Celebrating Romans*. Edited by Sheila McGinn. Grand Rapids, Mich.: Eerdmans, 2004.

———. "Beyond the New Perspective: Reflection on the Contemporary Evaluation of Sanders and Dunn" (paper presented at the British New Testament Conference, Manchester, U.K., 2001).

———. "The Contribution of Traditions to Paul's Theology." Pages 234–54 in *1 and 2 Corinthians*. Vol. 2 of *Pauline Theology*. Edited by David M. Hay. Minneapolis: Fortress, 1993.

———. "Divergent Images of Paul and His Mission." Pages 187–211 in *Reading Israel in Romans: Legitimacy and Plausibility of Divergent Interpretations*. Edited by Cristina Grenholm and Daniel Patte. Romans through History and Cultures Series. Harrisburg, Pa.: Trinity Press International, 2000.

———. "The Interpretation of Paul: Beyond the New Perspective" (paper given at the New Testament Postgraduate Seminar, Oxford, 2001).

———. "Martin Luther and Paul's Epistle to the Romans." Pages 103–14 in *The Bible as Book: The Reformation*. Edited by Orlaith O'Sullivan. London: British Library, 2000.

————. "Millennial Optimism for Jewish-Christian Dialogue." Pages 215–37 in *The Future of Jewish-Christian Dialogue*. Edited by Dan Cohn-Sherbok. Lampeter, U.K.: Mellen, 1999.

————. "Paul's Application of Scripture to Contemporary Events" (paper presented at the British New Testament Studies seminar on "Use of the Old Testament in the New," Hawarden, U.K., 1988).

————. *Paul's Gospel in an Intercultural Context: Jew and Gentile in the Letter to the Romans*. Berlin: P. Lang, 1992.

————. "The Place of Romans ix–xi within the Structure and Thought of the Letter." Pages 121–31 in *Studia Evangelica*, vol. 7: *Papers Presented to the 5th International Congress on Biblical Studies, Oxford, 1973*. Edited by Elizabeth A. Livingstone. Berlin: Akademie Verlag, 1982.

————. *The Purpose of Paul in the Letter to the Romans*. PhD thesis, University of Edinburgh, 1972.

————. "Romans III as a Key to the Structure and Thought of the Letter." *Novum Testamentum* 23 (1981): 22–40. Pages 25–42 in *Paul's Gospel in an Intercultural Context: Jew and Gentile in the Letter to the Romans*. By W. S. Campbell. Berlin: P. Lang, 1992.

————. "The Rule of Faith in Romans 12:1–15:13: The Obligation of Humble Obedience as the Only Adequate Response to the Mercies of God." Pages 259–86 in *Romans*. Vol. 3 of *Pauline Theology*. Edited by David M. Hay and E. Elizabeth Johnson. Minneapolis: Fortress, 1995.

————. "The Sociological Study of the New Testament: Promise and Problems." *Journal of Beliefs and Values* 14 (1990): 2–10.

Cancik, Hubert, H. Lichtenberger, and P. Schäfer, eds. *Geschichte—Tradition—Reflexion: Festschrift für Martin Hengel zum 70. Geburtstag*. Tübingen: Mohr/Siebeck, 1996.

Cargas, Harry James, ed. *Responses to Elie Wiesel*. New York: Persea, 1978.

Castelli, Elizabeth A. "Heteroglossia, Hermeneutics, and History: A Review Essay of Recent Feminist Studies of Early Christianity." *Journal of Feminist Studies in Religion* 10.2 (1994): 73–78.

————. *Imitating Paul: A Discourse of Power*. Louisville: Westminster/John Knox, 1991.

————. "Paul on Women and Gender." Pages 221–35 in *Women and Christian Origins*. Edited by Ross Shepard Kraemer and Mary Rose D'Angelo. Oxford: Oxford University Press, 1999.

————. "Romans." Pages 272–300 in *A Feminist Commentary*. Vol. 2 of *Searching the Scriptures*. Edited by Elisabeth Schüssler Fiorenza, A. Brock, and S. Matthews. New York: Crossroad, 1994.

Cavarero, Adriana. "Ansätze zu einer Theorie der Geschlechterdifferenz." Pages 66–102 in *Der Mensch ist zwei: Das Denken der Geschlechterdifferenz*. by Diotima, Philosophinnengruppe aus Verona. Vienna: Wiener

Frauenverlag, 1989. Original, *Il pensiero della differenza sessuale*. Milan: La Tartaruga, 1987.

Charlesworth, James H. *The Messiah: Developments in Earliest Judaism and Christianity*. Minneapolis: Fortress, 1992.

————. *The Old Testament Pseudepigrapha and the New Testament: Prolegomena for the Study of Christian Origins*. Society for New Testament Studies Monograph Series 54. Cambridge: Cambridge University Press, 1985.

————, ed. *The Old Testament Pseudepigrapha*. 2 vols. Garden City, N.Y.: Doubleday, 1983–85.

Chilton, Bruce, and Jacob Neusner. *Judaism in the New Testament: Practices and Beliefs*. London: Routledge, 1995.

Chodorow, Nancy. *The Reproduction of Mothering*. Berkeley: University of California Press, 1978.

Chopp, Rebecca S. "Theorizing Feminist Theology." Pages 215–31 in *Horizons in Feminist Theology: Identity, Tradition, and Norms*. Edited by Rebecca S. Chopp and Sheila G. Davaney. Minneapolis: Fortress, 1997.

Chopp, Rebecca S., and Sheila G. Davaney, eds. *Horizons in Feminist Theology: Identity, Tradition, and Norms*. Minneapolis: Fortress, 1997.

Christ, Carol P. "Embodied Thinking: Reflections on Feminist Theological Method." *Journal of Feminist Studies in Religion* 5.1 (1989): 7–15.

Ciampa, Roy E. *The Presence and Function of Scripture in Galatians 1 and 2*. Wissenschaftliche Untersuchungen zum Neuen Testament, 2. Reihe, 102. Tübingen: Mohr/Siebeck, 1998.

Clines, David J. A. *The Dictionary of Classical Hebrew*. Vols. 1–2. Sheffield: Sheffield Academic Press, 1993–95.

Cohen, Shaye J. D. *The Beginnings of Jewishness: Boundaries, Varieties, Uncertainties*. Berkeley: University of California Press, 1999.

————. *From the Maccabees to the Mishnah*. Library of Early Christianity 7. Edited by Wayne A. Meeks. Philadelphia: Westminster, 1987.

Cohn-Sherbok, Dan, *The Crucified Jew: Twenty Centuries of Christian Anti-Semitism*. London: HarperCollins 1992.

————. *The Hebrew Bible*. London: Cassell, 1996.

————. *Rabbinic Perspectives on the New Testament*. Lampeter, U.K.: Mellen, 1990.

————, ed. *The Future of Jewish-Christian Dialogue*. Lampeter, U.K.: Mellen, 1999.

Collins, Adela Yarbro, ed. *Feminist Perspectives on Biblical Scholarship*. Society of Biblical Literature Centennial Publications. Atlanta: Scholars Press, 1985.

Collins, John J. *The Apocalyptic Imagination*. New York: Crossroad 1984.

————. *Between Athens and Jerusalem: Jewish Identity in the Hellenistic Diaspora*. New York: Crossroad, 1986. 2d ed. Grand Rapids: Eerdmans, 2000.

————. *Jewish Wisdom in the Hellenistic Age*. Louisville: Westminster John Knox, 1997.

————, ed. *The Encyclopedia of Apocalypticism*. Vol. 1. New York: Continuum, 1999.

Collins, John J., and Gregory E. Sterling, eds. *Hellenism in the Land of Israel.* Notre Dame, Ind.: University of Notre Dame Press, 2001.

Corley, Kathleen E. "Feminist Myths of Christian Origins." Pages 51–67 in *Reimagining Christian Origins: A Colloquium Honoring Burton L. Mack.* Edited by Elizabeth A. Castelli and Hall Taussig. Valley Forge, Pa.: Trinity Press International, 1996.

————. *Private Women, Public Meals: Social Conflict in the Synoptic Tradition*. Peabody, Mass.: Hendrickson, 1993.

Cranfield, C. E. B. *The Epistle to the Romans*. 2 vols. 6th ed. International Critical Commentary. Edinburgh: T&T Clark, 1975–79.

Crüsemann, Marlene. "Unrettbar frauenfeindlich: Der Kampf um das Wort von Frauen in 1 Kor 14,(33b)34–35 im Spiegel antijudaistischer Elemente der Auslegung." Pages 199–226 in *Von der Wurzel getragen: Christlich-feministische Exegese in Auseinandersetzung mit Antijudaismus.* Edited by Luise Schottroff and Marie-Theres Wacker. Leiden: Brill, 1995.

Dabourne, Wendy. *Purpose and Cause in Pauline Exegesis: Romans 1.16–4.25 and a New Approach to the Letters*. Society for New Testament Studies Monograph Series 104. Cambridge: Cambridge University Press, 1999.

Dahl, Nils A. "The Neglected Factor in New Testament Theology." *Reflection* 73.1 (1975): 5–8. Reprinted, pages 153–63 in *Jesus the Christ: The Historical Origins of Christological Doctrine.* Edited by D. H. Juel. Minneapolis: Fortress, 1991.

————. *Studies in Paul: Theology for the Early Christian Mission*. Minneapolis: Augsburg, 1977.

Daube, David. *Collected Works of David Daube*. Vol. 1. Edited by Calum M. Carmichael. A Robbins Collection Publication. Berkeley: University of California, 1992.

————. *The New Testament and Rabbinic Judaism*. London: University of London, Athlone, 1956.

————. "Rabbinic Methods of Interpretation and Hellenistic Rhetoric." *Hebrew Union College Annual* 22 (1949): 239–64. Reprinted, pages 333–55 in *Collected Works of David Daube*. Vol. 1. Edited by Calum M. Carmichael. A Robbins Collection Publication. Berkeley: University of California, 1992.

Davaney, Sheila Greeve. *Pragmatic Historicism: A Theology for the Twenty-First Century*. Albany: State University of New York Press, 2000.

Davies, R. R., and R. T. White, eds. *A Tribute to Geza Vermes*. Sheffield: JSOT Press, 1990.

Davies, W. D. *Jewish and Pauline Studies*. Philadelphia: Fortress, 1984.

————. *Paul and Rabbinic Judaism: Some Rabbinic Elements in Pauline Theology*. London: SPCK, 1948. *Paul and Rabbinic Judaism: Some Elements in Pauline Theology*. 50th anniversary ed. Mifflintown, Pa.: Sigler, 1998.

Dawson, D. *Allegorical Readers and Cultural Revision in Ancient Alexandria*. Berkeley: University of California Press, 1992.

De Lauretis, Teresa, ed. *Feminist Studies/Critical Studies*. Theories in Contemporary Culture 8. Bloomington: Indiana University Press, 1986.

Derrida, Jacques. "Faith and Knowledge: The Sources of 'Religion' at the Limits of Reason Alone." Pages 42–101 in *Acts of Religion*. Edited by Gil Anidjar. New York: Routledge, 2002. Original, *La Religion*. Paris: Editions du Seuil, 1996 (papers presented at Capri, Feb. 28–Mar. 1, 1994).

————. "Force of Law: The Mystical Foundation of Authority." Pages 230–300 (232) in *Acts of Religion*. Edited by Gil Anidjar. New York: Routledge, 2002.

————. *Khôra*. Paris: Galilée, 1993.

————. *Negotiations: Interventions and Interviews, 1971–2001*. Edited by Elizabeth Rottenberg. Cultural Memory in the Present. Stanford: Stanford University Press, 2002.

————. *Points . . . : Interviews, 1974–1994*. Edited by Elisabeth Weber. Translated by Peggy Kamuf et al. Stanford: Stanford University Press, 1995.

————. *Writing and Difference*. Translated by Alan Bass. Chicago: University of Chicago Press, 1978. Original, *L'écriture et la différence*. Paris: Editions du Seuil, 1967.

Dietrich, Walter, Martin George, and Ulrich Luz, eds. *Antijudaismus—christliche Erblast*. Stuttgart: Kohlhammer, 1999.

Diner, Dan, ed. *Zivilisationsbruch: Denken nach Auschwitz*. Frankfurt: Fischer Taschenbuch, 1988.

Diotima, Philosophinnengruppe aus Verona (research group: Adriana Cavarero et al.). *Der Mensch ist zwei: Das Denken der Geschlechterdifferenz*. Vienna: Wiener Frauenverlag, 1989. Original, *Il pensiero della differenza sessuale*. Milan: La Tartaruga, 1987.

Dodd, C. H. *The Epistle to the Romans*. Moffatt New Testament Commentaries. London: Hodder & Stoughton, 1932.

Donaldson, Terence L. *Paul and the Gentiles: Remapping the Apostle's Convictional World*. Minneapolis: Fortress, 1997.

Donfried, Karl P., ed. *The Romans Debate*. Rev., expanded ed. Peabody, Mass.: Hendrickson, 1991.

Donfried, Karl P., and Peter Richardson, eds. *Judaism and Christianity in First Century Rome*. Grand Rapids: Eerdmans, 1998.

Dunn, James D. G. "The Formal and Theological Coherence." Pages 245–50 in *The Romans Debate*. Edited by Karl P. Donfried. Rev., expanded ed. Peabody, Mass.: Hendrickson, 1991.

———. *Jesus, Paul and the Law: Studies in Mark and Galatians*. London: SCPK, 1990.

———. *The Partings of the Ways between Christianity and Judaism and Their Significance for the Character of Christianity*. Philadelphia: Trinity Press International, 1991.

———. *Romans 1–8*. And *Romans 9–16*. Word Bible Commentary 38A–B. Dallas: Word, 1988.

———. *The Theology of Paul the Apostle*. Grand Rapids: Eerdmans, 1998.

Du Toit, André. "A Tale of Two Cities: 'Tarsus or Jerusalem?' Revisited." *New Testament Studies* 46.3 (July 2000): 375–402.

Eichholz, Georg. *Die Theologie des Paulus im Umriss*. Neukirchen-Vluyn: Neukirchener Verlag, 1981.

Eisenbaum, Pamela. "Is Paul the Father of Misogyny and Anti-Semitism?" *Crosscurrents* 50.4 (2000–2001): 506–24.

———. "Paul as the New Abraham." Pages 130–45 in *Paul and Politics: Ekklesia, Israel, Imperium, Interpretation*. Edited by Richard A. Horsley. Harrisburg, Pa.: Trinity Press International, 2000.

———. "A Remedy for Having Been Born of Woman: Jesus, Gender, and Genealogy in Romans" (paper presented at the Society of Biblical Literature, Nashville, 2000, seminar: "Romans through History and Cultures: Is Romans for Men Only?").

Elliott, Neil. *Liberating Paul: The Justice of God and the Politics of the Apostle*. Sheffield: Sheffield Academic Press, 1995.

———. "Paul and the Politics of the Empire." Pages 17–39 in *Paul and Politics: Ekklesia, Israel, Imperium, Interpretation: Essays in Honor of Krister Stendahl*. Edited by Richard A. Horsley. Harrisburg, Pa.: Trinity Press International, 2000.

———. *The Rhetoric of Romans: Argumentative Constraint and Strategy and Paul's Dialogue with Judaism*. Sheffield: Sheffield Academic Press, 1990.

Engberg-Pedersen, Troels. *Paul and the Stoics*. Louisville: Westminster John Knox Press, 2000.

———, ed. *Paul beyond the Judaism/Hellenism Divide*. Louisville: Westminster John Knox, 2001.

————, ed. *Paul in His Hellenistic Context.* Edinburgh: T&T Clark, 1994.

Evans, Craig A. "Paul and the Prophets: Prophetic Criticism in the Epistle to the Romans (with special reference to Romans 9–11)." Pages 115–28 in *Romans and the People of God, Essays in Honor of Gordon D. Fee.* Edited by Sven K. Soderlung and N. T. Wright. Grand Rapids: Eerdmans, 1999.

Evans, Craig A., and James A. Sanders, eds. *The Function of Scripture in Early Jewish and Christian Tradition.* Sheffield: Sheffield Academic Press, 1998.

————, eds. *Paul and the Scriptures of Israel.* JSNT Suppl. Series 83. Sheffield: Sheffield Academic Press, 1993.

Evans, Craig A., and Shemaryahu Talmon, eds. *The Quest of Context and Meaning: Studies in Biblical Intertextuality in Honor of James A. Sanders.* Leiden: Brill, 1997.

Evans, Judith. *Feminist Theory Today: An Introduction to Second-Wave Feminism.* London: SAGE Publications, 1995.

Fatum, Lone. "Image of God and Glory of Man: Women in the Pauline Congregations." Pages 50–133 in *Image of God and Gender Models in Judeo-Christian Tradition.* Edited by Kari E. Borresen. Oslo: Solum, 1991.

Finsterbusch, Karin. *Thora als Lebensweisung für Heidenchristen: Studien zur Bedeutung der Thora für die paulinische Ethik.* Göttingen: Vandenhoeck & Ruprecht, 1996.

Fishbane, Michael. *The Exegetical Imagination: On Jewish Thought and Theology.* Cambridge: Harvard University Press, 1998.

————. *The Garments of Torah: Essays in Biblical Hermeneutics.* Bloomington.: Indiana University Press, 1989.

Fitzmyer, Joseph A. *Romans.* Anchor Bible 33. New York: Doubleday, 1993.

Fredriksen, Paula. *Jesus of Nazareth, King of the Jews: A Jewish Life and the Emergence of Christianity.* London: Macmillan, 2000.

————. "Judaism, the Circumcision of Gentiles, and Apocalyptic Hope: Another Look at Galatians 1 and 2." *Journal of Theological Studies,* N.S., 42.2 (Oct. 1991): 532–64.

Frymer-Kensky, Tikva, David Novak, Peter Ochs, David F. Sandmel, Michael A. Signer, eds. *Christianity in Jewish Terms.* Radical Traditions: Theology in a Postcritical Key. Boulder, Colo.: Westview, 2000.

Fulkerson, Mary McClintock. "Contesting the Gendered Subject: A Feminist Account of the *Imago Dei.*" Pages 99–115 in *Horizons in Feminist Theology: Identity, Tradition, and Norms.* Edited by Rebecca S. Chopp and Sheila G. Davaney. Minneapolis: Fortress, 1997.

Fuller, Reginald H. *The New Testament in Current Study: Some Trends in the Years 1941–1962.* London: SCM, 1963.

Gadamer, Hans-Georg. *Truth and Method*. Translation revised by Joel Weinsheimer and Donald G. Marshall; 2d, rev. ed. New York: Crossroad, 1989. Original, *Wahrheit und Methode*. Tübingen: Mohr, 1960.

Gager, John G. "Paul's Contradictions—Can They be Resolved?" *Bible Review* 14 (Dec. 1998): 32–39.

———. *Reinventing Paul*. Oxford: Oxford University Press, 2000.

Gaston, Lloyd. "Faith in Romans 12 in the Light of the Common Life of the Roman Church." Pages 258–64 in *Common Life in the Early Church: Essays Honoring Graydon F. Snyder*. Edited by Julian V. Hills et al. Harrisburg, Pa.: Trinity Press International, 1998.

———. *Paul and the Torah*. Vancouver: University of British Columbia Press, 1987.

Georgi, Dieter. "God Turned Upside Down." Pages 148–57 in *Paul and Empire: Religion and Power in Roman Imperial Society*. Edited by Richard A. Horsley. Harrisburg, Pa.: Trinity Press International, 1997.

———. *Theocracy in Paul's Praxis and Theology*. Translated by David E. Green. Minneapolis: Fortress, 1991.

Gilligan, Carol. *In a Different Voice: Psychological Theory and Women's Development*. Cambridge: Harvard University Press, 1982.

———. "Woman's Place in a Man's Life Cycle." *Harvard Educational Review* 49 (1949): 431–46. Pages 5–23 in *In a Different Voice: Psychological Theory and Women's Development*. By Carol Gilligan. Cambridge: Harvard University Press, 1982. Chapter 12 in *The Second Wave: A Reader in Feminist Theory*. Edited by Linda Nicholson. New York: Routledge, 1997, 198–215.

Given, Mark D. *Paul's True Rhetoric: Ambiguity, Cunning, and Deception in Greece and Rome*. Harrisburg, Pa.: Trinity Press International, 2001.

Gnadt, Martina. "Abba Isn't Daddy—Aspekte einer feministische-befreiungstheologische Revision des Abba Jesu." Pages 115–31 in *Von der Wurzel getragen: Christlich-feministische Exegese in Auseinandersetzung mit Antijudaismus*. Edited by Luise Schottroff and Marie-Theres Wacker. Leiden: Brill, 1995.

Gollwitzer, Helmut. *Israel—und wir*. Berlin: Lettner, 1958.

Gössmann, Elisabeth. "The Image of God and the Human Being in Women's Counter Tradition." Pages 26–56 in *Is There a Future for Feminist Theology?* Edited by Deborah F. Sawyer and Diane M. Collier. Sheffield: Sheffield Academic Press, 1999.

Gössmann, Elisabeth, et al., eds. *Wörterbuch der feministischen Theologie*. Gütersloh: Gütersloher Verlagshaus, 1991.

Grenholm, Christina, and Daniel Patte, eds. *Reading Israel in Romans: Legitimacy and Plausibility of Divergent Interpretations*. Harrisburg, Pa.: Trinity Press International, 2000.

Grey, Mary. "Expelled Again from Eden: Facing Difference through Connection." *Feminist Theology* 21 (May 1999): 8–20.

———. *Introducing Feminist Images of God*. Sheffield: Sheffield Academic Press, 2001.

———. "Jesus—Einsamer Held oder Offenbarung beziehungshafter Macht? Eine Untersuchung feministischer Erlösungsmodelle." Pages 148–71 in *Vom Verlangen nach Heilwerden: Christologie in feministisch-theologischer Sicht*. Edited by Doris Strahm and Regula Strobel. Lucerne: Exodus, 1991.

———. *Redeeming the Dream: Feminism, Redemption and Christian Tradition*. London: SPCK, 1989.

———. *The Wisdom of Fools? Seeking Revelation for Today* (London: SPCK, 1993)

Gruen, Erich S. *Heritage and Hellenism: The Reinvention of Jewish Tradition*. Berkeley: University of California Press, 1998.

Haas, Peter J., ed. *Recovering the Role of Women: Power and Authority in Rabbinic Jewish Society*. Atlanta: Scholars Press, 1992.

Halivni, David Weiss. "Plain Sense and Applied Meaning in Rabbinic Exegesis." Pages 107–41 in *The Return to Scripture in Judaism and Christianity: Essays in Postcritical Scriptural Interpretation*. Theological Inquiries. Edited by Peter Ochs. New York: Paulist, 1993.

Hall, Sidney G. *Christian Anti-Semitism and Paul's Theology*. Minneapolis: Fortress, 1993.

Handelman, Susan. *The Slayers of Moses: The Emergence of Rabbinic Interpretation in Modern Literary Theory*. Albany: State University of New York Press, 1982.

Hanson, Anthony Tyrell. *The Living Utterances of God: The New Testament Exegesis of the Old*. London: Darton, Longman & Todd, 1983.

———. *The New Testament Interpretation of Scripture*. London: SPCK, 1980.

Harding, Sandra. "Is Gender a Variable in Conceptions of Rationality? A Survey of Issues." In *Beyond Domination: New Perspectives on Women and Philosophy*. Edited by C. C. Gould. Totowa, N.J.: Rowman & Allanheld, 1983.

Harnack, Adolf von. "Die Stellung des Apostels Paulus zum Judentum und Judenchristentum nach seinen Briefen; seine jüdischen Schranken." In

Beiträge zur Einleitung in das Neue Testament. Vol. 4: *Neue Untersuchungen zur Apostelgeschichte und zur Abfassungszeit der synoptischen Evangelien.* Leipzig: Hinrich, 1911.

Hawthorne, Gerald F., and Ralph P. Martin, eds. *Dictionary of Paul and his Letters.* Leicester, U.K.: Inter-Varsity Press, 1993.

Hay, David M., ed. *First and Second Corinthians.* Vol. 2 of *Pauline Theology.* Minneapolis: Fortress, 1993.

Hay, David M., and E. Elizabeth Johnson, eds. *Romans.* Vol. 3 of *Pauline Theology.* Minneapolis: Fortress, 1995.

Hays, Richard. *Echoes of Scripture in the Letters of Paul.* New Haven: Yale University Press, 1989.

Heidegger, Martin. *What Is Philosophy?* Translated from German by William Kluback and Jean T. Wilde. London: Vision, 1958.

Heine, Susanne. *Matriarchs, Goddesses, and Images of God: A Critique of Feminist Theology.* Translated by John Bowden. Minneapolis: Augsburg, 1988.

Hellholm, David, ed. *Apocalypticism in the Ancient Mediterranean World and the Near East.* Tübingen: Mohr/Siebeck, 1979.

Hengel, Martin. *Judaism and Hellenism: Studies in Their Encounter in Palestine during the Early Hellenistic Period.* Translated by John Bowden. 2 vols. Philadelphia: Fortress, 1981.

Heschel, Abraham J. *God in Search of Man: A Philosophy of Judaism.* New York: Farrar, Strauss & Cudahy, 1955. Reprinted, New York: Octagon Books, 1972.

Heschel, Susannah. *Abraham Geiger and the Jewish Jesus.* Chicago: University of Chicago Press, 1998.

————. "Anti-Judaism in Christian Feminist Theology." *Tikkun* 5.3 (1990): 25–28, 95–97. Original, "Jüdisch-feministische Theologie und Antijudaismus in christlich-feministischer Theologie." Pages 54–103 in *Verdrängte Vergangenheit, die uns bedrängt.* Ed. Leonore Siegele-Wenschkewitz. Munich: Chr. Kaiser, 1988.

————, ed. *On Being a Jewish Feminist: A Reader.* New York: Schocken, 1983.

Heyward, Carter. *The Redemption of God: A Theology of Mutual Relation.* Washington, D.C.: University of America Press, 1982.

————. *Touching Our Strength: The Erotic as Power and Love of God.* San Francisco: Harper & Row, 1989.

Hills, Julian V., et al., eds. *Common Life in the Early Church: Essays Honoring Graydon F. Snyder.* Harrisburg, Pa.: Trinity Press International, 1998.

Hoffmann, Hans-Werner, et al. *Hebräisches und aramäisches Wörterbuch zum Alten Testament.* Berlin: de Gruyter, 1997.

Hooker, Morna D., and S. D. Wilson, eds. *Paul and Paulinism: Essays in Honour of C. K. Barrett.* London: SPCK, 1982.

Horbury, William. *Jews and Christians in Contact and Controversy.* Edinburgh: T&T Clark, 1998.

Horsley, Richard A. "Rhetoric and Empire—and 1 Corinthians." Pages 72–102 in *Paul and Politics: Ekklesia, Israel, Imperium, Interpretation.* Edited by Richard A. Horsley. Harrisburg, Pa.: Trinity Press International, 2000.

————, ed. *Paul and Empire: Religion and Power in Roman Imperial Society.* Harrisburg, Pa.: Trinity Press International, 1997.

————, ed. *Paul and Politics: Ekklesia, Israel, Imperium, Interpretation: Essays in Honor of Krister Stendahl.* Harrisburg, Pa.: Trinity Press International, 2000.

Hurd, J. C. "Pauline Chronology and Pauline Theology." Pages 225–48 in *Christian History and Interpretation: Studies Presented to John Knox.* Edited by W. R. Farmer, C. F. D. Moule, and R. R. Niebuhr. Cambridge: Cambridge University Press, 1967.

Ilan, Tal. *Integrating Women into Second Temple History.* Peabody, Mass.: Hendrickson, 1999.

————. *Jewish Women in Greco-Roman Palestine: An Inquiry into Image and Status.* Texte und Studien zum antiken Judentum. Tübingen: Mohr/Siebeck, 1995.

Isherwood, Lisa, and Dorothea McEwan, eds. *An A to Z of Feminist Theology.* Sheffield: Sheffield Academic Press, 1996.

Janssen, Claudia, Luise Schottroff, and Beate Wehn, eds. *Paulus: Umstrittene Traditionen—lebendige Theologie: Eine feministische Lektüre.* Gütersloh: Chr. Kaiser/Gütersloher Verlagshaus, 2001. ET, *Journal for the Study of the New Testament* 79 (2000).

Jeremias, Joachim. *Abba: Studien zur neutestamentlichen Theologie und Zeitgeschichte.* Göttingen: Vandenhoeck & Ruprecht, 1966.

Jervis, L. Ann. "'But I Want You to Know . . .': Paul's Midrashic Intertextual Response to the Corinthian Worshipers (1 Cor 11:2–16)." *Journal of Biblical Literature* 112.2 (1993): 231–46.

Jewett, Robert. *Christian Tolerance: Paul's Message to the Modern Church.* Philadelphia: Westminster, 1982.

————. "Following the Argument of Romans." Pages 265–77 in *The Romans Debate.* Edited by Karl P. Donfried. Rev., expanded ed. Peabody, Mass.: Hendrickson, 1991.

————. "Paul, Phoebe, and the Spanish Mission." Pages 142–61 in *The Social World of Formative Christianity and Judaism: Essays in Tribute to Howard Clark Kee.* Edited by Jacob Neusner et al. Philadelphia: Fortress, 1988.

————. *Paul's Anthropological Terms: A Study of Their Use in Conflict Settings*. Leiden: Brill, 1971.

Johnson, E. Elizabeth. *The Function of Apocalyptic and Wisdom Traditions in Romans 9–11*. SBL Dissertation Series 109. Atlanta: Scholars Press, 1989.

————, ed. *Looking Back, Pressing On*. Vol. 4 of *Pauline Theology*. Atlanta: Scholars Press, 1997.

Johnson, Luke T. *The Writings of the New Testament: An Interpretation*. Philadelphia: Fortress, 1986.

Johnson, Mark. *The Body in the Mind: The Bodily Basis of Meaning, Imagination, and Reason*. Chicago: University of Chicago Press, 1987.

Jonas, Hans. *Philosophical Essays: From Ancient Creed to Technological Man*. Englewood Cliffs, N.J.: Prentice-Hall, 1974.

Jones, Serene. *Feminist Theory and Christian Theology: Cartographies of Grace*. Minneapolis: Fortress, 2000.

————. "Women's Experience between a Rock and a Hard Place: Feminist, Womanist, and Mujerista Theologies in North America." Pages 33–53 in *Horizons in Feminist Theology: Identity, Tradition, and Norms*. Edited by Rebecca S. Chopp and Sheila G. Davaney. Minneapolis: Fortress, 1997.

Jost, Renate, and Eveline Valtink, eds. *Ihr aber, für wen haltet ihr mich? Auf dem Weg zu einer feministisch-befreiungstheologischen Revision der Christologie*. Gütersloh: Chr. Kaiser/Gütersloher Verlagshaus, 1996.

Juel, Donald. *Messianic Exegesis: Christological Interpretation of the Old Testament in Early Christianity*. Philadelphia: Fortress, 1988.

Jüngst, Brigitta. *Auf der Seite des Todes das Leben: Auf dem Weg zu einer christlich-feministischen Theologie nach der Shoa*. Gütersloh: Chr. Kaiser/Gütersloher Verlagshaus, 1996.

Kahl, Brigitte. "Gender Trouble in Galatia? Paul and the Rethinking of Difference." Pages 57–73 in *Is There a Future for Feminist Theology?* Edited by Deborah F. Sawyer and Diane M. Collier. Sheffield: Sheffield Academic Press, 1999.

Kähler, Else. *Die Frau in den paulinischen Briefen*. Zurich: Gotthelf, 1960.

Kalsky, Manuela. *Christaphanien: Die Re-Vision der Christologie aus der Sicht von Frauen in unterschiedlichen Kulturen*. Gütersloh: Chr. Kaiser/ Gütersloher Verlagshaus, 2000.

Käsemann, Ernst. *Paulinische Perspektiven*. 2. Auflage. Tübingen: Mohr, 1972.

————. "Paul and Israel." Pages 183–87 in *New Testament Questions of Today*. London: SCM, 1969.

Keck, Leander E. *Paul and His Letters*. Philadelphia: Fortress, 1979. 2d ed., 1988.

Keesmaat, Sylvia C. *Paul and His Story: (Re)Interpreting the Exodus Tradition*. Sheffield: Sheffield Academic Press, 1999.

Kellenbach, Katharina von. *Anti-Judaism in Feminist Religious Writings.* Atlanta: Scholars Press, 1994.

Keller, Catherine. "Seeking and Sucking: On Relation and Essence in Feminist Theology." Pages 54–78 in *Horizons in Feminist Theology: Identity, Tradition, and Norms.* Edited by Rebecca S. Chopp and Sheila G. Davaney. Minneapolis: Fortress, 1997.

Kennedy, George A. *New Testament Interpretation through Rhetorical Criticism.* Chapel Hill: University of North Carolina Press, 1984.

King, Ursula. "Feminist Theologies in Contemporary Contexts: A Provisional Assessment." Pages 100–114 in *Is There a Future for Feminist Theology?* Edited by Deborah F. Sawyer and Diane M. Collier. Sheffield: Sheffield Academic Press, 1999.

———. *Woman and Spirituality: Voices of Protest and Promise.* Women in Society. Basingstoke, U.K.: Macmillan Education, 1989.

Kittredge, Cynthia Briggs. *Community and Authority: The Rhetoric of Obedience in the Pauline Tradition.* Harvard Theological Studies 45. Harrisburg, Pa.: Trinity Press International, 1998.

Kitzberger, Ingrid R., ed. *The Personal Voice in Biblical Interpretation.* London: Routledge, 1999.

Knight, George A. F. *Christ the Centre.* Edinburgh: Handsel, 1999.

Koch, Klaus. *Spuren des Hebräischen Denkens: Beiträge zur alttestamentlichen Theologie.* Vol. 1 of *Gesammelte Aufsätze.* Neukirchen-Vluyn: NeukirchenerVerlag,1991.

Kraemer, Ross Shepard. *Her Share of the Blessings: Women's Religions among Pagans, Jews, and Christians in the Greco-Roman World.* New York: Oxford University Press, 1992.

———. *Maenads, Martyrs, Matrons, Monastics: A Sourcebook on Women's Religions in the Greco-Roman World.* Philadelphia: Fortress, 1988.

Kraemer, Ross Shepard, and Mary Rose D'Angelo, eds. *Women and Christian Origins.* Oxford: Oxford University Press, 1999.

Kraus, Wolfgang. "'Volk Gottes' als Verheissungsbegriff bei Paulus." *Kirche und Israel: Neukirchener theologische Zeitschrift* 12 (1997): 134–47.

———. *Das Volk Gottes: Untersuchungen zur Ekklesiologie bei Paulus.* Tübingen: Mohr/Siebeck, 1996.

———, ed. *Christen und Juden: Perspektiven einer Annäherung.* Gütersloh: Gütersloher Verlagshaus, 1997.

Kristeva, Julia. "Woman Can Never Be Defined." Pages 137–41 in *New French Feminisms.* Edited by Elaine Marks and Isabelle de Courtivron. Translated by Marilyn A. August. New York: Schocken, 1981.

Kurth, Christina, and Peter Schmid, eds. *Das christlich-jüdische Gespräch: Standortbestimmungen.* Stuttgart: Kohlhammer, 2000.

Lampe, Peter. *Die stadtrömischen Christen in den ersten beiden Jahrhunderten.* Wissenschaftliche Untersuchungen zum Neuen Testament 2.18. Tübingen: Mohr/Siebeck, 1989.

Le Déaut, Roger. *La Nuit Pascale: Essai sur la signification de la Pâque juive à partir du Targum de Exode XII 42.* Analecta biblica 22. Rome: Institute Biblique Pontifical, 1963.

Lévinas, Emmanuel. *Totality and Infinity: An Essay on Exteriority.* Translated by Alphonso Lingis. Pittsburgh: Duquesne University Press, 1969. Original, *Totalité et infini: Essai sur l'extériorité.* The Hague: M. Nijhoff, 1961.

————. *Vier Talmud-Lesungen.* Frankfurt: Neue Kritik, 1993.

————. *Zwischen uns: Versuche über das Denken an den anderen.* Munich: C. Hanser, 1995.

Levine, Amy-Jill, ed. *Women Like This: New Perspectives on Jewish Women in the Greco-Roman World.* Atlanta: Scholars Press, 1991.

Lieberman, Saul. *Hellenism in Jewish Palestine.* 2d ed. New York: Jewish Theological Seminary of America, 1962.

Lieu, Judith M. "The 'Attraction of Women' in/to Early Judaism and Christianity: Gender and the Politics of Conversion." *Journal for the Study of the New Testament* 72 (1998): 5–22.

————. "'Impregnable Ramparts and Walls of Iron': Boundary and Identity in Early 'Judaism' and 'Christianity.'" *New Testament Studies* 48.3 (July 2002): 297–313.

Linafelt, Tod, ed. *Strange Fire: Reading the Bible after the Holocaust.* Sheffield: Sheffield Academic Press, 2000.

Lipsitz, George. *Time Passages: Collective Memory and American Popular Culture.* Minneapolis: University of Minnesota Press, 1990.

Lodge, John G. *Romans 9–11: A Reader-Response Analysis.* Atlanta: Scholars Press, 1996.

Lorde, Audre, and Adrienne Rich. *Macht und Sinnlichkeit: Ausgewählte Texte.* Edited by Dagmar Schultz. Berlin: Orlanda Frauenverlag, 1983.

Macdonald, Margaret Y. *Early Christian Women and Pagan Opinion: The Power of the Hysterical Woman.* Cambridge: Cambridge University Press, 1996.

————. "Reading Real Women through the Undisputed Letters of Paul." Pages 199–220 in *Women and Christian Origins.* Edited by Ross Shepard Kraemer and Mary Rose D'Angelo. Oxford: Oxford University Press, 1999.

MacFague, Sally. *The Body of God: An Ecological Theology.* Minneapolis: Fortress, 1994.

Mack, Burton L. *Rhetoric and the New Testament.* Minneapolis: Fortress, 1990.

Marcus, Marcel, Ekkehard W. Stegemann, and Erich Zenger, eds. *Israel und Kirche heute: Beiträge zum christlich-jüdischen Dialog: Für Ernst Ludwig Ehrlich.* Freiburg: Herder, 1991.

Marquardt, Friedrich-Wilhelm. *Das christliche Bekenntnis zu Jesus, dem Juden.* Vol. 1 of *Eine Christologie.* Munich: Chr. Kaiser, 1990.

Martin, Dale B. "Paul and the Judaism/Hellenism Dichotomy: Toward a Social History of the Question." Pages 29–62 in *Paul beyond the Judaism/Hellenism Divide.* Edited by Troels Engberg-Pedersen. Louisville: Westminster John Knox, 2001.

———. *Die Juden im Römerbrief.* Theologische Studien 107. Zurich: Theologischer Verlag, 1971.

Matlock, R. Barry. *Unveiling the Apocalyptic Paul: Paul's Interpreters and the Rhetoric of Criticism.* Sheffield: Sheffield Academic Press, 1996.

Mattila, Sharon Lee. "Where Women Sat in Ancient Synagogues: The Archaeological Evidence in Context." In *Voluntary Associations in the Greco-Roman World.* Edited by John S. Kloppenborg and Stephen G. Wilson. London: Routledge, 1996.

McGinn, Sheila E. "Feminist Approaches to Romans: Rom 8:18–23 as a Case Study" (paper presented at the Society of Biblical Literature, Nashville, 2000, seminar: "Romans through History and Cultures").

Meeks, Wayne A. *The First Urban Christians: The Social World of the Apostle Paul.* New Haven: Yale University Press, 1983.

———. "Judaism, Hellenism, and the Birth of Christianity." Pages 17–28 in *Paul beyond the Judaism/Hellenism Divide.* Edited by Troels Engberg-Pedersen. Louisville: Westminster John Knox Press, 2001.

———. "Judgment and the Brother: Romans 14:1–15:13." Pages 290–300 in *Tradition and Interpretation in the New Testament: Essays in Honor of E. Earle Ellis.* Edited by Gerald F. Hawthorne and Otto Betz. Grand Rapids: Eerdmans; Tübingen: Mohr, 1987.

———. *The Origins of Christian Morality: The First Two Centuries.* New Haven: Yale University Press, 1993.

———, ed. *The Writings of St. Paul.* New York: Norton, 1972.

Meier-Seethaler, Carola. *Gefühl und Urteilskraft.* Munich: C. H. Beck, 1997.

Meissner, Stefan. *Die Heimholung des Ketzers: Studien zur jüdischen Auseinandersetzung mit Paulus.* Tübingen: Mohr, 1996.

Mendes-Flohr, Paul R. *German Jews: A Dual Identity.* New Haven: Yale University Press, 1999.

Metz, Johann Baptist. "Kirche nach Auschwitz." In *Israel und Kirche heute: Beiträge zum christlich-jüdischen Dialog: Für Ernst Ludwig Ehrlich.* Ed. Marcel Marcus, Ekkehard W. Stegemann, and Erich Zenger. Freiburg: Herder, 1991.

Michel, Otto, et al., eds. *Studies on the Jewish Background of the New Testament*. Assen: Van Gorcum, 1969.

Miller, James C. *The Obedience of Faith, the Eschatological People of God, and the Purpose of Romans*. Atlanta: Society of Biblical Literature, 2000.

Mitchell, Margaret M. *The Heavenly Trumpet: John Chrysostom and the Art of Pauline Interpretation*. Tübingen: Mohr, 2000.

———. *Paul and the Rhetoric of Reconciliation: An Exegetical Investigation of the Language and Composition of 1 Corinthians*. Tübingen: Mohr, 1991.

Moltmann-Wendel, Elisabeth. *I Am My Body: New Ways of Embodiment*. London: SCM, 1994.

———. *A Land Flowing with Milk and Honey: Perspectives on Feminist Theology*. Translated by John Bowden. New York: Crossroad, 1986.

Moo, Douglas J. *The Epistle to the Romans*. Grand Rapids: Eerdmans, 1996.

Moore, George F. "Christian Writers on Judaism." *Harvard Theological Review* 14 (1921): 197–254.

Mosès, Stéphane. *Der Engel der Geschichte: Franz Rosenzweig, Walter Benjamin, Gerschom Scholem*. Frankfurt: Jüdischer Geschichte, 1994. Original, *L'ange de l'histoire: Rosenzweig, Benjamin, Scholem*. Paris: Edition du Seuil, 1992.

Moxnes, Halvor. *Theology in Conflict: Studies in Paul's Understanding of God in Romans*. Supplements to Novum Testamentum 53. Leiden: Brill, 1980.

Muilenburg, James. "Form Criticism and Beyond." *Journal of Biblical Literature* 88 (1969): 1–18.

Mulder, Martin J., ed. *Mikra: Text, Translation, Reading, and Interpretation of the Hebrew Bible in Ancient Judaism and Early Christianity*. Assen: Van Gorcum, 1988.

Müller, Karlheinz. *Studien zur frühjüdischen Apokalyptik*. Stuttgart: Katholisches Bibelwerk GmbH, 1991.

Munck, Johannes. *Christ and Israel: An Interpretation of Romans 9–11*. Philadelphia: Fortress, 1967.

———. *Paulus und die Heilsgeschichte*. Acta Jutlandica: Teologisk serie 6. Copenhagen: Munksgaard, 1954. ET, *Paul and the Salvation of Mankind*. Translated by Frank Clarke. London: SCM, 1959.

Nanos, Mark D. "The Inter- and Intra-Jewish Political Context of Paul's Letter to the Galatians." Pages 146–59 in *Paul and Politics: Ekklesia, Israel, Imperium, Interpretation*. Edited by Richard A. Horsley. Harrisburg, Pa.: Trinity Press International, 2000.

———. *The Irony of Galatians: Paul's Letter in First-Century Context*. Minneapolis: Fortress, 2002.

————. "The Jewish Context of the Gentile Audience Addressed in Paul's Letter to the Romans." *Catholic Biblical Quarterly* 61.2 (Apr. 1999): 283–304.

————. *The Mystery of Romans: The Jewish Context of Paul's Letter to the Romans.* Minneapolis: Fortress, 1996.

Neusner, Jacob. *Invitation to Midrash: The Workings of Rabbinic Bible Interpretation.* San Francisco: Harper & Row, 1989.

————. *The Rabbinic Traditions about the Pharisees before 70.* 3 vols. Leiden: Brill, 1971.

————, ed. *The Study of Ancient Judaism.* New York: Ktav, 1981.

Neusner, Jacob, et al., eds. *The Social World of Formative Christianity and Judaism: Essays in Tribute to Howard Clark Kee.* Philadelphia: Fortress, 1988.

Neusner, Jacob, and Bruce Chilton. *The Intellectual Foundations of Christian and Jewish Discourse: The Philosophy of Religious Argument.* London: Routledge, 1997.

Neyrey, Jerome H. *Paul, in Other Words: A Cultural Reading of His Letters.* Louisville: Westminster/John Knox Press, 1990.

Nicholson, Linda, ed. *Feminism/Postmodernism.* New York: Routledge, 1990.

————, ed. *The Second Wave: A Reader in Feminist Theory.* New York: Routledge, 1997.

Nicholson, Linda, and Maggie Humm, eds. *Modern Feminisms: Political, Literary, Cultural.* New York: Columbia University Press, 1992.

Nickelsburg, George W. E., and George W. MacRae, eds. *Christians among Jews and Gentiles: Essays in Honor of Krister Stendahl on His Sixty-Fifth Birthday.* Philadelphia: Fortress, 1986.

Niebuhr, Karl-Wilhelm. *Heidenapostel aus Israel: Die jüdische Identität des Paulus nach ihrer Darstellung in seinen Briefen.* Tübingen: Mohr, 1992.

Ochs, Peter. *Peirce, Pragmatism, and the Logic of Scripture.* Cambridge: Cambridge University Press, 1998.

————, ed. *The Return to Scripture in Judaism and Christianity: Essays in Postcritical Scriptural Interpretation.* New York: Paulist, 1993.

Osiek, Carolyn. "The Oral World of Early Christianity in Rome: The Case of Hermas." Pages 151–72 in *Judaism and Christianity in First-Century Rome.* Edited by Karl P. Donfried and Peter Richardson. Grand Rapids: Eerdmans, 1998.

————. "Women in House Churches." Pages 300–15 in *Common Life in the Early Church: Essays Honoring Graydon F. Snyder.* Edited by Julian H. Hills. Harrisburg, Pa.: Trinity Press International 1998.

Osiek, Carolyn, and David Balch, eds. *Families in the New Testament World: Households and House Churches.* Louisville: Westminster John Knox Press, 1997.

Osten-Sacken, Peter von der. *Christian-Jewish Dialogue: Theological Foundations.* Translated by Margaret Kohl. Philadelphia: Fortress, 1986.

Page, Ruth. "Has Feminist Theology a Viable Long-Term Future?" Pages 193–97 in *Is There a Future for Feminist Theology?* Edited by Deborah F. Sawyer and Diane M. Collier. Sheffield: Sheffield Academic Press, 1999.

Pagels, Elaine. *The Gnostic Paul.* Philadelphia: Trinity Press International, 1992.

Patte, Daniel. *Early Jewish Hermeneutic in Palestine.* Society of Biblical Literature Dissertation Series 22. Missoula, Mont.: Scholars Press, 1975.

———. *Paul's Faith and the Power of the Gospel: A Structural Introduction to the Pauline Letters.* Philadelphia: Fortress, 1983.

Perelman, Chaïm, and Luci Olbrechts-Tyteca. *The New Rhetoric: A Treatise on Argumentation.* Translated by John Wilkinson and Purcell Weaver. Notre Dame, Ind.: University of Notre Dame Press, 1969. Original, *Traité de l'argumentation: La nouvelle rhétorique.* 2 vols. Paris: Presses universitaires de France, 1958.

Pieper, Annemarie. *Gibt es eine feministische Ethik?* Munich: W. Fink, 1998.

Plaskow, Judith. "Blaming the Jews for the Birth of Patriarchy." Pages 250–54 in *Nice Jewish Girls.* Edited by Evelyn T. Beck. Watertown, Mass.: Persephone, 1982.

———. "Feminist Anti-Judaism and the Christian God." *Journal of Feminist Studies in Religion* 7.2 (1991): 99–108. Original, "Feministischer Antijudaismus und der christliche Gott." *Kirche und Israel: Neukirchener theologische Zeitschrift* 5.1 (1990): 9–25.

———. *Standing Again at Sinai: Judaism from a Feminist Perspective.* San Francisco: Harper & Row, 1990.

Poirié, François. *Emmanuel Lévinas.* Lyon: La Manufacture, 1987.

Polaski, Sandra Hack. *Paul and the Discourse of Power.* Sheffield: Sheffield Academic Press, 1999.

Pomeroy, Sarah B. *Goddesses, Whores, Wives, and Slaves: Women in Classical Antiquity.* New York: Schocken, 1975.

Porter, Stanley E. "Paul as Epistolographer and Rhetorician?" Pages 222–48 in *The Rhetorical Interpretation of Scripture: Essays from the 1996 Malibu Conference.* Edited by Stanley E. Porter and Dennis L. Stamps. Sheffield: Sheffield Academic Press, 1999.

Porter, Stanley E., and Dennis L. Stamps, eds. *The Rhetorical Interpretation of Scripture: Essays from the 1996 Malibu Conference.* JSNT Suppl. Series 180. Sheffield: Sheffield Academic Press, 1999.

Porton, Gary. "Defining Midrash." Pages 55–103 in *The Study of Ancient Judaism*. New York: Ktav. 1981.

Räisänen, Heikki. *Paul and the Law*. 2d ed. Tübingen: Mohr, 1987.

———. "Paul, God, and Israel: Romans 9–11 in Recent Research." Pages 178–206 in *The Social World of Formative Christianity and Judaism: Essays in Tribute to Howard Clark Kee*. Edited by Jacob Neusner et al. Philadelphia: Fortress, 1988.

Raphael, Melissa. *Thealogy and Embodiment: The Post-Patriarchal Reconstruction of Female Sacrality*. Sheffield: Sheffield Academic Press, 1996.

Reasoner, Mark. *The Strong and the Weak: Romans 14:1–15:13 in Context*. Society for New Testament Studies Monograph Series 103. Cambridge: Cambridge University Press, 1999.

Rendtorff, Rolf. "Nach Auschwitz." *Kirche und Israel: Neukirchener theologische Zeitschrift* 10 (1995): 5–7.

———. *Theologie des Alten Testaments: Ein kanonischer Entwurf*. Vol. 1 of *Kanonische Grundlegung*. Neukirchen-Vluyn: Neukirchener Verlag, 1999.

Rendtorff, Rolf, and Ekkehard Stegemann, eds. *Auschwitz—Krise der christlichen Theologie:* Munich: Chr. Kaiser, 1980.

Ricoeur, Paul. *Freud and Philosophy: An Essay on Interpretation*. Translated by Denis Savage. New Haven: Yale University Press, 1970.

———. *The Symbolism of Evil*. Boston: Beacon, 1969.

Riesner, Rainer. *Paul's Early Period: Chronology, Mission Strategy, Theology*. Translated by Doug Stott. Grand Rapids: Eerdmans, 1998.

Robbins, Vernon K. *The Tapestry of Early Christianity: Discourse, Rhetoric, Society and Ideology*. London: Routledge, 1996.

Roetzel, Calvin J. *The Letters of Paul: Conversations in Context*. 4th ed. Louisville: Westminster John Knox, 1998.

Rosenzweig, Franz. *Der Mensch und sein Werk, Gesammelte Schriften*. Edited by Reinhold Mayer and Annemarie Mayer. Dordrecht: Martinus Nijhoff, 1984.

———. *Zweistromland: Kleinere Schriften zur Religion und Philosophie*. Berlin: Philo, 1926.

Ruddick, Sara. *Maternal Thinking: Toward a Politics of Peace*. Boston: Beacon, 1989.

Ruether, Rosemary Radford. *Faith and Fratricide: The Theological Roots of Anti-Semitism*. New York: Seabury, 1974.

———. "Feminism and Jewish-Christian Dialogue: Particularism and Universalism in Search for Religious Truth." Pages 137–48 in *The Myth of Christian Uniqueness: Toward a Pluralistic Theology of Religions*. Edited by John Hick and Paul Knitter. Maryknoll, N.Y.: Orbis, 1987.

————. *Gaia and God: An Ecofeminist Theology of Earth Healing*. London: SCM, 1993.

————. *Women and Redemption*. Minneapolis: Fortress, 1998.

Ruether, Rosemary Radford, and Eleanor McLaughlin, eds. *Women of Spirit: Female Leadership in the Jewish and Christian Traditions*. New York: Simon & Schuster, 1979.

Russell, Letty M., and Shannon Clarkson, eds. *Dictionary of Feminist Theologies*. Louisville: Westminster John Knox Press, 1996.

Rutgers, L. V. *The Hidden Heritage of Diaspora Judaism*. Leuven: Peeters, 1998.

Rutledge, David. *Reading Marginally: Feminism, Deconstruction, and the Bible*. Leiden: Brill, 1996.

Sacks, Jonathan. "The Other—Jews and Christians." *The Other as Mystery and Challenge* (Martin Buber House, Baylor University Center for American and Jewish Studies) 25 (spring 1998): 31–41.

Safrai, Hannah. "Women and the Ancient Synagogue." In *Daughters of the King: Women and the Synagogue: A Survey of History, Halakhah, and Contemporary Realities*. Edited by Susan Grossman and Rivka Haut. Philadelphia: Jewish Publication Society, 1992.

Sampley, Paul. "The Weak and the Strong: Paul's Careful and Crafty Rhetorical Strategy in Romans 14:1–15:13." Pages 40–52 in *The Social World of the First Urban Christians: Studies in Honor of Wayne A. Meeks*. Edited by L. Michael White and O. Larry Yarbrough. Minneapolis: Fortress, 1995.

Sanders, E. P. *Paul and Palestinian Judaism: A Comparison of Patterns of Religion*. Philadelphia: Fortress, 1977.

————. *Paul, the Law, and the Jewish People*. Philadelphia: Fortress, 1985.

Sawyer, Deborah F. *Women and Religion in the First Christian Centuries*. London: Routledge, 1996.

Sawyer, Deborah, and Diane M. Collier, eds. *Is There a Future for Feminist Theology?* Sheffield: Sheffield Academic Press, 1999.

Schaumberger, Christine, and Luise Schottroff. *Schuld und Macht: Studien zu einer feministischen Befreiungstheologie*. Munich: Chr. Kaiser, 1988.

Schiffman, Lawrence H. *Reclaiming the Dead Sea Scrolls: The History of Judaism, the Background of Christianity, the Lost Library of Qumran*. Philadelphia: Jewish Publication Society, 1994; reprinted, New York: Doubleday, 1995.

Schmuckli, Lisa. *Differenzen und Dissonanzen: Zugänge zu feministischen Erkenntnistheorien der Postmoderne*. Königstein im Taunus, Germany: U. Helmer, 1996.

Schottroff, Luise. *Befreiungserfahrungen: Studien zur Sozialgeschichte des Neuen Testaments.* Munich: Chr. Kaiser, 1990.

———. "'Gesetzesfreies Heidenchristentum'—und die Frauen? Feministische Analysen und Alternativen." Pages 227–46 in *Von der Wurzel getragen: Christlich-feministische Exegese in Auseinandersetzung mit Antijudaismus.* Edited by Luise Schottroff and Marie-Theres Wacker. Leiden: Brill, 1995.

———. "Die Lieder und das Geschrei der Glaubenden: Rechfertigung bei Paulus." *Evangelische Theologie* 60.5 (2000): 332–47.

———. *Lydias ungeduldige Schwestern: Feministische Sozialgeschichte des frühen Christentums.* Gütersloh: Chr. Kaiser/Gütersloher Verlagshaus, 1994. ET, *Lydia's Impatient Sisters: A Feminist Social History of Early Christianity.* Translated by Barbara and Martin Rumscheidt. Louisville: Westminster John Knox, 1995.

———. "Die Schreckensherrschaft der Sünde und die Befreiung durch Christus nach dem Römerbrief des Paulus." *Evangelische Theologie* 39 (1979): 497–510.

———. "Women as Followers of Jesus in New Testament Times: An Exercise in Sociohistorical Exegesis of the Bible." Pages 453–61 in *The Bible and Liberation: Political and Social Hermeneutics.* Edited by Norman K. Gottwald and Richard A. Horsley. New York: Orbis, 1993.

Schottroff, Luise, and Marie-Theres Wacker, eds. *Kompendium feministische Bibelauslegung.* Gütersloh: Chr. Kaiser/Gütersloher Verlagshaus, 1998.

———, eds. *Von der Wurzel getragen: Christlich-feministische Exegese in Auseinandersetzung mit Antijudaismus.* Biblical Interpretation Series 17. Leiden: Brill, 1995.

Schottroff, Luise, Silvia Schroer, and Marie-Theres Wacker, eds. *Feministische Exegese: Forschungsbeiträge zur Bibel aus der Perspektive von Frauen.* Darmstadt: Wissenschaftliche Buchgesellschaft, 1995. ET, *Feminist Interpretation: The Bible in Women's Perspective.* Translated by Barbara and Martin Rumscheidt. Minneapolis: Fortress, 1998.

Schroer, Silvia. "Auf dem Weg zu einer feministischen Rekonstruktion der Geschichte Israels." Pages 83–172 in *Feministische Exegese: Forschungsbeiträge zur Bibel aus der Perspektive von Frauen.* Edited by Luise Schottroff, Silvia Schroer, and Marie-Theres Wacker. Darmstadt: Wissenschaftliche Buchgesellschaft, 1995; Primus, 1997. ET, *Feminist Interpretation: The Bible in Women's Perspective.* Translated by Barbara and Martin Rumscheidt. Minneapolis: Fortress, 1998.

———. "Feminismus und Antijudaismus: Zur Geschichte eines konstruktiven Streits." Pages 28–39 in *Antijudaismus—christliche Erblast.* Edited by Walter Dietrich, Martin George, and Ulrich Luz. Stuttgart: Kohlhammer, 1999.

————. *Die Weisheit hat ihr Haus gebaut: Studien zur Gestalt der Sophia in den biblischen Schriften.* Mainz: Matthias-Grünewald, 1996.

Schubert, Paul. *Form and Function of the Pauline Thanksgivings.* Beihefte zur Zeitschrift für die neutestamentliche Wissenschaft 20. Berlin: A. Töpelmann, 1939.

Schüssler Fiorenza, Elisabeth. "Biblical Interpretation and Critical Commitment." *Studia Theologica* 43 (1989): 5–18.

————. *Bread Not Stone: The Challenge of Feminist Biblical Interpretation.* Boston: Beacon, 1984.

————. *But She Said: Feminist Practices of Biblical Interpretation.* Boston: Beacon 1992.

————. "The Ethics of Interpretation: De-Centering Biblical Scholarship." *Journal of Biblical Literature* 107 (1988): 3–17.

————. *In Memory of Her: A Feminist Theological Reconstruction of Christian Origins.* New York: Crossroad, 1983.

————. *Jesus: Miriam's Child, Sophia's Prophet: Critical Issues in Feminist Christology.* New York: Continuum, 1995.

————. "Liberation: A Critical Feminist Perspective." *Theology Digest* 46.4 (winter 1999): 327–36.

————. "Missionaries, Apostles, Coworkers: Romans 16 and the Reconstruction of Women's Early Christian History." *Word and World* 6 (1986): 420–33.

————. "Paul and the Politics of Interpretation." Pages 40–57 in *Paul and Politics: Ekklesia, Israel, Imperium, Interpretation.* Edited by Richard A. Horsley. Harrisburg, Pa.: Trinity Press International, 2000.

————. *Rhetoric and Ethic: The Politics of Biblical Studies.* Minneapolis: Fortress, 1999.

————, ed. *The Power of Naming: A Concilium Reader in Feminist Liberation Theology.* London: SCM, 1996.

Schüssler Fiorenza, Elisabeth, and S. Matthews, eds. *Searching the Scriptures.* Vol. 1: *An Introduction.* New York: Crossroad, 1993.

Schüssler Fiorenza, Elisabeth, A. Brock, and S. Matthews, eds. *Searching the Scriptures.* Vol. 2: *A Feminist Commentary.* New York: Crossroad, 1994.

Schwartz, Daniel R. *Studies in the Jewish Background of Christianity.* Tübingen: Mohr, 1992.

Schwartz, Regina, ed. *The Book and the Text: The Bible and Literary Theory.* Oxford: Blackwell, 1990.

Schweitzer, Albert. *Geschichte der paulinischen Forschung von der Reformation bis auf die Gegenwart.* Tübingen: Mohr, 1911. ET, *Paul and His*

Interpreters: A Critical History. Translated by W. Montgomery. New York: Macmillan, 1951.

————. *Die Mystik des Apostels Paulus*. Tübingen: Mohr, 1930. ET, *The Mysticism of Paul the Apostle*. Translated by W. Montgomery. London: A. & C. Black, 1931.

Scott, James M. *Paul and the Nations: The Old Testament and Jewish Background of Paul's Mission to the Nations with Special Reference to the Destination of Galatians*. Tübingen: Mohr/Siebeck, 1995.

Segal, Alan F. *Paul the Convert: The Apostolate and Apostasy of Saul the Pharisee*. New Haven: Yale University Press, 1990.

————. "Paul's Experience and Romans 9–11." In *The Church and Israel: Romans 9–11*. Edited by Daniel Migliore. *Princeton Seminary Bulletin*, Suppl. Issue no. 1 (1990): 56–70.

————. "Response: Some Aspects of Conversion and Identity Formation in the Christian Community of Paul's Time." Pages 184–90 in *Paul and Politics: Ekklesia, Israel, Imperium, Interpretation*. Edited by Richard A. Horsley. Harrisburg, Pa.: Trinity Press International, 2000.

Siegele-Wenschkewitz, Leonore. "The Discussion of Anti-Judaism in Feminist Theology—A New Area of Jewish-Christian Dialogue." *Journal of Feminist Studies in Religion* 7.2 (fall 1991): 95–99. Original, "Antijudaismus in feministischer Theologie." *Kirche und Israel: Neukirchener theologische Zeitschrift* 5.1 (1990): 5–8.

————, ed. *Verdrängte Vergangenheit, die uns bedrängt: Feministische Theologie in der Verantwortung für die Geschichte*. Munich: Chr. Kaiser, 1988.

Smith, Jonathan Z. *Map Is Not Territory: Studies in the History of Religion*. Chicago: University of Chicago Press, 1993.

Soderlund, Sven K., and N. T. Wright, eds. *Romans and the People of God: Essays in Honor of Gordon D. Fee on the Occasion of His Sixty-Fifth Birthday*. Grand Rapids: Eerdmans, 1999.

Sölle, Dorothee. *Träume mich, Gott: Geistliche Texte mit lästigen politischen Fragen*. Wuppertal: P. Hammer, 1994.

Soulen, R. Kendall. *The God of Israel and Christian Theology*. Minneapolis: Fortress, 1996.

Stamps, Dennis. "The Theological Rhetoric of the Pauline Epistles: Prolegomenon." Pages 249–59 in *The Rhetorical Interpretation of Scripture: Essays from the 1996 Malibu Conference*. Edited by Stanley E. Porter and Dennis L. Stamps. Sheffield: Sheffield Academic Press, 1999.

Stanley, Christopher D. *Paul and the Language of Scripture: Citation Technique in the Pauline Epistles and Contemporary Literature*. Cambridge: Cambridge University Press, 1992.

————. "'Pearls before Swine': Did Paul's Audiences Understand His Biblical Quotations?" *Novum Testamentum* 41 (Apr. 1999): 124–44.

Stanton, Elizabeth Cady, et al. *The Woman's Bible.* 2 vols. New York: European Publishing Co., 1895–98. Reprint, Boston: Northeastern University Press, 1993.

Stegemann, Ekkehard W., ed. *Messiasvorstellungen bei Juden und Christen.* Stuttgart: Kohlhammer, 1993.

Stegemann, Ekkehard W., and Wolfgang Stegemann. *The Jesus Movement: A Social History of Its First Century.* Edinburgh: T&T Clark, 1999.

Stegemann, Hartmut. *Die Essener, Qumran, Johannes der Täufer und Jesus.* Freiburg: Herder, 1993.

Stendahl, Krister. *Final Account: Paul's Letter to the Romans.* Minneapolis: Fortress, 1995.

————. *Paul among Jews and Gentiles and Other Essays.* Philadelphia: Fortress, 1976.

————. "Paul and the Introspective Conscience of the West." Pages 78–96 in *Paul among Jews and Gentiles and Other Essays.* By K. Stendahl. Philadelphia: Fortress, 1976. GT, "Der Apostel Paulus und das 'introspektive' Gewissen des Westens." Translated by Wolfgang Stegemann. *Kirche und Israel: Neukirchener theologische Zeitschrift* 11 (1996): 19–33.

Stone, Michael E., ed. *Jewish Writings of the Second Temple Period.* Vol. 2 of Literature of the Jewish People in the Period of the Second Temple and the Talmud. Section 2 of Compendia rerum Iudaicarum ad Novum Testamentum. Assen: Van Gorcum, 1984.

Stowers, Stanley K. *A Rereading of Romans: Justice, Jews, and Gentiles.* New Haven: Yale University Press, 1994.

————. "Social Status, Public Speaking, and Private Teaching: The Circumstances of Paul's Preaching Activity." *Novum Testamentum* 26 (1984): 59–82.

Strack, Hermann L., and Günther Stemberger. *Einleitung in Talmud und Midrasch.* 8th ed. Munich: C. H. Beck, 1992. ET, *Introduction to the Talmud and Midrash.* Translated by Markus Brockmuehl. Edinburgh: T&T Clark, 1991.

Strahm, Doris. *Vom Rand in die Mitte: Christologie aus der Sicht von Frauen in Asien, Afrika und Lateinamerika.* Lucerne: Edition Exodus, 1997.

Strahm, Doris, and Regula Strobel, eds. *Vom Verlangen nach Heilwerden: Christologie in feministisch-theologischer Sicht.* Fribourg: Edition Exodus, 1991.

Sutter Rehmann, Luzia. *Geh, frage die Gebärerin: Feministisch-befreiungstheologische Untersuchungen zum Gebärmotiv in der Apokalyptik.* Gütersloh: Chr. Kaiser/Gütersloher Verlagshaus, 1995.

———. "German-Language Feminist Exegesis of the Pauline Letters: A Survey." *Journal for the Study of the New Testament* 79 (2000): 5–18.

Talbert, Charles H. "Paul, Judaism, and the Revisionists." *Catholic Biblical Quarterly* 63.1 (2001): 1–22.

Talmon, Shemaryahu. "Bilanz und Ausblick nach 50 Jahren Qumranforschung." Pages 137–58 in *Die Schriftrollen von Qumran: Zur aufregenden Geschichte ihrer Erforschung und Deutung.* Edited by S. Talmon. Regensburg: F. Pustet, 1998.

———. *Juden und Christen im Gespräch.* Vol. 2 of *Gesammelte Aufsätze.* Neukirchen-Vluyn: Neukirchener Verlag, 1992.

———, ed. *Jewish Civilization in the Hellenistic-Roman Period.* Sheffield: Sheffield Academic Press, 1991.

———, ed. *Die Schriftrollen von Qumran: Zur aufregenden Geschichte ihrer Erforschung und Deutung.* Regensburg: F. Pustet, 1998.

Tamez, Elsa. *The Amnesty of Grace: Justification by Faith from a Latin American Perspective.* Nashville: Abingdon, 1993.

———. "Der Brief an die Gemeinde in Rom: Eine feministische Lektüre." Pages 557–73 in *Kompendium feministische Bibelauslegung.* Edited by Luise Schottroff and Marie-Theres Wacker. Gütersloh: Chr. Kaiser/ Gütersloher Verlagshaus, 1998.

Taubes, Jacob. *Die Politische Theologie des Paulus.* Munich: W. Fink, 1993.

Thiselton, Anthony C. *New Horizons in Hermeneutics.* Grand Rapids: Zondervan, 1992.

———. *The Two Horizons: New Testament Hermeneutics and Philosophical Description with Special Reference to Heidegger, Bultmann, Gadamer, and Wittgenstein.* Grand Rapids: Eerdmans, 1980.

Tomson, Peter J. "Christologie aus jüdischem Wurzelgrund: Jesus in Bezug auf die Schrift, die Tradition und die Geschichte Israels." *Analecta Bruxellensia* 4 (1999): 142–55.

———. *"If This Be from Heaven . . .": Jesus and the New Testament Authors in Their Relationship to Judaism.* Sheffield: Sheffield Academic Press, 2001.

———. *Paul and the Jewish Law: Halakha in the Letters of the Apostle to the Gentiles.* Minneapolis: Fortress, 1990.

Tracy, David. *Plurality and Ambiguity: Hermeneutics, Religion, Hope.* San Francisco: Harper & Row, 1987.

Unnik, W. C. van. *Tarsus or Jerusalem, the City of Paul's Youth?* Translated by George Ogg. London: Epworth, 1962.

Valentin, Joachim, and Saskia Wendel, eds. *Jüdische Traditionen in der Philosophie des 20. Jahrhunderts.* Darmstadt: Wissenschaftliche Buchgesellschaft, 2000.

Valtink, Eveline. "Feministisch-christliche Identität und Antijudaismus." Pages 1–28 in *Von der Wurzel getragen: Christlich-feministische Exegese in Auseinandersetzung mit Antijudaismus.* Edited by Luise Schottroff and Marie-Theres Wacker. Leiden: Brill, 1995.

Van Buren, Paul M. *According to the Scriptures: The Origins of the Church's Old Testament.* Grand Rapids: Eerdmans, 1998.

———. *A Theology of Jewish-Christian Reality.* Part 1: *Discerning the Way.* San Francisco: Harper & Row, 1980. Reprint ed., Lanham, Md.: University Press of America, 1995.

Vermes, Geza. *The Changing Faces of Jesus.* London: Penguin, 2001.

———. *The Complete Dead Sea Scrolls in English.* New York: Penguin, 1997.

———. *Post-Biblical Jewish Studies.* Leiden: Brill, 1975.

———. *The Religion of Jesus the Jew.* Minneapolis: Fortress, 1993.

Wacker, Marie-Theres. "Der/dem anderen Raum geben: Feministische-christliche Identität ohne Anti-Judaismus." Pages 247–70 in *Von der Wurzel getragen: Christlich-feministische Exegese in Auseinandersetzung mit Antijudaismus.* Edited by Luise Schottroff and Marie-Theres Wacker. Leiden: Brill, 1995.

———. "Feminist Theology and Anti-Judaism: The Status of the Discussion and the Context of the Problem in the Federal Republic of Germany." *Journal of Feminist Studies in Religion* 7.2 (fall 1991): 109–16. First published in *Kirche und Israel: Neukirchener theologische Zeitschrift* 5.2 (1990): 168–76.

Walker, Alice. *In Search of Our Mothers' Gardens: Womanist Prose.* San Diego: Harcourt Brace Jovanovich, 1983.

Walters, James C. *Ethnic Issues in Paul's Letter to the Romans: Changing Self-Definitions in Earliest Roman Christianity.* Valley Forge, Pa.: Trinity Press International, 1993.

Waschke, E.-J. "Die Einheit der Theologie heute als Anfrage an das Alte Testament—ein Plädoyer für die Vielfalt." Pages 339–41 in *Alttestamentlicher Glaube und biblische Theologie: Festschrift für Horst Dietrich Preuss zum 65. Geburtstag.* Edited by Jutta Hausmann and Hans-Jürgen Zobel. Stuttgart: Kohlhammer, 1992.

Watson, Francis B. *Paul, Judaism and the Gentiles: A Sociological Approach.* Cambridge: Cambridge University Press, 1986.

Weber, Elisabeth, ed. *Points . . . : Interviews, 1974–1994.* By Jacques Derrida. Translated by Peggy Kamuf et al. Stanford: Stanford University Press, 1995.

Wegner, Judith Romney. *Chattel or Person? The Status of Women in the Mishnah.* New York: Oxford University Press, 1988.

Weiler, Gerda. *Ich verwerfe im Lande die Kriege*. Munich: Frauenoffensive, 1984.

Wengst, Klaus. *Pax Romana: Anspruch und Wirklichkeit*. Munich: Chr. Kaiser, 1986.

White, John L. "Introductory Formulae in the Body of the Pauline Letter." *Journal of Biblical Literature* 90 (1971): 91–97.

———, ed. *Studies in Ancient Letter Writing*. Semeia 22. Chico, Calif.: Scholars Press, 1981.

White, L. Michael, and O. Larry Yarbrough, eds. *The Social World of the First Urban Christians: Studies in Honor of Wayne A. Meeks*. Minneapolis: Fortress, 1994.

Wire, Antoinette C. *The Corinthian Women Prophets: A Reconstruction through Paul's Rhetoric*. Minneapolis: Fortress Press, 1990.

Wolfson, H. A. *Philo: Foundations of Religious Philosophy in Judaism, Christianity, and Islam*. 2 vols. Cambridge: Harvard University Press, 1948.

Woodhead, Linda. "Feminist Theology—Out of the Ghetto?" Pages 198–206 in *Is There a Future for Feminist Theology?* Edited by Deborah F. Sawyer and Diane M. Collier. Sheffield: Sheffield Academic Press, 1999.

Wuellner, Wilhelm. "Paul's Rhetoric of Argumentation in Romans: An Alternative to the Donfried-Karris Debate over Romans." *Catholic Biblical Quarterly* 38 (1976): 330–51. Reprinted, pages 128–46 in *The Romans Debate*. Edited by Karl P. Donfried. Rev., expanded ed. Peabody, Mass.: Hendrickson, 1991.

Yerushalmi, Yosef Hayim. *Ein Feld in Anatot: Versuche über jüdische Geschichte*. Berlin: Wagenbach, 1993.

———. *Zachor: Erinnere Dich! Jüdische Geschichte und jüdisches Gedächtnis*. Berlin: Wagenbach, 1988. Original, *Zakhor, Jewish History and Jewish Memory*. Seattle: University of Washington Press, 1982.

Young, Iris Marion. "The Ideal of Community and the Politics of Difference." Pages 300–23 in *Feminism/Postmodernism*. Edited by Linda Nicholson. New York: Routledge, 1990.

———. *Justice and the Politics of Difference*. Princeton: Princeton University Press, 1990.

Young, Pamela Dickey. *Feminist Theology/Christian Theology: In Search of Method*. Minneapolis: Fortress, 1990.

Zenger, Erich. *Am Fusse des Sinai: Gottesbilder im Ersten Testament*. Düsseldorf: Patmos, 1993.

Ziesler, John. *Paul's Letter to the Romans*. London: SCM, 1989.

ᥣ᥆ **INDEX** ᥆᥎